Faith & Practice in Conflict Resolution

Faith & Practice in Conflict Resolution

Toward a Multidimensional Approach

edited by
Rachel M. Goldberg

A Division of Lynne Rienner Publishers, Inc. • Boulder & London

Published in the United States of America in 2016 by
Kumarian Press
A division of Lynne Rienner Publishers, Inc.
1800 30th Street, Boulder, Colorado 80301
www.rienner.com

and in the United Kingdom by
Kumarian Press
A division of Lynne Rienner Publishers, Inc.
3 Henrietta Street, Covent Garden, London WC2E 8LU

Library of Congress Cataloging-in-Publication Data
Names: Goldberg, Rachel M., editor, author.
Title: Faith and practice in conflict resolution : toward a
  multidimensional approach / edited by Rachel M. Goldberg.
Description: Boulder, Colorado : Kumarian Press,
  A Division of Lynne Rienner Publishers, Inc., 2016. |
  Includes bibliographical references and index.
Identifiers: LCCN 2015038775 |
  ISBN 9781626372740 (hardcover : alk. paper)
Subjects: LCSH: Peace-building—Religious aspects. |
  Conflict management—Religious aspects.
Classification: LCC BL65.P4 F35 2016 | DDC 303.—dc23
  LC record available at http://lccn.loc.gov/2015038775

British Cataloguing in Publication Data
A Cataloguing in Publication record for this book
is available from the British Library.

Printed and bound in the United States of America

♾ The paper used in this publication meets the requirements
    of the American National Standard for Permanence of
    Paper for Printed Library Materials Z39.48-1992.

5   4   3   2   1

Contents

Acknowledgments

I MUST FIRST THANK BRIAN BLANCKE, MY PARTNER IN SO MUCH
of this. Brian has an extraordinary ability to look inside things and see
truth there, but an even more extraordinary ability to be open, nonjudg-
mental, and loving about the truth when he sees it. He's done that with
me as colleague and friend over many years, and as a coauthor. The first
two chapters owe much of their passion, eloquence, and depth to him,
not just as a writer and extraordinary scholar and researcher, but by eliciting and supporting those things in myself, as well. Thank you, Brian.

My family was also extraordinarily supportive as I struggled with
a long illness and a challenging idea of scholarship. Clearly, if I'd had
any sense I'd have written something safe and easily publishable, but I
had to write this kind of work, so I am incredibly grateful to Danny,
Peter, Lola, Rosemary, Katie, Ben, and Max, not to mention my patient
and ever-loving friends—without whom I would have long ago been
dead or insane or possibly both—for many things, but most of all for
enduring, year after year, with love. These include Catherine Benedict,
Patty Hassett, Stacy Ciufo, and Chris Kopeck. Also, thanks to Moth and
Dad—no longer on the Earth, but who made this, and so many other
things, possible.

Also, I need to thank Ron Cherubino, a friend and amazing healer,
and the extraordinary professors and mentors I have had in my academic journey, including Frank Blechman, for always telling the truth,
and better than that, living it; John Burdick, who hung in there with his
first dissertation chairship and myself; Wallace Warfield, whom I miss;
and Chris Mitchell, Juliana Birkhoff, and all the other ICAR and Syracuse greats, including Lou Kriesberg and Neil Katz. I must also mention
my wonderful friends and colleagues at Eastern Mennonite University,

who have consistently fostered and supported some of the most multi-dimensional work in this field. And Jeannette J. Jansky, who helped me learn to read by doing pioneering work in dyslexia and working with me long before most people even understood these kinds of challenges.

Finally, I want to thank my colleagues and students, especially the Restorative Justice-eers, who are amazing, and my wonderful friends and colleagues here at DePauw, and at my previous academic and practical settings, too numerous to mention, who have been with me as we and this field have grown. DePauw is truly an institution that supports wide-ranging thinking in a dynamic world and is deeply student-centered in a way that supports extraordinary teaching and amazing faculty and staff. I would also like to thank the exceptional practitioners who contribute whole practice to this book, who have been so extraordinary to work with, and who, with others, continue to transform this field for the better.

*　*　*

This book has an accompanying website intended to be a place where articles and other resources can be collected; practice and case examples stored; and community brought together to think and question. I have spaces to post articles, case stories, reflections and discussions, syllabuses, exercises, tools, processes, and more. I have already posted poems that John Paul Lederach uses in his teaching, as well as copies of his syllabuses and case stories from practitioners. Please visit www.rmgresilience.com.

—*R. M. Goldberg*

1

Faith and Multidimensional Practice in Conflict Resolution

Rachel M. Goldberg

THIS BOOK INCLUDES MOMENTS OF BOTH ORDINARY AND extraordinary practice by excellent practitioners who intervene in conflicts professionally. Crossing a military checkpoint with her companions at risk, Louise Diamond believes she was able to bring her presence to bear in a way that transformed hostility into humanity in the soldier on guard. Daniel Bowling, with characteristic artistry and humility, reflects on what happened when he lost mindfulness in a particular case, and also how he regained it, and how he changed himself in a way that changed the case. M. Brandon Sipes talks about coaching a party in a congregational conflict to approach one of the other and most difficult parties, not with arguments or facts, but with an inquiry into his deep commitments, in a way that transformed the conflict. Julia Morelli shares a moment of body awareness that enabled her to change her physical presence in a way that shifted everyone else in the conflict. Christopher Fitz describes a time when physically playing through incidents using Playback Theatre gave the community he was working with new insight into tense racial dynamics. Joy Meeker describes following powerful emotional cues into a deeper layer of conflict to reveal the heart of a workplace dispute, and gently revealing structural inequality playing itself out in the conflict, so it became visible to all parties and was engaged positively. John Paul Lederach, Louise Diamond, and myself in my role as editor invite the field to take a step beyond understanding that moments of artistry like this exist, to asking what some of the elements producing them may be, and how we can support, teach,

1

and train students and trainees to do more profound, meaningful, and transformative practice intervention.

This is not a small task. Practitioners in the field of conflict engagement take on an extraordinary job. We have the amazing task of helping people find the capacity in themselves to believe they can talk to their enemies, recover from their wounds, and rebuild their lives and their societies, when all around them are the signs of their previous (or current) destructive circumstances (Lederach 2005). What enables participants and practitioners to transcend their situations, their norms of conflict, and move to engage something unknown but potentially better? How do we find it in ourselves to support and foster this? How do we develop this capacity in ourselves and how can it be taught?

I believe that what creates this kind of profound and important practice, in part, is practitioners bringing their whole selves, including their spiritual resources, to bear. Let me give you one more example. Volkan (1997) tells a story from an early problem-solving workshop in 1980 with Israelis and Egyptians that highlights one of those transformative moments. When Ebd El Azim Ramadan, an Egyptian scholar, talked about the need for a Palestinian state, Nechama Agmon, an Israeli child psychologist, asked him how he could convince her not to fear a Palestinian state. Ramadan answered, "I do not believe that you Israelis are afraid; Israelis are never afraid." Agmon was appalled, and the exchange quickly ended (Volkan 1997, 33).

The next day Ramadan asked to speak. He had not slept the night before, grappling with what had happened and whether he could trust that Agmon was sincere. He decided to consult the Quran and found three passages that spoke of Moses's fear. "He read these passages to the group in Arabic and English. He then added, 'I never thought that Moses was afraid. But now I know that since Moses was afraid, you can be, too. So I believe you, Nechama" (Volkan 1997, 34). Volkan comments that one might expect Ramadan to be pleased that an enemy was afraid, except that it might have been hard to share a sense of victimhood with her. Part of what made his hate possible was a belief that Israelis didn't have emotions, that they were inhuman. This interaction humanized her.

> As a result of coming face-to-face with his "enemy" and discovering some unexpected empathy for Agmon, he consulted the Qur'an for help. Then he experienced the sudden connection between emotional experience and intellectual understanding that rehumanized the Israelis. In acknowledging their human identity, Ramadan also had to acknowledge that they had a grievance and negative emotions pertaining to it. (Volkan 1997, 34)

Here, Volkan connects a cognitive shift with an emotional one, and it is logical to assume, given the story, that there was a spiritual shift as well, although that aspect is not mentioned. I believe, as do the other authors in this book, that these kinds of shifts originate in multiple levels of human experience, and that to foster them and embody the kind of practice described above, we need more than skills, techniques, and reason; although these are a natural beginning of practitioner development, they are not the end.

In this volume we attempt to do two things: (1) to recognize and support the kind of work that comes from practitioners who bring their developed, complex, whole selves to bear, rather than trying to cut parts of themselves off (which so much of the early work of this field encouraged us to do in order to be neutral), and (2) to show that this mastery or artistry in conflict engagement can be consciously supported and fostered in practitioners. The book includes case examples, concrete practical skills and techniques, and clear recommendations for teaching and training the development of what I have termed *multidimensional practice*. My hope is that this book begins the critical work of documenting not just case examples of what many call artistry or mastery but practitioners' theories-in-action and usable techniques.

Conflict and a sense of threat can push parties and practitioners into simplistic thinking and reactive, limbic-brain, fight-flight-freeze responses (Rubin, Pruitt, and Kim 1994; Yoder 2005; Coleman 2011). In conflict situations people often become their worst, least resourceful, least rational selves. Our job as conflict specialists is to help people who are feeling vulnerable, threatened, and without resources to pull themselves back together enough to reengage their rational, long-term, planning brain, while not shutting down parts of themselves or becoming rigid. Research on trauma and abuse survivors shows that cutting parts of oneself off, disassociation, distancing, and removing oneself from an abused body and shattered emotions, while not an uncommon response to trauma, is only temporarily functional and is a damaging and unhealthy way to live (Thompson 1994; Yoder 2005). Eventually the abuse survivor needs to reintegrate the mind, body, and emotions in order to live a healthy life.[1] I have seen the same shattering and need for reintegration in many conflicts where the parties might not characterize themselves as traumatized.

This need for wholeness also applies to ourselves, as practitioners and interveners, both in a moment of confrontation that sets us off balance and as part of our lifelong development. Part of what we can offer is to bring our own emotional balance and maturity to a chaotic, reactive interaction, supporting the conflict to move beyond simplistic dichotomies into productive ambiguity, complexity, and paradox (Mayer 2015; Nan 2011). Diamond recalls how people have told her, "It's not what you did, no matter how useful that was, but *how* you are that made the difference" (Chapter 2). I argue that our ability to develop wholeness and embrace and use our multiple intelligences, supports powerful presence. Leaders in this field, including Daniel Bowling, Louise Diamond, and John Paul Lederach make an eloquent case for the importance of presence and wholeness in conflict engagement practice.

For many practitioners of conflict engagement, including myself, this means we need to accept and listen to the parts of ourselves that permit the transcendence of our own limitations, doubts, fears, and current states of consciousness in order to support parties to do the same. Doing so can mean accessing and using what I am calling spiritual or transcendent intelligence, as well as using emotional and somatic intelligences. This allows me, and the other practitioners in this book, to take in data on many levels, integrate them, and make an intuitive leap in a way that brings our *presence* to bear transformatively. The time has come to reject the old objectivist norms that teach us to cut off key parts of ourselves in order to be neutral and that new scientific discoveries are rapidly repudiating. Instead, we need to work on being multidimensional and whole, bringing the integrated self to bear as an asset, and doing it in a way that scrupulously respects the self-determination of disputing parties.

For many of the authors in this book, the root of this kind of transformative work is their spiritual development, although we also refer to emotional intelligence, and somatic or body awareness. We have all watched great practice, or had moments of it ourselves, and know the real transformational work that leaps beyond the bedrock skills and processes we are all taught. For much of our history, we have written this off as personal characteristics—"you got it or you don't." We wonder if that amazing practitioner is just a deeper person or more charismatic than ourselves. This attitude increases the mystique of our successes but impoverishes our practice. Much of what pushes us to look away from the apparent magic is rooted in the objectivist norms of the past. Although there are truly extraordinary people in this field, there is more in the way of really understanding them than our hero or heroine worship or insecurities. I hope this book can begin to pull back the curtain hiding some of the older intellectual machinery that masquerades as truth. The book goes further to show that despite those obstacles, we have both the theory and practical skills necessary to begin to train and support the development of extraordinary practice. Transformative practice can be supported and learned.

This chapter introduces the rationale for this book, presents some background—including a review of those old norms that have guided much of our practice and professional development, while mentioning what is replacing them—briefly reviews how our sibling disciplines of psychology and law have been engaging spirituality in practice, presents some definitions that help shape the overall conversation of the book, and then introduces the overall content. As you see, I have begun with the rationale.

I was inspired to write this book because, in the dynamic flux of a conflict intervention, the most effective work I do as a practitioner often comes from that transcendent leap-beyond kind of work, a leap into the elusive soft spot where angry, fearful people can open and shift. One of my mentors, Frank Blechman, surprised (and inspired) me when I was a graduate student by telling me, "We are in the business of providing hope and love." Frank, as ever, cut through the rhetoric and pointed right at the heart of our work, in a way we almost never discuss, or train, or teach. The heart of what I do that makes a difference, and why I love this work, lies there. Through my research on the topic of spirituality and conflict and multidimensional work (work engaging cognitive, spiritual, somatic, and emotional intelligences), I came to see more clearly that, for me, the leap-beyond is informed by deep experiential and theoretical knowledge. It is guided by emotional calibration and intelligence by feeling my way with an attitude of caring (Frank's focus on love), all of which was rooted, for me, in years of spiritual and personal development.

As a professor, I regularly see some of my students develop this leap-beyond level of ability. How do they move from mechanically using skills in processes to integrating and holding their presence in a way that can change the conflicts for the people involved? Am I part of what fosters the growth from a mechanical to an artistic mediator, or am I just privileged to see some students reach that new level on their own? I am very clear, from having watched hundreds of students learn the skills and processes, that this leap-beyond work is actually much of what makes a difference in real conflicts. In my experience, when transformation and shift happens for parties, mediators often bring themselves to bear in this way.

Of course, there are times when skills and processes alone can change a situation. For instance, unproductive meetings can be transformed by simply having an agenda, thinking about who needs to be at the meeting, and recording who said they would do what by when. But in deep conflict, when people are enmeshed in trouble that pushes them into a dichotomous, reactive state, I have rarely seen mechanical solutions produce anything but mechanical, short-term solutions. Our world is full of just that, and deteriorating in ways that bring more human pain. So our ability to support this leap-beyond work, what others have called mastery or artistry, is critical to our ability to bring deep peace and enduring change that transforms violence and suffering. The book includes chapters by interveners, discussing how they do multidimensional work in their practice, and also chapters by two exceptional leaders in this field, John Paul Lederach and Louise Diamond, on how we can go beyond understanding to begin to intentionally educate, train, and support multidimensional peacebuilders.

The spiritual development of excellent practitioners can be an asset that helps them make space for hope in hopeless situations and believe in the new with love—in other words, the capacity to imagine humanity in our broken selves and our enemies, to be a *wounded healer* (Lederach 2005; and Barr 2006). That is largely supported by the engagement of the transcendent in us, which defines the work of whole, emotionally mature practitioners who listen to their reason, emotions, spirit, and bodies. And a great deal of how it operates is through what has been called presence.

This book builds on pathbreaking work like *Bringing Peace Into the Room* (Bowling and Hoffman 2003), which focuses on the impact of the mediator's presence, and Lederach's *The Moral Imagination* (2005), which describes the potential of human creativity to imagine new possibilities when surrounded by the old. Many, including LeBaron et al. (2013), Fox (2004), Gold (2003), Schirch (2005, 2015), and Nan (2011), have been working to explore what supports leap-beyond shifts in consciousness that allow transformation.

Earlier waves of development in the field, such as *Getting to Yes* (Fisher et al. 1991), focused on problem-solving techniques, such as moving from positions to interests, and on how to manage strong emotions and fragile identities (*Difficult Conversations*, Stone et al. 1999). The newest wave, of which this book is a part, focuses not on the parties directly, nor on mediator techniques, but on the artistry of the work, the intervener's *presence*, who they are in the work, and how that impacts the process.

My work also builds on other research, which shows that wholeness and the engagement of multiple intelligences, as well as self-development (like mindfulness and spiritual practices), lead to better conflict engagement. Research suggests that those who practice regular meditation, for instance, have a developed frontal cortex, and are less likely to draw entirely from the lizard brain when responding to trauma and threats, instead showing a capacity for rationality rather than engaging a flight-fight-avoid response (Cahn and Polich 2006; Siegel 2007). This means that when under stress or threat, they are more creative and open, less reactive, and more centered, and more productive in their conflict engagement (Lederach 2015). Schirch argues that faith traditions have used rituals for centuries for "cognitive transformation and trauma healing" (2015, 528) that support the ability to shift perspective and make new meaning out of experiences of conflict. She says, " . . . relying only on direct, rational forms of communication to arrive at negotiated solutions or manage tensions in conflict is a mistake. Solving complex problems requires the full capacity of the human brain, including the parts responsible for emotions and senses" (2015, 530). It stands to reason that if this is true of conflict parties, it is true for practitioners. Similarly, Nan argues that shifts in consciousness require an ability to gain some distance from and perspective on prior thinking patterns, a location or a space where transitional frameworks can be built that allow the old to be shifted (which faith traditions excel at creating), and "the creation of new structures of consciousness" (2011, 253). She adds that "mindfulness practices and other contemplative traditions . . . may help support that transitional space" (253).

Powerful work has been developing in other arenas, which also informs and shapes this book. Following Daniel Goleman's (1995 and 2006) work on emotional intelligence and Kahneman's *Thinking Fast and Slow* (2011), both Bernie Mayer in his recent publication (2015) and Morelli and Fitz in Chapter 5 point to how emotions are used by humans to calibrate our *fast thinking*, or rapid intuitive responses to conflict based on experience. Schön (1983) is credited with being one of the early thinkers to give credence to this kind of insight, which he called *knowing-in-practice* and *reflection-in-action*. In other words, cognition is supported by emotions in ways that help us read situations and respond rapidly and well in ways beyond our *slow thinking* or rational, cognitive processes. All of these are abstract but powerful indications that what supports real transformative work, what allows us and our clients to transcend our mental schemas and conflict-patterned responses, includes but also goes beyond rational, cognitive skills and responses. In this book I ask us to move a step or two beyond some of the abstraction and into concrete approaches and to explore ways to develop these abilities.

Despite decades of excellent work, and some shining lights of the kind mentioned already, we have been slow to document these efforts. However, we often recognize and respect them. For instance, most of us revere the examples Martin Luther King Jr. and Mohandas Gandhi, who are complex, emotionally mature leaders who saw their work as deeply rooted in, and fueled by, their faiths. Both dealt with large-scale, complex conflicts and exerted a disproportional influence more because of who and what they were than because of specific resources they could use as carrots or sticks. For Gandhi, satyagraha's power was an inherently spiritual one. This *truth-force* was truth as God, or God as truth (Scalmer 2012):

> Voluntary suffering was no "meek submission" to the will of the "evil-doer," but rather an attempt to pit "one's whole soul" against "the will of the tyrant." . . . Gandhi believed that suffering, "bravely born," had the capacity to melt "even a heart of stone." . . . Sacrifice, nobly endured, might convince an opponent to "see the error of their ways" . . . promoting "introspection," "rethinking" . . . and even "moral transformation." (Scalmer, 340)

Using satyagraha, Gandhi led India to transcend generations of colonization and literally changed the world. This quote beautifully captures the multidimensional nature of his work and reflects that developed maturity that supports complexity and ambiguity as well as paradox. He talks about cognitive, emotional, somatic, and spiritual engagement, all unified in an understanding of his most important belief. On some level, most of us recognize an authenticity and power in bringing this kind of wholeness into conflict resolution work.

I argue that developing our emotional maturity, somatic awareness, and an ability to harness the transcendent in ourselves—what many see as the power of spirituality and the resources of faith traditions—supports leap-beyond work. After researching the history of the debates about these concepts in this field, and what is being done in psychology and law (Goldberg and Blancke 2011), Brian Blancke and I developed a framework for thinking about how to practice in a more multidimensional way than currently exists in the field's models and theories, which is presented in Chapter 2. This book includes chapters by several practitioners who are already creating extraordinary practice by engaging multiple dimensions of conflict, and themselves, as they work to transform conflicts. In doing so, their practice respects the self-determination of parties in a deeper, more sophisticated way than is often seen in our traditional methods. The practitioner chapters include their authors' theories, orientations, and principles, narratives from their cases showing how they embody those ideas, and practical advice and exercises that readers can apply in their own work to cultivate their own multidimensional work.

This is a book about how conflict resolvers, peacebuilders, theologians who work with conflict, students and professors of conflict resolution and peace studies, and parties to conflicts which have spiritual aspects can explore how those who intervene in conflicts can use their multidimensional abilities and intelligences—that is, their whole selves and their presence—as an asset.

This represents advanced work. It is unreasonable to expect participants in a forty-hour mediation training to develop this leap-beyond or multidimensional capacity based on just one training. Sometimes trainees who have had many years of experience developing themselves, as therapists, community leaders, or religious leaders, come in with this depth and can immediately bring conflict resolution skills to a profound level. But, if in our field we aim to support mediators and peacebuilders at all levels (including students and novices), who we want to learn to bring themselves to bear in conflict situations with centered intelligence, emotional resonance, and what Cloke calls *calibrated intuition* (see Chapter 2), then we need to conceive of our work, and how we support and develop practitioners, in a new way.

Although these aspects of artistry are gaining importance within the field, perplexingly, we rarely think about how to develop this or how to support students and trainees to find this in themselves, except through pointing to examples in people like Lederach and Diamond. This book is full of practitioners modeling multidimensional, integrated, transformational work. Although the modeling is powerful, I have asked these authors to go further, presenting some practical skills and explaining their theoretical frameworks as well.

With examples like Gandhi and King, we might have expected a book like this earlier in our history. However, it is also notable that all of the authors in this book (including myself) struggled with how to communicate on this topic in a genuine, academic, and practical way. We lurched between dry but rigorous writing and analytic thinking on the one hand and passionate but unclear and unsubstantiated rhetoric on the other. Perhaps the difficulty is one of talking rationally about something that is often treated as beyond rationality, and talking concretely about something transcendent. We have all struggled to bring these two worlds of understanding together into something cogent and multidimensionally rich. This challenge comes from a long history lauding the separation of cognition, emotion, soma, and spirit, which this chapter reviews briefly. As Joy Meeker pointed out to me, the very fact of the difficulty of engaging this topic signaled its value and the need for further exploration.

So what keeps us from talking or writing about this easily? For most of us, our early mediation training focused on being neutral, which often meant suppressing or cutting off parts of ourselves. The only trustworthy protection for party self-determination and empowerment was seen as neutrality, which was interpreted as avoiding faith, and often emotion, altogether as Meeker's training to be like Mr. Spock demonstrates (see Chapter 6). In fact, one mediation trainer I know tells new mediators to pretend they are aliens from another planet, and it is hoped through this mental exercise that they will not bring anything of their own culture or experience to bear in their work, lest they damage the self-determination of the parties. I cannot help but imagine the alien mediators and Mr. Spock trying to work with New York Jews like myself, and thinking what a complete disaster it would very likely be.

Another obstacle comes from some modern resistance to faith. When I meet people at conferences in the quintessential elevator moment and mention that I am writing about religion and conflict resolution, the first reaction is often "Wonderful!"—and then they tell me a story about religiously based violence. This is part of why I avoid the use of the word "religion" in this book (a discussion of my choice follows later in this chapter). I do acknowledge that the transcendent, because of its emotional power, can be used to as a motivator for hatred. It is often seen as a driver of intolerance and violence. As I write this, the Islamic State of Iraq and Syria (ISIS) is imposing what it interprets as Islamic spiritual laws in the regions it has conquered, saying in the words of one imam, "We will take you to paradise, even if we have to drag you in chains on the way there" (Aarja 2014). The specter of this kind of manipulation seems totally antithetical to the norms of pluralism and self-determination that are core to many in this field. Such norms are why most of us are taught to reframe the conflict away from spiritual values, which are framed as irreconcilable, and away from emotional causes, to specific issues that are seen as more manageable and negotiable.

Moreover, we have been remarkably reluctant to write and talk about what we all experience when the "magic," or leap-beyond work, happens. The more I researched this topic, the more I realized that Enlightenment thinking, fading though it is, has been standing in the way of the field engaging in a serious, thoughtful conversation about who we are when we do our best. Emotions, the body, the spiritual resources of the practitioner, all fell long ago into the category of "other" in a way that made them suspect. This characterization has rendered some of our capacities invisible and mysterious and tempted theorists to gloss over the human complexity of the journey to excellence. Lederach aptly reflects that this means "we lose sight of ourselves, our deeper intuition, and the source of our understandings of *who we are* and *how we are* in the world. In doing so we arrive at a paradoxical destination: We believe in the knowledge we generate but not in the inherently messy and personal process by which we acquired it" (2005, viii).

The history of objectivism has silenced us about what we do best. Literally. In this book I hope to encourage us in the field to start talking, logically and rationally, as well as emotionally, somatically, and spiritually, about how we do what we do best—clearly and well enough that practitioners at all levels can begin reflecting on the multidimensional nature of their own work.

As I mentioned earlier, this avoidance is often done in the name of party self-determination and neutrality, two bedrock principles of conflict resolution processes like mediation. Although this can seem field specific, these ideas have deep taproots. Our field of conflict resolution has been shaped, since the early days of its professional journey, by the legacy of our struggle to legitimize ourselves through standards like those that seemed to validate the legal profession. Like many seeking professional credibility, we relied on the norms of expert neutrality and objectivism, which are an extremely problematic foundation on which to build our professional house. The idea that legitimacy comes from objectivity is connected to a very long attempt to find truth by separating mind and body, reason and emotion, science and faith, which is also problematic though understandable.

Historically, knowledge has been gathered in three modes (Nachmias and Nachmias 1992): the authoritarian mode, where truth was only accessible though certain socially sanctioned authorities like kings and their appointed advisers; the mystical mode, where truth came from divine authorities like prophets, gods, their chosen mediums; and, since the Enlightenment, the rationalistic mode, where truth was derived from pure logic. The enterprise of moving beyond a world defined entirely by superstition and fear was a noble one. Unfortunately, a lot of the baby was thrown out with the bathwater in a way that simultaneously enriched and impoverished our understanding of our capacities and ourselves.

The original divisions between science, religion, reason, and emotion can actually be traced back to pre-Socratic times when the word *Logos*, which at that time meant story, reason, discourse, or thought, was later differentiated by Plato and Aristotle into two separate categories: *Logos* and *mythos* (Fisher 1987). Logos was the philosophical discourse of logical and scientific thought associated with the rational, abstract functions of the mind. Mythos was the poetic and rhetorical discourse that was considered inferior. Although modern scientific inquiry is rooted in the ability to separate knowledge based on myth and impression from knowledge based on testable and generalizable information—which has real value, for it enriched our understanding of our-selves and our world—the division also elevated logic over all other forms of information gathering and assessment, which impoverished us as well (Fisher 1987). This division was then carried into the field of law, where we found our legitimacy norms:

> In order to justify law as a separate discipline and science that could be understood and applied logically and rationally there was a con-certed effort to deplete it of feelings, emotions, and thus, of spirit . . . The application of . . . positivism to the study and practice of law cre-ated a moral . . . vacuum. Law became its own morality. (Hall 2005, 72–73)

This split developed over time, as Jones and Hughes describe (2003), into the current paradigm shaping most modern science and thought, as well as the professions that grew out of them like the legal profession. They are rooted in the concepts of objectivism, reductionism, and deter-minism. Descartes brought us objectivism, the idea that we can use rea-son to separate us from our environment and reactions in a way that produces objective knowledge. Reductionism was inspired by the new mechanical age which led scientists to believe that the way to under-stand any system was to reduce it to its parts and study the parts, just like a machine. Determinism states that every cause has an effect. "Combined with objectivism and reductionism, it should always be pos-sible to determine the cause of every phenomenon by tearing it apart and analyzing those pieces in an objective and observer-independent manner" (Jones and Hughes 2003, 487). The key was keeping mind, body, heart, and spirit separate; and, it was believed, this process led to the truth.

You can see how appealing and useful this has been. In our field we have used the concepts of outside (separate) mediators who are neutral (setting aside their emotions and values from their processing of the case) to present ourselves as trustworthy and fair. We use the concept of neutrality and objectivity ostensibly to protect parties from mediators, so that the parties, as the experts in their own situation, own the prob-lem and the solution (i.e., can exercise their self-determination). Cobb and Rifkin, in their groundbreaking article on neutrality, cited mediation texts as representing impartiality as "equivalent to the absence of feel-ings, values, or agendas" (1991, 42), or as I mentioned earlier, the alien-from-another-planet goal for mediators. Neutrality has been seen as the parties' best protection, and also as the bedrock of our role legitimacy—why it is appropriate for us to intervene, following legal concepts of avoiding a conflict of interest.

The very basis of these original separations, however, is now under attack in most disciplines. There is increasing evidence, for instance, that there is no real way to separate the knower and the known, the cornerstone of objective, empirical scientific investigation. Jones and Hughes also summarized recent research and thought that shows that "the human mind is inherently embodied, and no separate and objective reasoning facility exists" (2003, 487), that most of our thought is unconscious, and that humans navigate our understanding about abstract concepts largely through metaphors. The authors go on to add that human systems are complex and adaptive and are nonlinear, nondeterminative (cause and effect are not uniquely coupled), and integrated wholes (which cannot be understood by breaking them down into any sort of essential elements) (2003). Lincoln and Guba chronicle this cutting-edge thinking in their book *Naturalistic Inquiry* and say old paradigms are collapsing and new paradigms are emerging in " . . . physics, chemistry, brain theory, ecology, evolution, mathematics, philosophy, politics, psychology, linguistics, religion, consciousness, and the arts" (1985, 51).

Even before this, however, many questions have been raised about the objective stance of neutrality. These include Laue and Cormick attacking neutrality as working *against* self-determination, saying that "claims to neutrality on the part of the intervener . . . almost always work to the advantage of the party in power" (1978, 221). Other theorists have said neutrality does not protect parties, and holding a stance of neutrality can actually blind you to your own biases in a way that can unconsciously disempower clients (Gunning 1995; LeBaron et al. 1998; Cobb 1993; Rack 2000; Wing 2008, 2009; Goldberg 2009).

What if, conversely, by holding to rigid norms of neutrality, we are actually ignoring or silencing needs that are core to the parties? For instance, by sidestepping the parties' faith as an aspect of a conflict because, we, as interveners, were taught to avoid it or are uncomfortable with it ourselves, despite the fact that the parties feel it is important. By doing so, we may be missing how parties either make sense of the conflict or how they would like to resolve it (through spiritual forgiveness, for example, in used in Rwandan restorative justice processes[2]). Similarly, what is missed by ignoring parties' strong emotions, which often signal what is at the heart of the matter for them (Gopin 2004), in order to get back to the task of problem solving? These actions also undermine the self-determination of the parties.

In doing research in this area, I found that the two other disciplines that are most related to ours and against whom we frequently measure ourselves—psychology and law—were asking similar questions, with psychology well ahead of us in the development of their answers.

Although this research is summarized in Goldberg and Blancke (2011), I will highlight some key findings here. It is striking, for instance, that therapists do not attempt to pretend they are neutral, but instead acknowledge the impact of their values: "Research has provided evidence that therapists' values influence every phase of psychotherapy, including the theories of personality and therapeutic change, assessment strategies, goals of treatment, the design and selection of interventions, and evaluations of therapy outcome" (Richards, Rector, and Tjeltveit 1999, 135). Client self-determination is, if anything, more important for psychologists than it is for us. They protect it, not through mythical neutrality (quixotically attempting to pretend they have no values), but by developing a great deal of self-awareness, so their values do not drive them unconsciously, by working to maintain healthy boundaries with clients, and by training therapists to respect the multidimensional needs of their clients. This has led to a major subfield focus on spirituality, and, in fact, eight peer-reviewed journals in the field are "dedicated to spiritual topics" (Aten and Leach 2009, 15).

Self-awareness helps them understand how they might unconsciously impose their own religious views (countertransference). Richards and Bergin (2004), however, feel that spiritually oriented therapists are *less* likely to "violate their clients' value autonomy" (302) by addressing the issue with an "explicit minimizing valuing approach," which simply means that therapists are open about their values and beliefs when appropriate, while prioritizing client needs and making it easy for clients to express their own needs and values.

It is also key, of course, to find out how much, if at all, spirituality is important to the client. Pargament and Krumrei (2009) have developed a number of instruments and approaches that could be useful in our field, for instance, adding a regular assessment question like "Has your spirituality or religion been involved in the way you dealt with your problem? If so, in what way?" (2009, 100) As Blancke mentions in Chapters 2 and 9, this most basic level is often something we ignore or avoid, again, running on the old objectivist norm that spirituality is somehow tainted terrain. This is an extraordinarily irrational fear coming from a rationalist framework. I love this particular point, because it is at this level that objectivism actually *becomes* a faith object, not an exercise in cognition. Spirituality in this case is scary only because it is associated with so many outdated narratives about truth and reason, not because there is anything objectively, inherently wrong with it.

Psychologists can teach us a great deal in terms of self-awareness. They recommend various self-reflective exercises like working with an expert from the therapist's religion to engage unresolved issues, creating a spiritual genogram, writing a spiritual autobiography, or using guided journaling. For example, a genogram is a common therapeutic tool showing "transmission of family patterns across generations" (Wiggins 2009, 60) and is a way for therapists to look at their own intergenerational spiritual patterns and their own responses. Doing so helps them be aware of when they might engage in countertransference, or what triggers their responses.

For example, "some therapists may have been raised in orthodox religious homes and disassociated themselves with their family's religion . . . [and] continue to wrestle with unresolved theological questions that make them anxious when religious or spiritual topics arose. When such anxiety strikes therapists, they may (consciously or unconsciously) redirect a therapy session toward another topic" because of their own feelings, not in response to the needs of the client (Wiggins 2009, 55). Of course, another risk is that therapists can be too invested in clients' taking a particular direction, in a way that is spiritually inappropriate for the client, as, of course, could be the case with proselytizing. Both of these are clearly an issue in terms of client self-determination. Instead, therapists are trained to stay focused on the purpose of the process and on the needs and goals of the client, and to keep good boundaries (Wiggins 2009, 57). If this is a problem for the therapist, Wiggins suggests "supervision, personal counseling, or client referral" (2009, 57). All of these responses could work well for conflict resolvers and support parties.

When it comes to faith and spirituality, writers from the legal world tend to focus on ethics and lawyer burnout (Hall 2005; Rickard 2008). In terms of ethics, both law and psychology have, in the development of their standards, struggled with the difference between ethics and rules and how to support real ethics in practice (Hall 2005; Sibley 1984; Hathaway and Ripley 2009). One of main authors in this area, Hall, recalls one of his colleagues who put it best when discussing how being a good person connects to following the legal rules: " . . . one can be a complete sleazeball, from the standpoint of morality, and never violate a single rule in the law governing lawyers" (Hall 2005, 23). Hall wanted to know why people do or do not live by their principles. He argues that shutting off emotions, values, and spirituality does not support ethical practice. His response is an intriguing one. He grounds his own practice in what he calls spiritual love because "to love spiritually gives us more objectivity and allows us to see within the person and not just respond to what they present. When we detach ourselves from the person, then we view them so superficially that we cannot honestly serve them" (Hall 2005, 26). Although this may feel alien to some mediators, it is worth noting that this attempt to ground work in something beyond our own immediate reactions is similar to what Bowling demonstrates in his chapter on mindfulness (see Chapter 3), which is not necessarily either religious or rooted in a particular conception of love.

Hall also argues that it is important for lawyers to care for and value themselves, saying that a failure to do so makes it easy to "overwork and adopt negative coping mechanisms" (2005, 31), which is a risk in our profession as well. He argues that authentic practice springs from a deep engagement with, and an ability to "articulate and commit" to (2005, 33), the deepest meaning in our lives. Hall thinks this engagement translates into more fulfilling work as well, a life rooted in purpose:

> Faith, in its deepest and most meaningful sense, involves a sincere . . . belief in the ultimate goodness within the universe and people. . . . For lawyers it means a rejection of the cynicism that pervades the profession, and the resurrection of our individual responsibility to change the situations we encounter. To have faith in our clients' ability to benefit from their interactions with us cannot be determined by whether they win or lose. We must begin to believe in them as much as we believe in their case . . . to have this level of faith requires that we bring more of ourselves to the process, and that we transform sterile business encounters into life affirming relationships. (Hall 2005, 41)

Hall argues that his own spiritual rootedness both helps him be a better, more ethical lawyer and reconnects him to the values that make the law a tool for justice in society.

I believe that the best, most transformative work we do can often be connected to our self-development and self-awareness. That includes the ability to attend to our emotional intelligence, the signals being sent by our fast-thinking, experience-based intuition, which is often a *felt-sense* in the body long before it is a formed thought, calibrated through our analytic and reasoning capacities, and transferred through our presence in a way that can allow us to touch that in ourselves and the parties that allows us to transcend our context—that is transcendent. We need to stop looking away from and start looking *at* all these multiple engines and calibrators of deep understanding, insight, and response. We have remarkable resources and models in this field of creative, compassionate, insightful, intuitive, powerful, transformative work. Other disciplines and fields have begun to integrate spirituality and multiple intelligences, and our own interveners in their practice are doing so as well, which the practitioner chapters showcase. However, the field has not yet documented this kind of work being done in other fields, connecting it to our own, nor have we documented our own advances. This book begins to document that work.

A Few Words, or Definitions

This section explains some of the words used, as well as how I have framed them for myself and the authors of this book (although the other authors were free to use whatever words they wanted). First, I want to explain briefly why so much of the book focuses on one aspect of multidimensional work. To begin with, the history of our Western relationship with faith has marginalized the topic in some extraordinary ways, rendering it a "voice" very hard to hear as legitimate, as mentioned in the previous sections. Faith traditions have supported alternative knowledge systems in a way that Enlightenment thinking has rejected, which is one reason I focus on them here, although the divide persists. Much of the book also focuses on what I am calling spiritual or transcendent intelligence because faith traditions serve as one of the mechanisms for transferring an integrated sense of meaning, from one generation to another, that accesses multiple intelligences and attempts to help us create an integrated sense of self.

Some of the practitioner authors (Bowling and Sipes) refer explicitly to a self-identified faith tradition that they draw on to transform their practice, while others (Lederach et al., Morelli and Fitz, Meeker, and Diamond) do not. Some of the latter, in fact, identify with and are shaped by their faith traditions but chose to be obscure in their references in order to support readers to take the work in whatever direction is best for them. For still others, spiritual intelligence is not the most transformative resource for them, and they model multidimensional practice in other ways. From the standpoint of the mission of this book, it is less important, for instance, to know if Daniel Bowling is a Buddhist than to know that his chapter models how a practitioner intentionally develops methods to work with and respect multiple capacities in ways that can change him as a practitioner and the quality of his work.

I do not use the word "religion" in this book (although some of the practitioners do) for several reasons, the first of which deals with ways that word could confuse or mislead readers who might be working with different literatures. The word "religion" combined with "conflict" immediately conjures up the conversation in the field about religious terrorism and violence (remember my elevator conversations?), which is not what I am focusing on. The word "religion" is also being hotly contested in theological circles as actually referring to forms of worship modeled after the Abrahamic religions.[3] This argument tends to marginalize non-Western faiths in a way that is completely inappropriate for this book, and could also derail readers into focusing on other topics.

The third reason is to avoid confusing the focus of the book with the excellent work that has been done in faith-based diplomacy, which has helped shape my thinking, but is not what this book is about.

I have chosen to use the word "spirituality" and refer to "faith traditions," both of which connect more congruently with the focus on multiple intelligences and multidimensional work. For those who seek them, here are definitions that informed my thinking about the differences between religion and spirituality. "In general, religion involves the allegiance of an individual to the specific beliefs and practices of a group or social institution, whereas spirituality is the personal, subjective experience of the divine" (Abernethy et al. 2006; Frasier and Hansen 2009, 81). I would add to those definitions something of transcendence, reaching for or inspired by things that are bigger than one's self, "transcending one's locus of centricity," in Hall's words (2005, 20) This is a goal not only for theists, as Carrie Menkel-Meadow argues, but also for secular humanists (2001).

Emmonds connects spirituality, which he feels is about "an ultimate concern," to the way humans make and pursue goals:

> One of the functions of a religious belief system and a religious world view is that it provides "an ultimate vision of what people should be striving for in their lives . . . as providing a guide to "the most serious and far-ranging goals there can possibly be. . . . Spiritual strivings, then, as personal goals focused on the sacred, become the way in which ultimate concerns are encountered in people's lives. Ultimate concerns are bridges linking motivation, spirituality, and intelligence." (2000, 4)

Another set of important terms involves the concept of multiple intelligences. Blancke and I use the concept of multiple intelligences in our framework for considering how to be multidimensional practitioners, which is introduced in Chapter 2. As such, I thought it would also be helpful to briefly define the intelligences we refer to in this section of the book. Gardner (2011) defines intelligence as " . . . basic information-processing operations or mechanisms which can deal with specific kinds of input" (68). These are related to specific parts of the brain, develop in skill from novice to expertise, and respond to a particular environment to produce, in Gardner' view, "forms of memory, attention, or perception" (2011, 70) that respond to specific kinds of stimulus. They are also developed in human communication through a symbol system like language (Gardner 2011, 71).

Gardner is credited as one of the first to explore the concept that there are multiple forms of intelligence. Blancke and I draw on this concept of multiple intelligences to get at the concept of multidimensionality in conflict resolution practice. It is, more than anything, a metaphor for that, as we expect that wholeness and integration of capacities includes things beyond intelligence, however defined. Still, it does help us begin to explore what it would look like to consciously bring more parts of ourselves to bear in our work. Most readers, I assume, have some familiarity with cognitive intelligence, so I will not go too deeply into that, but I will briefly explain how we use the terms *spiritual* and *emotional intelligences*. Somatic intelligence is discussed in depth in Chapter 5.

Emmonds argues that spiritual intelligence is indeed a form of intelligence as defined by Gardner because, among other reasons, it functions as a diagnostic and analytic tool in problem solving "where problem solving is defined with respect to practical goal attainment and some sort of positive developmental outcome" (2000, 5). Gardner was uncomfortable with the concept, finding it controversial, and toyed with a concept of *existential intelligence*, relating to a "capacity to locate oneself with respect to such existential features of the human condition as the significance of life, the meaning of death, the ultimate fact of the physical and psychological worlds, and such profound experiences as love of another" (Sisk 2002).

In this book I also use the term *transcendent* to refer to that which gets us beyond our own limitations; something implicit in our capacity to transcend our circumstances and limitations. Sisk hypothesizes that this form of intelligence would include skills such as an ability to access a sense of higher knowing or connectedness with something beyond ourselves, intuition, a sense of relationship with other humans and the natural environment, and, as Emmonds did, problem solving (2002). In fact, a better term might be *transcendent intelligence*, but I largely use *spiritual intelligence* as this is becoming more a widely recognized term.

Other aspects of definitions of spiritual intelligence include Vaughan (2002) and Zohar and Marshall's (2000) version:

> Vaughan's (2002) model [has] components [including]: (a) power to form a meaning that is rooted on a profound knowledge of existential questions; (b) responsiveness in the utilization of multiple consciousness levels aimed to properly address the problems; (c) attentiveness regarding the interconnection of each individual as well as to the transcendent. Zohar and Marshall (2000) have defined [it] as coping with/handling, and answering, problems of meaning and value. It has also been referred to as an intelligence in which people can survive and take actions in a broader, richer, meaningful context. (Hosseini et al. 2010, 182–183)

I also want to briefly touch on emotional intelligence. Joy Meeker's chapter deals with emotions in depth, but it may also be useful here to briefly reference Goleman's (1995 and 2006) concept of emotional intelligence, which builds on Gardner's concepts of multiple intelligences. Emotional intelligence involves awareness of one's own and other's emotions, and the capacity to manage those emotions well personally and in relationships. Those capacities have turned out to play a larger role in success rates in the workplace than cognitive intelligence or expertise (Goleman 2006). Emotional intelligence includes a number of skills and competencies, which Goleman feels can be learned and developed consciously. They include competency in various aspects of emotional self-awareness, self-management, social awareness, and social skills.

Overview of the Book

I finish here with an overview of the content of the book. Chapters 1 and 2 introduce the larger goals and rationale for the book and explain some key terminology and frameworks that shape the overall goal Blancke and I set out to accomplish by developing the multidimensional framework. Chapter 1 sets the tone and makes the overall case, including a brief review of my research on how psychology and law are engaging similar issues. It also includes some definitions of key terms and reviews the overall content of the book. Chapter 2 details the larger arguments of the book in more depth as well as explains the concept of multidimensional work and presents the multidimensional practice framework. The framework provides a way to consider wholeness in practice using the idea of multiple intelligences and intervention as a form of change-making ritual. Blancke and I use the framework for thinking through what multidimensional practice might look like and use it to compare classic mediation with a traditional Hawaiian conflict resolution process called Ho'oponopono, which actively engages the spiritual understanding of the parties. The chapter also includes practice examples from interviews with Louise Diamond and Kenneth Cloke, showing how excellent practitioners incorporate faith and spirituality into their conflict resolution processes while protecting and enhancing the self-determination of parties.

Chapters 3, 4, 5, 6, 7, and 8 contain the practitioner chapters, which start the work of documenting this kind of practice as it is now being developed. Chapters 3 through 6 include the work of scholars-practitioners who present practical theories and case examples showing how they are working with wholeness and presence. Chapters 7 and 8 are focused specifically on how to train and teach multidimensional practice. These chapters present diverse examples of how practitioners' spirituality, emotional intelligence, and somatic intelligence transform their practice. I asked these chapter writers to describe their work in concrete as well as poignant language, and to go beyond describing a technique to talking about how it works, when it works, and when it does not. The practitioner chapters cover a wide spectrum of practice—we have seasoned masters of the field like John Paul Lederach, Louise Diamond, and Daniel Bowling, and new leaders, like Myla Leguro, Kathryn Mansfield, Laura Taylor, Maria Zapata, and M. Brandon Sipes. They include a chapter by a theologian (Sipes) and explorations by those pushing us to engage the field in deeper and new ways like Meeker, Morelli, and Fitz. I will briefly introduce the focus of each one.

Chapter 3, by Daniel Bowling, reviews several key aspects of Buddhist thinking, including the Four Noble Truths, as ways to train the mind. Bowling shows how he achieved, and lost, mindfulness in ways that affected a conflict in his own practice, leading the reader through the application and value of mindful techniques in a detailed example the reader can use to reflect on his/her own practice. Chapter 4 is from theologian M. Brandon Sipes. He reflects on three Christian concepts: repentance, forgiveness, and the new creation, or the hope of a better future, which motivate and support him in his work in the Middle East using the Kumi method (Brashear et al. 2012), which focuses on structural change as well as conflict transformation. In Chapter 5, Julia Morelli and Christopher Fitz describe a complex dynamic between physiological actions and reactions to conflict, and dispute resolution processes. They argue a need for increased somatic intelligence for practitioners and review three areas of useful application: mind-body practices like meditation and yoga, somatic approaches (awareness of embodied responses) used in psychology and coaching, and creative arts, including applied theater. Joy Meeker reflects on and develops an understanding of emotionally intelligent conflict resolution work in Chapter 6. She argues that emotions can create a gap between current realities and preferred realities—creating a liminal *space-in-between*, "an uncomfortable place full of the potential of personal and social transformation." Using a story from her conflict practice, she demonstrates how staying with emotions deepens the socially just and personally transformative potential of our work.

Chapters 7 and 8 build on the examples of practitioners who are doing nuanced, multidimensional work to ask: How do we train and educate multidimensional peacebuilders and practitioners? What kind of education do we need to support the development of this kind of practice? I feel privileged to include in this section the insights of extraordinary leaders who have shaped the field: John Paul Lederach and Louise Diamond. John Paul Lederach et al.'s Chapter 7 shares insights from the results of a pilot program at three institutions, including the Kroc Institute at the University of Notre Dame, that are designed to "nurture the rise of peacebuilders with sustaining, transformative presence capable of making a constructive difference in violence habituated systems." In this apprenticeship-focused program, four trainees worked with Lederach, and their reflections are part of the chapter. His work focused on supporting transformational development through walking and talking in depth with his apprentices about their vocational calling, and engaging creativity and profound reflection through poetic listening. The results were deep and transformative for all parties and point to a very different kind of educational relationship and set of goals. Louise Diamond, in Chapter 8, describes three key principles she believes define the *inner spirit* of peacemaking and their implications for the kind of training that practitioners need in order to do deeper, whole, transformative work. For her, peacebuilding and transformation is, inherently, a spiritual process, and the presence of the practitioner a transformative resource. She relates her deep principles to practice stories from her extensive and diverse practice and explains what she did to embody peace in her presence in ways that transformed the conflicts.

Brian Blancke concludes the book, using our framework to reflect on the body of work represented in the book as a whole and to suggest some generalizable conclusions and applications, offering some synthesis that we hope will advance the field in this area. The reflections suggest real insights and potential in this kind of work and draw the diversity of work here into coherence of lessons learned.

My goal in this book has been to wrestle with and attempt to begin to document and share some of what the field has referred to as artistry and mastery and presence—the work beyond skills, techniques, and process—specifically, to begin to consciously develop and use our multiple capacities, including our capacity to access the transcendent. For many practitioners, what allows us to develop this kind of meaningful presence is to use our faith traditions and spirituality to draw on something larger than ourselves. I hope this book begins to chronicle not just what but how we draw on this and also somatic and emotional intelligences. Lederach and Diamond go further, discussing how we train and educate for this kind of mediator development. All of us involved in this project understand that we are at the beginning of a conversation that will far exceed this book, and that what creates the artistry, the mastery, the leap-beyond, is complex, multifaceted, and beyond the scope of any one book or set of theorists and practitioners. However, my hope is that this will start a conversation in the field that will make space for multi-dimensional consideration of the complex, nuanced, and transcendent nature of what we do best. I am deeply grateful for the opportunity to have taken this journey with the extraordinary leaders represented in this book and those who read this and make the new paths that lead to our multidimensional future.

Notes

1. This section and others in this chapter were originally published in *Conflict Resolution Quarterly* 28 (4) (2011): 377–398, and they are reprinted with permission from John Wiley and Sons (license number 2951891021836).

2. For instance, see examples portrayed by Christian parties in the documentary *As We Forgive*, Laura Walters Hinson (2009), Mpower Pictures.

3. For an example see Daniel Dubuisson (2007).

2

A Possible Framework
for Multidimensional Practice

Rachel M. Goldberg and Brian Blancke

BUILDING ON CHAPTER 1, THIS CHAPTER GOES INTO MORE DEPTH setting up the academic background and argument for multidimensional practice. The discussion also delves more deeply into the importance of how we bring ourselves to the table as interveners, and what it would look like to create practice that supported bringing more of ourselves (rather than less) into our work. It asks what it would look like to bring something of wisdom, or Lederach's "below and beyond" (Chapter 7), into our processes. The chapter presents a framework for thinking through what multidimensional practice can look like and uses that framework to compare classic mediation with a traditional Hawaiian conflict resolution process called Ho'oponopono, which actively engages the spiritual understanding of the parties. We ground the discussion in practice examples from the authors and conclude by presenting extraordinary practitioners who are already bringing their whole selves to bear in a way that is extremely respectful of the self-determination of the parties.

What's the Problem? What Happens
When We Leave Part of Ourselves Behind

We began to address the risks of cutting parts of ourselves off in Chapter 1. Here we develop that further. What happens when we enact cognitive orientations so strongly that we prevent parties from prioritizing emotional or even spiritual understanding? What happens to self-determination if we are afraid to listen to our whole selves, or if we ask parties to ignore or dismiss part of their realities? There is significant evidence that we run the risk of shutting down or delegitimizing parties' experiences in a way that seriously undermines self-determination (Gunning 1995; Cobb 1993; Wing 2008, 2009; Goldberg 2009; Rack 2000). Rack revealed that good mediators (who were Anglo in this instance), despite being as neutral as they could, still disenfranchised Latino parties through failing to understand key aspects of the culture of the participants. In this case, as in the church case below, neither a stance of neutrality nor a process designed to be unbiased was sufficient to support party self-determination.

In order to examine what we think is missing in current practice, we present two examples from Brian Blancke's research and practice. The first describes the work of a dedicated intervener who used his skills to influence a conflict toward reason and resolution. Unfortunately, his efforts were not successful. Although there may have been many contextual and case-specific reasons for the eventual failure, we think there are several instructive questions that can be raised about this intervention.

In December 1998, the Oneida Indian Nation, after more than a decade of negotiation on their land claim (to 250,000 acres of upstate New York land) and frustrated by a lack of any clear progress, moved to amend its twenty-five-year lawsuit to include the 20,000 nonnative property owners in the claim area. This meant they were actively challenging the rights of those individuals to own the land in question (which included homes and businesses) in order to increase pressure on the state to negotiate a settlement. This, not surprisingly, escalated the conflict significantly. At the same time, the judge in the case appointed a new settlement master for the negotiations—Dean Ronald Riccio of Seton Hall Law School—in an attempt to (yet again) settle the Oneida claim (Blancke and Wulff 2002). Dean Riccio met with the litigation parties— the state of New York, the federal government, Madison and Oneida counties, and the Oneidas—and announced that within four months a draft agreement would be reached. But that did not happen, in part because of angry citizen resistance to the settlement talks. Dean Riccio held public meetings to discuss the land claim and the status of the negotiations and to involve area citizens in the settlement process. But, as the citizens had been excluded from most previous negotiation attempts, this process was dismissed as a public relations gimmick by the local property owners' association, Upstate Citizens for Equality, and the situation continued to deteriorate. Anonymous death threats were made against

Oneidas and anyone who patronized Oneida businesses. Luckily, the threats were never acted upon (Blancke and Wulff 2002).

A few months later, Dean Riccio, clearly frustrated, wrote an angry progress report to the judge, circulating it among the parties prior to sending it, in order to push them toward settlement. Here are some of the key parts of the report:

> Although I have no doubt all the parties have negotiated in good faith, the settlement talks have been sidetracked by rhetoric, posturing, bickering, and maneuvering. For example, one party recently explained a complete reversal of a long held position on a crucial settlement issue by saying, "that was then and this is now." Such arbitrary responses are neither helpful nor indicative of a significant commitment to the settlement process . . . The settlement talks have been more like oral arguments in court than efforts to amicably resolve outstanding conflicts. Further, most parties have not been willing to subordinate their own self-interest to the overriding interest of the innocent Oneida and non-Oneida members of the public who are daily suffering fear and anxiety as a result of the pendency of this litigation . . . there are literally thousands of totally innocent Oneida and Non-Oneida alike who . . . deserve a better outcome than this. I am sorely disappointed the parties during the settlement process have not appeared to be as concerned about [the effected] innocent persons as they should have been. . . . I remain willing to assist the Court and the parties whatever way I can. But I believe the process is at an impasse. (Riccio 2000, 2, 4)

Any mediator could sympathize with Riccio's frustration. However, he was, in essence, accusing the parties of being childish, arbitrary, oblivious to the cost of the conflict to their relative communities, and insincere. He used his power to threaten to declare an impasse as a tactic to force the parties into making concessions, but this failed to move them and the mediation was terminated.

What troubles us about this was that it was an attempt to move the parties toward settlement by threatening and shaming them. We were left with the following questions: When we use our intellectual techniques, such as agent of reality, what is the intent of doing so, and what is the impact? Is there something missing in our practice that might have made better sense of this situation and, perhaps, elicited a better response from the parties?

The parties' opposition to a settlement was rooted in anger and fear, and distrust about what a settlement meant for both local property owners and the tribe members. We think some of the dimensions missing from this mediator's approach are the emotional and spiritual realities of the parties. This tactic on his part, we feel, shows a failure to understand the heart of the matter for either side. The mediator in this case drew largely on cognitive skills and addressed the intellectual dimension of the conflict through agent of reality or case evaluation tactics. The basic premise was that the parties were being irrational and needed to "see reason." However, using the threats and eliciting a fear of not settling as a strategy to overcome the fear of settling (which existed largely in an emotional dimension) was unsuccessful. We think the intervener might have failed to think about the likely emotional impact of this kind of tactic in this emotional context. We also found ourselves wondering if there was a way to use or elicit compassion to motivate these parties to change or reexamine their positions. Would this case have developed differently if the mediator had engaged greater emotional intelligence and empathy, and shown greater respect for the spiritual and emotional needs of the parties?

Even if the settlement master had been successful with this ploy and the parties had reached a settlement, how would he have overcome the public's anger and fear to implement the solution in a way that created a sustainable resolution? The Navajo have an expression, "You can't get to a good place in a bad way, ever."[1] Albert Einstein echoed this when he said, "We can't solve problems by using the same kind of thinking we used when we created them" (Harris 1995). For the Navajo, conflict is a symptom that things are out of place or in dissonance, and the goal is to return the individual and the community to a state of harmony (Brown 2002). Many traditional, indigenous conflict resolution methods work within multiple dimensions of understanding to accomplish this, moving beyond pure reason to engage emotional, somatic, and spiritual needs (LeResche 1993).

As mediators, we are equipped with all sorts of cognitive tools and techniques to help parties in conflict to settle their dispute. But how attentive are we to *how* we use these tools and techniques to motivate disputants, in terms of the intent that shapes the actions we take? As Crumb notes, "We begin to understand that all people are operating out of one of two modes: fear or love. Actions [including the mediator's] that are injurious or create disharmony and distress result from fear—from a contracted mind that is limited in its ability to see alternatives" (1987, 215). In fact, research has shown that evoking fear in parties, because of the way the brain processes this emotion, causes "egocentric and mal-adaptive patterns of reactions to situations that require creative and novel solutions for coping" (Jarymowicz and Bar-Tal 2006, 372).

To connect this to the example, consider when Dean Riccio used the strategy of agent of reality. Did he do so from an intention of threatening the parties and shaming them, which would evoke fear and resistance, or from compassion, which can open the mind to a transformational shift? Certainly, fear has not settled the Oneida land claim.

Nor do we think that this is an isolated incident. In fact, we have struggled with the same issues ourselves. For instance, both of us do conflict resolution with religious congregations, and in the following case example the issue of fear (and spirituality) came up again. After conducting eighteen to twenty individual hour-long intake sessions to assess the issues and willingness to mediate a divided congregation, Blancke scheduled a large group mediation. He and his comediator opened with the standard introductory remarks when one of the parties interrupted them. That party wanted to offer a prayer to start the mediation. The two mediators exchanged glances and Blancke thought, "Oh, G#d no. They will use it to attack the other side!" He could tell that his comediator felt the same way, and they replied, "Why don't we stick with the process as we discussed it during the intake session, and everyone will have a chance to speak?" Then another party, from the other side of the dispute, chimed in: "We would like to offer a prayer, too, and if we can't, we won't continue." Facing the prospect of dueling prayers (and starting the mediation out on a negative note), the mediators looked at each other, and Blancke crossed his fingers, hunched his shoulders, and said ok. They were very pleasantly surprised and relieved when both sides offered a genuine prayer. The mediation got off to a great start as a result. But in that moment before, the mediators were acting out of fear, attempting to take control to prevent the parties from offering heartfelt prayers. The mediators were trying to create a safe space where no one would be attacked, but they ended up seizing control and shutting down what the parties wanted to do (which was to bring their spiritual intelligence to the table)—until there was a revolt. What happens to the process when mediators act out of fear? What happens when mediators use fear to motivate parties (as in the Oneida dispute)?

To us, the issue of intention, or looking at it another way, emotional orientation is not a naïve platitude, but essential. To quote Martin Luther King Jr., "Upheaval after upheaval has reminded us that modern man is traveling along a road called hate. Far from being the pious injunction of a Utopian dreamer, the command to love one's enemy is an absolute necessity for survival" (1981, 3). He goes on to say, "Returning hate for hate multiplies hate, adding deeper darkness to a night already devoid of stars. Darkness cannot drive out darkness; only light can do that. Hate cannot drive out hate; only love can do that" (7). In the Oneida example, we wonder if a process that aimed at eliciting compassion from parties might have had more success than one designed to move them through fear, adding to their already present fears, or one motivated by our own fears, as we saw with the congregation and the opening prayers.

Wholeness

The discussion so far highlights two problems with current conflict resolution practice. Something is missing that we want—wisdom, love? And we are drawing on something we don't want—threats and fear, intimidation. Why is this happening? As we mentioned in the previous chapter, we feel this may go back to the ancient division of logos and mythos that was the beginning of a long journey separating mind and body, thought and emotion, intuition, religion, values, and facts, into superior and inferior substances. Maybe the crack we feel in our own work comes from this ancient splitting. We also wanted to examine our belief that something is missing. Janell Hale worked with us for this chapter and created Table 2.1 by surveying key skills from two "bibles" of the field, Moore's *Mediation Process* (2003) and Kaner's *Facilitator's Guide to Participatory Decision Making* (2007). As the table shows, although relatively strong in cognitive and emotional components, they are relatively weak on somatic and spiritual ones. While far from exhaustive, even in terms of the full list of skills in each book, the table is suggestive that maybe the field is weak in these areas.

Does this really matter in practice? To connect this back to the Oneida example, we think one possible explanation for the failure of

Table 2.1 Key Skills Distribution—Are We Missing Something?

Skill	Cognitive	Emotional	Somatic	Spiritual
Active Listening[a]	An exact statement or paraphrase of what the member said	Focuses on the emotional content of the message		
Brainstorming[b]	Ideas are listed without discussion or evaluation	Members suspend judgment, creativity is valued		
Building Relationships[b]	Creates context for members to overcome their differences and find common ground	Reduces isolation		
Caucuses[a]	Members are separated from each other and direct communication is restricted		Physical separation changes the dynamic of the conversation	

(continues)

Table 2.1 continued

Skill	Cognitive	Emotional	Somatic	Spiritual
Empowerment[a]	Mediators can work to minimize the negative effects of unequal distribution of power between parties			
Humor[a]		Can allow members to vent while limiting the negative effects of anger		
Mirroring[b]	Highly structured, the facilitator repeats the speaker's words verbatim	Builds trust	Imitates the posture and positioning of the speaker	
Naming Feelings[b]		Helps members and the group identify what they are feeling		
Open-ended Questions[b]	Helps members clarify, develop, and refine their ideas	Helps the speaker feel understood		
Paraphrasing[b]	Demonstrates to a speaker that his or her thoughts were heard and understood	Is nonjudgmental and validating; people feel that their ideas are respected and legitimated.		
Reflection[b]	Gives members a chance to collect their thoughts	Allows time to regain control over emotions		Members may use this time to connect spiritually
Reframing[b]	Identifies core assumptions and deliberately replaces or reverses them in order to gain an alternative perspective	Involves a significant change in outlook		
Roleplays[b]	Allows for rough-draft thinking	Allows members to express feelings in a nonthreatening manner	Involves the body in assuming a new character	
Stacking[b]	Creates a sequence so that all who want to speak have an opportunity	Members know their input is valued and that they will have a turn to speak		

Notes: a. These concepts are from Moore's *Mediation Process* (2003).
b. These are taken from Kaner's *Facilitator's Guide to Participatory Decision-Making* (2007).

Riccio's ploy is that he drew his solution exclusively from one aspect of human experience and understood the case from that single dimension. He seems, like so many of us are taught, to have assumed emotions were a distraction and not relevant to the settlement of the case, and seems to have underestimated the Oneida's spiritual commitment to the land and the nonnative parties' emotional commitment to their homes. He asked, in essence, "Why can't these people just be rational (and compromise)?" We believe that was the wrong question.

But, if rationality and objectivity don't lead where we want to go, what does? What orientation would lead a mediator to understand more deeply the experience of the parties? Martin Luther King Jr. suggested "*agape*, understanding and creative, redemptive goodwill for all men" (King 1981, 6, emphasis in original). His key message in the sermon on Loving Your Enemies was that we are all abused and abusers, and that there is no way to heal except through love. He said, "Every word and deed must contribute to an understanding with the enemy and release those vast reservoirs of goodwill which have been blocked by impenetrable walls of hate" (King 1981, 6). What would it be like to put logos and mythos back together, to practice more holistically, and to root work in love? The goal of this chapter is to begin to think about how to access multiple dimensions of knowledge, or wisdom, in a way that uses our whole selves and seeks to engage the four dimensions (somatic, emotional, cognitive, and spiritual understanding) in our work.

These are not unexplored ideas, by any means. LeBaron (2003), Kelly (2000), Cloke (2006), Diamond (2004), Bowling and Hoffman (2003), and Riskin (2002) have all been working with these concepts in various ways. Mary Clark hypothesized that, in addition to the basic human needs listed by authors like Burton, there was a basic human need for what she called sacred meaning (Clark 1993). Erica Ariel Fox, through the Global Negotiation Insight Institute (GNII), has been exploring "what mindfulness and the great wisdom traditions have to teach us in the negotiation and dispute resolution field" (Harvard Law Bulletin 2004, 5). Many in the field are trying to put wisdom (the original Logos) back into conflict resolution. Kenneth Cloke and Louise Diamond, who we interviewed for this chapter, and the other authors in this book are only a few of the practitioners who are already doing multidimensional work.

Wisdom and Working in All Four Dimensions

We want to build on the wonderful work being done by these practitioners and scholars and others, and begin to think about what it might look like to design and work with logos and mythos, with wisdom and love intentionally, and in all four dimensions of human knowledge: somatic, emotional, cognitive, and spiritual. One way to begin to look at this is to learn from other cultures' intervention processes and approaches. Several, including many indigenous, traditional, have long had conflict resolution models that integrate multiple intelligences. Diane LeResche said, concerning Native American perspectives on peacemaking:

> At its core, Native American peacemaking is inherently spiritual; it speaks to the connectedness of all things; it focuses on unity, on harmony, on balancing the spiritual, intellectual, and physical dimensions of a community of people. A peacemaking process tends to be viewed as a "guiding process," a relationship healing journey . . . it brings peace through good feelings, not through fear. Peacemaking involves deep listening, not defending, arguing, forcing. (LeResche 1993, 321)

She goes on to discuss the concept of *sacred justice:*

> Peacemaking is generally not as concerned with distributive justice or "rough-and-wild justice" (revenge, punishment, control, determining who is right) as it is with "sacred justice." Sacred justice is that way of handling disagreements that helps mend relationships and provides healing solutions . . . it involves going to the heart. It includes speaking from the heart, from one's feelings . . . It is helping them reconnect with the higher spirits, or seeing the conflict in relation to the higher purposes." (LeResche 1993, 322)

We have created a framework to challenge ourselves and the field to start considering "the bones" of a new model that engages all four dimensions, as indigenous peacemaking often does, that could be adapted to various traditions and cases. In an attempt to map out how this can be done (and to expand our awareness of what the field is already doing), we looked at the universal facets and functions of third-party intervention as defined by John Paul Lederach (1995) and connected them to the concept of wisdom, which we define as learning and understanding your situation using many aspects of human knowing, with openness and humility.

Lederach details a number of components of any third-party intervention: entry ("who will emerge as an acceptable third party and how the process and forum for dealing with conflict will be constructed"), gathering perspectives ("what happened?"), locating the conflict ("the process of attaching meaning to events and people's actions and situating what the conflict is about in order to know how to deal with it"), arranging and negotiating ("how do we get out" of this problem?), and finding a way out and agreement ("who will do what, when?") (Lederach 1995, 93–95). We also explore how and when we use cognitive, emotional, somatic, and spiritual intelligences with each of these components. But there is more to wisdom than just employing our various intelligences at each stage. The larger question is: What are we trying to accomplish in mediation by doing so?

Sara Cobb, in her groundbreaking article on empowerment, hypothesized that what we can best accomplish as mediators, in terms of how to empower parties, is to help them destabilize their conflict narratives enough to allow a change in how they see themselves, each other, and the problem (Cobb 1993). We see this as essentially what mediation can do—we help parties unmake the status quo. They come to us because they feel trapped in their sense of the way things are in a way that allows no resolution or forward motion. We help them unmake that reality and make a new one, and reintegrate it into their lives, supporting them to engage Lederach's *moral imagination* (2005) or the kind of leap-beyond transitions discussed in Chapter 1. In short, we help them move through the separation, transition, and incorporation stages of a ritual of change. Davidheiser (2006) synthesizes the insights of Turner (1969) and Van Gennep (1960) in describing these stages of ritual and applies them to mediation. What makes that change possible? The liminality of the ritual space. As Davidheiser says, "The efficacy of much third party peacemaking or mediation is linked to the creation of a special social space in which the conventions and scripts of everyday life are loosened, enabling personal and social transformation" (2006). He uses Nordstrom's example of Mozambicans' use of rituals to reintegrate veterans into society after war. Powerfully, in that example, violence is seen not as a fixed entity or truth but as a "social, political, and cultural construction" (Davidheiser 2006). This means, of course, that even as we make soldiers, violence, and war through ritual, (for instance, through military boot camp and hazing), we can similarly unmake them, or transition from a culture of war to one of peace.

Turner and Van Gennep describe rituals as having three parts: separation, transition, and incorporation. Separation is the movement from regular life to the sacred and is a way of marking the beginning of the ritual. Davidheiser says that "transition represents what scholars term a 'liminal state', [or] a special social space in which the usual customs and conventions do not apply. . . . the liminal state [is] 'anti-structure,' or the relaxation of the mores and rules of everyday social structure" (2006, 1). He argues that this liminal space is what rituals are created for and how they allow change. Nan (2011) makes the same point about how conflict resolution processes can help support shifts in consciousness, and Schirch has written extensively about the power of ritual and in her latest article also talks about Mozambique (2015). Incorporation is the point where changes are reintegrated into normal life, and participants are returned to day-to-day living. These stages are often what we experience when a mediation goes really well, when something powerful and apparently magical happens, and a long-standing conflict is dissolved—the transformation discussed in Chapter 1.

Example: Ho'oponopono

What might multidimensional practice look like—one that deliberately moves through separation, transition, and incorporation? We decided the best way to understand this would be to find an example of a conflict resolution process already working in all multiple dimensions. One particularly interesting example, for our purposes, is the traditional Hawaiian conflict resolution process of Ho'oponopono, which demonstrates a number of the issues we want to engage here and helps show how these ideas can be translated into our conflict resolution process.[2] We do want to note that we are not making a claim that all conflict resolvers should now incorporate aspects of Ho'oponopono, or that it is necessarily a superior process. We only wanted to show one way that a process can be designed to incorporate different dimensions, demonstrating, at least, that such a thing is possible, and, at most, a model that could inspire new thinking in our practices.

Ho'oponopono is a traditional Hawaiian conflict resolution process that has been used by the United Nations Educational, Scientific, and Cultural Organization (UNESCO), the World Health Organization (WHO), the Hawaii State Teachers Association, and various healing institutions all over the world (King 1989; Shook 2000; Saunders n.d.). Ho'oponopono means "setting to right" (Shook 2000, 1) and is rooted in traditional Hawaiian belief "in a universe that operates on principles of harmonious relationships" (6). The goal of the process is thus to restore harmony and make things right with yourself, your ancestors, and the people with whom you have relationships (What is Huna: Basic Huna, Ho'oponopono 2006; King 1989). The focus is on repairing the family and relationships, not on compromise (Merry 1987). Moreover, "Ho'oponopono 'is getting the family together to find out what is wrong. . . . Then, with discussion and repentance and restitution and forgiveness—and always with prayer—to set right what was wrong'" (Pukui et al. 1971; Hurdle 2002). The focus of the process is internal, seeking self-knowledge and change for all, including the intervener (King 1989; Saunders n.d.; Hew Len and Brown 1999).

The process includes a *pule*, or opening prayer, a statement of the problem, "self-scrutiny and discussion of individual conduct, attitudes and emotions, absolute truthfulness and sincerity . . . honest confession to the gods (or God), and to each other of wrong-doing, grievances, grudges and resentments," discussion, and also *kúkulu kumuhana*, where the problem is identified and the strength of the group is brought together for a shared purpose, until all aspects of the matter have been revealed. Then parties engage in some form of restitution, mutual forgiveness, and a closing prayer (Pukui et al. 1971; Shook 2000). The process is led by a kahuna *lapa'au* (a healer) or a family senior, and when emotions are negative, that person directs that all questions be channeled through them. They nearly always also call for cooling-off periods of silence called *ho'omalu*, which can serve to "calm tempers, encourage self-inquiry" or give participants a chance to rest (Pukui et al. 1971; Shook 2000).

Many of the basic premises are counterintuitive for North American mediators. The intervener is known by all parties—an *insider-partial* (Lederach 1986)—and frames the goal as "to set things right with each other and the Almighty" or ancestor gods (Pukui et al. 1971). They are seen as able to transform the relationships through a connection to "that original Source" (Hew Len and Brown 1999). The work also focuses on forgiveness and is premised on the belief that the job of the intervener is not one of accepting a case but of being drawn to a problem created by the intervener now or in their soul's past. The spiritual focus includes framing the work with the opening prayer, or *pule,* that is seen as laying the foundation for the sincerity and truthfulness of the work (Shook 2000). This is one way that Ho'oponopono integrates emotional and spiritual intelligence. Despite how counterintuitive this process is for many North American mediators, it is very effective. For instance, Stanley Hew Len spent several years as a consulting clinical psychologist at the Hawaii State Hospital and achieved profound results by using this process with the most violent and dangerous criminals in Hawaii (King 1989).

Ho'oponopono, like classic mediation, can allow parties to unmake destructive conflict through ritual. As argued earlier, through emotion, ritual, myth (think of propaganda), and action, we make war, violence, pain, and destruction. It makes sense that unmaking them takes more than logic, assessment, and analysis. Haleakala Hew Len says of Ho'oponopono that you need to get the intellect out of the way to hear the Divinity (King 1989). Maybe, at least, mediators need to be able to hear their hearts as well as their minds to help parties unmake and make anew in multiple dimensions.

As practitioners, we often struggle to help parties see that change is possible. One way might be the creation of a new kind of space where change is supported—that liminal space that destabilizes conflict narratives and unmakes current reality. That leaves us with two questions: How can that space be created, and what is possible within it? We do want to acknowledge that in some ways classic mediation already creates a transformational space, and the mediator leads those involved to unmake and make anew their relationships and understandings. Here we are pursuing two goals: (1) to understand what we already do well more deeply and, (2) to learn how to consciously engage multidimensional practice. Practitioners of Ho'oponopono say that how you approach things, who you are in the moment, and how you live your life is key to what you can do in the work. This seems to directly connect to the larger conversation about mediator presence noted in Chapter 1.

Practitioners of Ho'oponopono say one key is the separation, how you enter into the antistructure or liminal space. Setting the right intention is considered essential. This is a key concept in Ho'oponopono and parallels work being done, for instance, by Gold (2003) and LeBaron (2003). In Ho'oponopono, parties must approach the work with a true resolve to correct wrongs and a determination to speak with complete honesty and sincerity (Pukui et al. 1971). As we discussed in Chapter 1, one can follow the rules and still be a "complete sleazeball." Any process can be mechanically followed, or alternatively followed with passion and a higher intention. In Ho'oponopono, the spiritual framing is considered essential for supporting parties and the intervener to enter the work with honesty, sincerity, and a transformative resolve.

It is also considered important for the leader to do self-reflective work, which connects to the call for self-awareness from psychology. Long before Freud, the ancient Hawaiians conceptualized the conscious and unconscious mind (What is Huna: Basic Huna 2006; King 1989). How you work with your unconscious and higher self are large parts of preparation to do change work (What is Huna: Basic Huna 2006). Intention is important in Ho'oponopono because thoughts are seen as change agents; in essence, your intentions shape the world around you. This is why the actions of the intervener, in doing their internal work, changes the conflict or situation for the parties; internal work creates the external world. Recent work in quantum physics and cell biology seems to back up the idea that our thoughts have a greater impact in our experience of reality than we previously thought possible.[3]

In Ho'oponopono, change involves cleansing inner patterns, with the sense that the work occurs internally for the intervener and simultaneously within the parties (King 1989). Their practitioners believe the only way to make the work effective and untainted is to do it in a sacred context. In the words of Morrnah Simeona, a traditional kahuna and practitioner of Ho'oponopono:

> The main purpose of the process is to discover the Divinity within oneself. The Ho'oponopono is a profound gift which allows one to develop a working relationship with the Divinity within and learn to ask that in each moment, our errors in thought, word, deed or action be cleansed. The process is essentially about freedom, complete freedom from the past. . . . Connect with the Divinity within on a moment-to-moment basis . . . [and] ask that that moment and all it contains, be cleansed. Only the Divinity can do that. Only the Divinity can erase or correct memories and thoughtforms. (King 1989)

So, in this process, to enter liminal space and create change, you need to learn to speak to the divine in yourself, or in the terms of another tradition, learn to create a dialogue with your subconscious and have clear intentions as you create the liminal space. Referring back to Chapter 1, this would mean having a strong self-awareness.

Again, although this may be counterintuitive for some conflict resolvers, it is clear that even the act of taking a moment to stop and listen, to center yourself, in and of itself, can change the rhythm and impact of a process. Particularly if interveners and parties set an intention to come to the work from their highest or best self (Dukes et al. 2009), together with parties they could create joint liminal space, supporting all to move beyond their day-to-day understandings, and status quo "reality" into the new, into change, into remaking the status quo.

Finally, Ho'oponopono leaders ask parties to reflect on what kind of person they want to be and why they do what they do (Pukui et al. 1971). They also ask themselves the same things. This uses a kind of agent of reality that is self-reflective: is the work I am doing consistent with the practitioner I want to be? This kind of reflection motivates parties through love, not fear; through respect, not control. Ho'oponopono teaches that internal self-knowledge and seeking to understand the higher parts of ourselves could have a profound effect on our ability to foster real change through the quality of the ritual's liminal space, and on our ability to be truly respectful to one another. We believe this may be an important aspect of bringing wisdom to conflict resolution processes. Wisdom encompasses not just the wielding of conflict resolution skills but an examination of who we are being in our lives, which, of course, connects back to presence.

The transition section involves using *mahiki*, or discussion, to figure out what went wrong, discuss individual roles, and uncover the multiple layers of the conflict. The goal here is for the parties to use *mihi*, an honest confession to the gods and each other about wrongdoing, which leads to forgiveness, restitution, and a mutual release from the negative entanglements of the conflict.

The process ends with a *pani*, or closing, where the family's strengths and enduring bonds are reaffirmed, and a *pule ho'opau*, or closing prayer, is performed, giving thanks to all involved, including the Divine. After the ceremony, the participants and the kahuna share a snack or meal to which all have contributed, showing the bonds between family members and transitioning back into normal routines (Shook 2000).

Ho'oponopono engages multiple intelligences to move parties and the intervener through separation, transition, and incorporation. The process functions in a context of love, not fear, asking all, including the leader, to approach understanding and change through self-reflection and forgiveness, and through a connection to the highest self or divine. Table 2.2 outlines our framework and shows how we think Ho'oponopono demonstrates multidimensional work. As you can see, Ho'oponopono engages multiple intelligences throughout the process. The conclusion of the book considers the ways in which the framework may contribute to our overall movement forward in the field, and reflects on the practitioner chapters in terms of the framework.

Practice: Four-Dimensional Work— What Is Being Done Now

A reader might wonder, at this point, how to translate such work into his or her own local context. There is already a thriving core of practitioners who are not only doing so, but who have been doing exceptional work for many years in this manner, as this book shows. They do this not by imposing a spiritual ideology on parties but by intense dedication to refining themselves, as conflict resolvers and peacemakers. Erica Fox explains why this is so important: ". . . as mediators, we ourselves are the resource; *we* are the vessel, *we* ourselves—not a scalpel, a gavel, a wrench, or a keyboard—are the tools we use when parties turn to us with their delicate, intimate conflicts" (Fox 2004, 463).

We were privileged to interview two of the most well-known and influential practitioners in the field who are doing multidimensional work: Kenneth Cloke and Louise Diamond. Their stories below demonstrate integrated, spiritually rooted practice.

Louise Diamond, who cofounded the Institute for Multi-Track Diplomacy (IMTD), has worked as a peacebuilder all over the world, "helping adversaries bridge political, historical, cultural, and psychological divides . . . [She has] also trained hundreds of peacebuilders from dozens of countries" (Diamond n.d.) and created some of the formative theories of the field such as multitrack diplomacy (Diamond and McDonald 1996).

Diamond's spirituality is fully integrated into her practice. For her, understanding and knowing the connectedness of all things is core to her spiritual beliefs: "Where we have separated into warring factions,

Table 2.2 Multidimensional Practice Framework, Using the Example of Ho'oponopono

Separation

Stage	Cognitive Dimension	Somatic Dimension	Emotional Dimension	Spiritual Dimension
Entry/ Who should be involved? What is needed?	The process is led by a kahuna lapa'au (a healer) or a family senior The leader is known by all parties The goal is to set things right with each other and the Almighty or ancestor gods	?[a]	In this process, how you approach things shapes the shift; a determination to speak with complete honesty and sincerity is essential A true resolve to correct wrongs is key	The kahuna has spiritual as well as healing expertise, and reflects on how they live their lives Intention is important because thoughts create the world The leader must do self-reflective work in order to work well with their higher self to prepare Connect to the source
Gather Perspectives/ Dialogue to build joint understanding	Kūkulu Kumuhana, identifying the problem and also pooling strengths for a shared purpose	?	All parties engage in self-scrutiny When emotions are negative, all comments are directed to the leader	Opening prayer, *pule*, which lays the foundation for sincerity and truthfulness It is important to get intellect out of the way in order to hear the Divinity

(continues)

that's our woundedness, how we have forgotten our wholeness, and peacebuilding is the healing of that woundedness" (L. Diamond, pers. comm., July 12, 2010). For her, healing the separation and helping par-

Table 2.2 continued

Transition

Stage	Cognitive Dimension	Somatic Dimension	Emotional Dimension	Spiritual Dimension
Locate conflict/ What are the core concerns? Create common meanings and frameworks	Using *mahiki*, or discussion, to figure out what went wrong, discuss individual roles Leaders often call for cooling-off periods of silence called *ho'omalu*, which encourages self-inquiry	*Ho'omalu* also gives participants a chance to rest	*Ho'omalu* also calms tempers	*Mihi*, an honest confession to the Gods and each other about wrong doing, resentments until all is revealed The kahuna thinks about how they contributed to the problem
Arrange-Negotiate	Repentance Reflect on what kind of person you want to be Restitution	?	The focus is on forgiveness *Mihi*, loosening of negative entanglements, or a mutual release by both parties	Working with the Divine to cleanse internal patterns Set things right with others and with the gods

Incorporation

Stage	Cognitive Dimension	Somatic Dimension	Emotional Dimension	Spiritual Dimension
Way Out-Agreement: Who will do what, when, and how the relationship will continue?	Determine restitution terms	*Pani*, or closing, where the family's strengths and enduring bonds are reaffirmed	After the ceremony all share a snack or meal to which all have contributed, showing the bonds between family members and transitioning back into normal routines	*Pule ho'opau*, or closing prayer, giving thanks to all

Notes: As a thought experiment, it may be interesting to the reader to compare this chart with Lederach's summary of classic community mediation, using the same stages (although not the multiple intelligences), found in his book *Preparing for Peace* (1995).

a. The symbol "?" stands for data unknown.

ties understand that "there is only one family of life" is what spirituality and peacebuilding are about. The root of her ability to do this work is regular meditation and spiritual practice that allows her to bring the energy of peace into a conflict situation:

> I think peacebuilders need training to reach the vibration of peace. That's what we're there [for] . . . there is pain, and sorrow, and anger, and grief, and hate, and we're there to bring a vibration of peace. I can't tell you how many people in how many parts of the world have told me, "it's not what you did, no matter how useful that was, but *how* you are that made the difference." (L. Diamond, pers. comm., July 12, 2010)

Here is one example of how Diamond does this. She was making a film "during a period of high tension and sporadic outbursts in a country racked by decades of recurring violence . . . At that time, individuals from that faction who cooperated with foreign media were often placed in detention by the government authorities" (Diamond 2004, 51). As she approached a military checkpoint at night, she realized that she had forgotten to put the studio-sized camera in the trunk where it would be hidden:

> It was only as we approached the midnight checkpoint that I remembered the extent to which the presence of such a camera could cause trouble for my evening's hosts, who had put their own safety at stake to cooperate with my project.
>
> I had the briefest of moments to prepare myself. Physically I reacted by placing the folds of my skirt over the camera, knowing full well that this would be futile in the likely event that the soldiers asked everyone in the car to get out. Emotionally, I tuned in to the courage and kindness of my hosts, who had so willingly risked their safety for the opportunity to speak a message of peace . . . At the same time, I tuned in to the soldiers manning the outpost. Their highest goal, too, came from a place of internal logic and integrity. Their mission was to protect the people in the city, and to screen the possible import of anything or anyone that could fuel fires of violence already burning so close to the surface.
>
> Holding that thought of the dignity of both sides, I slipped into a place I have learned to go when things get difficult. I opened my heart to the flow of love and appreciation for all in this conflict who were struggling to find a better way . . . As we drove up to the solider at the gate, I simply sat and radiated that light. The soldier began to question the driver sternly, while he looked inside the car, sweeping into its corners with his watchful eyes. When he saw me, something softened. He straightened, smiled, and waved us through. (Diamond 2004, 51–53)

For Diamond, who we are and how we are as peacemakers influences the situation and the people in it. She says, "The implication . . . is that the energy and hate that we, ourselves as peacemakers generate, will affect others. If I'm approaching a situation like this soldier who can affect a lot of lives, I can approach it with fear, but I approached it with love. I can't prove this, but it appears his energy changed when it met my energy field" (L. Diamond, pers. comm., July 12, 2010). If it seems strange to view the power of the intervener this way, it is notable that this is far from unique. Rollins recalled hearing a similar story from Cesar Chavez, who said that on "the mornings of those days on which he would be meeting about workers' rights with the owners of huge grape farms, he would rise at 4 A.M. to meditate and pray, preparing to love everyone in the room that he would enter that day, [saying]: 'It changed me and changed them'" (Rollins 2007, 226).

Kenneth Cloke has also had a deep impact on the field. He has a long and diverse practice experience, and has taught, trained, and written several very influential books, including *Mediating Dangerously* (2001). He was also the founder of *Mediators Beyond Borders*, for which volunteers work to "partner with communities worldwide to build their conflict resolution capacity for preventing, resolving and healing from conflict" (Mediators Beyond Borders n.d.).

Cloke also embodies a spiritual peacemaker, and for him as well, spirituality is not a specific activity, but how he is a mediator:

> My definition of spirituality means being completely present and with both people simultaneously, as deeply as I possibly can . . . and . . . [to] invite them to do the same with each other . . . What spirit consists of for me, is energy. And what we are searching for is the unobstructed flow of energy, of heart, mind, body and spirit, between us. So, if I can create an open channel through which this energy flows inside myself and if I can find a place where that energy will flow more freely within them, it will circulate more freely between us. (K. Cloke, pers. comm., July 7, 2010)[4]

He also meditates, as Diamond does, and explains why that enables him to be completely present during mediations: "I do daily meditation, which doesn't sound like it has much to do with mediation, but if you are emotionally exhausted, mentally preoccupied, or physically distracted or in pain, you are not able to be present in a way that elicits that same kind of presence from them."

Cloke opens blocked energy by moving "in the direction of anything that is profound or poignant or both for [the parties], asking a question that moves them in that direction." The idea is to get at something that is meaningful, heartfelt, touching, funny, core for them, and if you do, " . . . it will increase their energy."

An example from Cloke's practice shows how he does this. He was working with a teacher's union and a large, urban school district with a long history of adversarial conflict. He said:

> The first thing I did was to go up to the flipchart and draw the [nego-tiation] table. And I drew x's on one side and o's on the other, and I asked: "What is going to happen to any conversation, predictably and inevitably, at a table like this one?" and they told me, because they all knew. There would be polarization, and the teams would need to unify, and only the leaders would be able to speak, and new ideas would be shut down.

Cloke then elicited how they would have to sit to avoid that. He said, "'Ok, so pick up all your papers and go do that.' And they did. 'OK, what has shifted?' They didn't use [words like] energy or a spiritual change, but they [said they] felt alive and awake and aware of the peo-ple right next to them. They said it was much easier to talk this way and felt less defensive and positional" (Cloke, 2006, 88).

Then Cloke asked, "'What's at stake, what will change as a result of this conversation?' The response to [this question was] heartfelt and profound" (Cloke 2006, 88). A key theme was "'lives of children.' I asked them to imagine that all the children in their schools . . . were present in the room watching what [they] were about to do today" (Cloke 2006, 89).

> And the next question was, "So how can we guarantee that the issues we talk about will be in a way that will benefit the lives of children?" So they all agreed to a single principle that all decisions would be held to: how this would impact the lives of children, and they were all tear-ing up. There were around 60 people in the room, all experienced, sen-ior negotiators, reacting now from a profound, heartfelt orientation. Their process worked, partially because it opened with relationally oriented . . . personal communication that set the stage for dialogue, clear and open communications, and a more trust-based, collaborative, consensus-based relationship. None of these topics were traditional topics for bargaining, yet by touching people's hearts, the parties rebuilt their trust in each other . . . and nourished consensus. (Cloke 2006, 93)

Of course, one could imagine using such relationally based interven-tions and having them backfire. The challenge, says Cloke, is to move into places in a conflict that trap the most energy, which means touching the deepest, most potentially explosive parts of the conflict. However, those places are also the source of the deepest transformation. How can you do this without triggering an explosion? Cloke had two answers: "You show up with as much sensitivity to them as you can possibly muster, with as much freedom as you can muster to move where they want to move but are afraid to [go], even if it's counter intuitive . . . The only way to do it right is to feel your way into it." The way to do this is to use what he calls a well-calibrated intuition. We feel this gets at one of the possible concerns about drawing on other ways of understanding: What makes an intuitive, emotional, or spiritual insight reliable? Cloke recommends *calibrating* intuition by essentially testing it against the individuals you are working with. He says, "Ask yourself how you would answer the question you just asked [them]." If you correctly predict the answer given, you are well-calibrated. If you are wrong, you need to either get better information about them or understand what is blocking your understanding. You can "ask questions that lead you to a deeper level of truth" or figure out "if something in you is so loud that you can't really pay attention."

Conclusion

Both Diamond and Cloke, like practitioners of Ho'oponopono, engage cognitive, emotional, somatic, and spiritual knowledge to move parties and the intervener through separation, transition, and incorporation. Both have developed an awareness of what their emotions and body can teach them about the situations they are in, and have learned how to use somatic, emotional, and spiritual intelligence to hold and bring peace into the conflicts they touch. Diamond moved into liminal, transformative space, to open her situation to love. Cloke elicited profound insights and movement from negotiators, just by allowing them to tell him what their physical location said about the conflict they were in (which was also a somatic intervention). By working to move parties to a more profound, emotional place, he was able to elicit from them criteria that moved the negotiation to a different level. Both create processes that support and prioritize party self-determination. Both practitioners believe that the core of their effectiveness is their ability to access something transcendent in themselves, and that is what allows them to support extraordinary shifts.

What would an integrated, multidimensional intervention in the Oneida land claim look like? One radical approach would be to return to how treaties were first conducted between European settlers and the Haudenosaunee[5] (to whom the Oneida belong). Those treaties were, in the

eyes of one scholar, "diplomatic dramas" that were prescribed by Haudenosaunee ritual, the condolence ceremony, "which imparted its structure to treaty protocol" (Fenton 1985, 6). The ritual refers to a time in
tribal history when violence was transformed by a ceremony that healed
loss and helped parties return to "the good mind" to speak honestly with
one another for peace. It used what they called "bare words" to clear tears
from the eyes, for unplugging the ears, and for clearing the throat after the
loss of a chief or leader (27). This treaty protocol emphasized "clearing
the path" of any boulders (i.e., obstacles) and "polishing" the covenant
chain or relationship between the parties before exchanging proposals and
negotiating. It is, in fact, a traditional form of trauma healing. By following prescribed spiritual practices, the Haudenosaunee and the white
colonists would address any emotional and relational disturbances prior to
addressing substantive differences. Perhaps this is what needs to be done
for both the Oneidas and the present-day property owners. There are
many grievances and pains that need to be healed after 200 years.

Alternatively, a mediator in the Oneida land claim might draw lessons from the Allagash Wilderness Waterway dispute (Reitman 2003a).
Besides having all the parties at the table (including the property owners) and having strong state and federal leadership, this case shows that
what was needed as part of a larger consensus-building process were
small group exercises that allowed parties to recognize their shared values for the land. What if, like the parties in that case, Oneidas and local
citizens walked the reservation together and talked about the significance of the land for them and for their communities (i.e., why they
love the land and what their connection is to it)? What if they had dialogues[6] with each other over meals cooked with locally grown produce
(where they might open with, for example, the Haudenosaunee Thanks-
giving Address/Prayer)? Perhaps they would then begin to see each
other as people who appreciate the land for many of the same reasons,
and who in the past (and present) have a lot of experience with peaceful
coexistence (as in the condolence ceremony above). This could result in
the same kind of breakthrough that happened in Maine over the Allagash River—a dispute that had been raging for decades—as people are
moved, out of commonality and compassion, rather than out of fear and
hatred. Both processes also move parties out of their status quo reality
into liminal, change-making space.

As for the congregational dispute, what might a multidimensional
approach look like? One thing we could have done with the parties during the intake process was to explore if they wanted to include their
faith in the process and how, as mentioned in Chapter 1. (Also, if I had
been more spiritually grounded, perhaps I would not have reacted out of

fear.) The question as practitioners is, are we open to having this conversation or do we ignore it? If we ignore or avoid it, are we respecting the self-determination of the parties?

We believe the work of Ken Cloke and Louise Diamond demonstrates that we can do profound, integrated practice in this field that deeply engages our spiritual, cognitive, emotional, and somatic intelligences in such a way that, if anything, is more respectful of party self-determination than that of classic mediation. These conflict resolvers seem to do so in ways that match the recommendations of those in psychology doing similar work. Cloke and Diamond do continuous, rigorous work to be deeply self-reflective and self-aware, so they may, more profoundly, respect parties.

We are aware the work presented here blurs the line between the art and the science of conflict resolution. Maybe another way to calibrate, or reinforce, the reliability of multiple intelligences is to triangulate one with the others. If you are simultaneously uncomfortable emotionally, have a bad "gut feeling" and feel "off" spiritually, then the chances are that something is seriously wrong and needs to be addressed. And, maybe, as Louise Diamond suggests in Chapter 8, mediators would need additional training to engage these multiple ways of knowing, with skill.

The framework we have presented is, we hope, a way for practitioners to consider their own practice in a new way. We hope it also stands as a recommendation to the field to expand our models to meaningfully engage human experience more completely. We also hope it will lead to more work focused on mediator self-awareness; training in somatic, emotional, and spiritual intelligences; and new models of practice that take seriously the transformative potential of faith for practitioners and parties. The rest of the book is composed of chapters written by practitioners about how they are using these concepts and the successes and challenges they have faced.

Notes

This chapter was originally published in the *Cardozo Journal of Conflict Resolution* 13 (2): 437–465. Although it has been revised for this book, it is reprinted here with permission.

1. From the notes from the training handout *Training for Restorative Justice Trainers*, Community Justice Institute, Florida Atlantic University, July 2002, p. 10.

2. We would like to note that we do not claim to be experts in this process, and we have gained our understanding of it through bibliographic research and an interview with one of the major researchers in this area. We were not suc-

cessful in our multiple attempts to contact and speak to native practitioners to be sure we have represented the process correctly. We believe that a long history of researchers essentializing behavior has unfortunately, though understandably, left practitioners reluctant to talk to outsiders.

3. See, for instance, Fred Alan Wolf (1986) or Bruce Lipton (2005).

4. All further quotes in this section are from the same interview, July 7, 2010, except where noted otherwise.

5. This is the term the confederation uses in reference to themselves. Most North Americans are more familiar with the term "Iroquois."

6. There was a dialogue program called Voices on the Land, regarding the Onondaga land claim (another tribe in the same region), that reflected many of the same issues. Both authors worked on these dialogues. The dialogues brought together Native Americans, local citizens, and leadership of the landowners group, Upstate Citizens for Equality. These dialogues presented several moments of real connection and transformation that, we believe, could have had a major impact on the conflict if they had been extended beyond the half-day program we were involved in. Other dialogues, although successful, were also hampered by lack of funds. See Blancke and Wulff (2002).

3

The Buddha's Teachings on the Personal Qualities of a Conflict Resolver

G. Daniel Bowling

THROUGHOUT FORTY-FIVE YEARS OF TEACHING, THE BUDDHA taught how to deal with conflicts among the *sangha,* or community, of monks and lay practitioners. Twenty-five-hundred years later, his teachings remain powerfully relevant for conflict resolution practitioners, who wish to bring all of who they are into their practice, including all ways of "knowing" or intelligences.

The Buddha never asked anyone to believe his teachings; rather, he urged practicing his methods for training in mindfulness and relying on personal experience to evaluate their effectiveness. Drawing not on belief but on my thirty-five-year meditation practice, I consistently see a clear connection between my own lapses of mindfulness and the conflict that arises in my life as well as a connection to my clarity and presence in my role as neutral. The impact of those lapses and of my moments of clarity encourages my confidence in the Buddha's teachings as a way to develop the personal qualities required for conflict resolution (Bowling and Hoffman 2003).

To understand his conflict teachings, we must examine them within the framework of his foundational principles—the Four Noble Truths—enunciated in his first *sutta* (sermon), "Setting in Motion the Wheel of the *Dhamma*" (Bodhi 2000, Number 56.11).[1] This chapter uses a court-connected mediation as the context for analyzing the Four Noble Truths and examples of the Buddha's teachings about conflict.

49

Conflict, Ignorance, and Mindfulness

The Buddha is more appropriately understood as the first psychologist, with profound insights into the mind, rather than a religious teacher. He focused on freeing the mind from our acute ignorance that causes suffering rather than joy, conflict and violence rather than connection, saying, "I do not perceive even one other thing . . . that leads to such great harm as an undeveloped mind." (Thera and Bodhi 1999, Number 1.iii, 2). When asked why we fight constantly, he pointed to our untrained minds and our obsessive attachment to experiences we like, resistance to experiences we do not like, and attachment to views arising from our ignorance (Number 2.iv, 6) that generates unwholesome thoughts and actions, such as compulsively craving power instead of relationships (Number 3.69). He taught, "Speak or act with a corrupted mind, and suffering follows as the wagon wheel follows the hoof of the ox. . . . Speak or act with a peaceful mind, and happiness follows like a never-departing shadow" (Fronsdal 2008). He compared our untrained minds to a dog tied on a leash bound to a strong post. The dog (our mind) runs around the post, without the mindfulness necessary to gain freedom, through insight into life (Bodhi 2000, Number 22. 99).

The Buddha taught mindfulness to free the mind and acquire the ability to be present and aware in each moment (Moffitt 2008). Mindfulness is a universal human capacity—a way of paying attention—that can be cultivated, sustained, and integrated into everyday life through deep inquiry with a disciplined meditation practice. Mindfulness means paying attention to whatever is happening or arising in the present moment. Through practice, we learn awareness, moment by moment, of physical sensations, thereby developing somatic intelligence; of the feeling tone of those sensations, developing somatic and emotional intelligence; of our mental states, the unending stream of repetitive and compulsive thoughts that determine how we experience life, developing somatic, emotional, cognitive, and spiritual intelligence; and of the fundamental laws that govern human behavior and life as it unfolds, again developing all four intelligences.

Mindfulness purifies the mind from defilements—unwholesome mental forces running below the surface of consciousness vitiating our thinking, values, attitudes, and actions. The Buddha termed three defilements as the "roots of evil"—greed, hatred, and delusion—from which emerge numerous offshoots, such as anger, cruelty, violence, conflict, avarice, arrogance, hypocrisy, and vanity—the multitude of unskillful filters through which we inaccurately view our world (Bodhi 1998–

2012). The Buddha taught numerous practices for mindfulness both in daily life and in meditation,[2] leading to clear comprehension, that is, the ability to see clearly how to relate skillfully to life and the inevitable conflicts that arise (Moffitt 2008), and providing insight into three fundamental entrapments of life. These are (1) an identification with beliefs about the self that cause us to cling fearfully to experiences we like and to resist experiences we do not like, even though (2) every experience is impermanent, thereby (3) causing us to cling to that which is impermanent but is necessarily unsatisfactory, leaving us unfulfilled, revolving endlessly in a vicious cycle.

Mindfulness is essential for developing conflict resolution skills and the personal qualities required of a conflict resolver. Unfortunately, conflict resolution literature and training focus on two stages of professional development, leaving out the crucial third stage. David Hoffman and I introduced these three stages (Bowling and Hoffman 2000) as the process for gaining mastery in any endeavor and for generating extraordinary conflict resolution, true peacemaking.

As beginning mediators, we focus on the first stage, learning skills and techniques for resolving conflicts, for example, reframing. As we gain skill proficiency and move to the next stage, most of us explore the underlying theories. This second stage augments our intellectual understanding of various conflict resolution theories (Shaw 2005). In *Bringing Peace Into the Room* (Bowling and Hoffman 2003) we asserted that our professional development fails until we incorporate the third stage—acquiring the personal qualities essential to master conflict resolution. This chapter focuses on third-stage development.

A Court-Connected Mediation

As program staff attorney/mediator in the Alternative Dispute Resolution (ADR) program for the United States District Court's Northern District of California, I assist in running the program, and mediate cases. In a call the day before the mediation of a mortgage foreclosure case regarding a plaintiff's claims of mortgage fraud, the plaintiff's attorney, "Mr. James," asked to postpone for reasons that did not ring true. Plaintiffs have little hope of winning these cases, because relevant statutes strongly favor financial institutions. They are usually seeking to delay a foreclosure sale or obtain a favorable modification of their mortgage loan. Even though I suspected Mr. James' motives, based on his conduct in many previous mediations, after reading the parties' mediation statements, I became concerned neither side was actually ready to mediate, because the bank had filed a motion to dismiss, but the court had not yet ruled. In my experience, whenever attorneys are not prepared—lacking not only a firm grasp of the factual and legal strengths and weaknesses of their case, but also a strategically sound negotiation plan—mediation is unlikely to be successful. So I initially agreed that the mediation should be postponed but told Mr. James I would call "Ms. Waters," the bank's attorney and find out whether she agreed also.

When I called, I was surprised to learn the bank was prepared to consider a loan modification—the relief the plaintiff was seeking—and would not rely on the arguments in the motion to dismiss. She did not want to postpone but instructed me not to reveal this change in position to Mr. James, so she could choose the most strategically appropriate time to announce this important shift in the bank's position.

I had a problem, especially given that Mr. James was the most challenging lawyer I had ever experienced in twenty-eight years of mediation. As mediator, I cannot order parties to do anything. Mediation, as a voluntary process, requires agreement from both sides. I told Ms. Waters I would call Mr. James and conference her into the call, so they could decide what to do. She agreed.

I called Mr. James, learning he had left for the day. His secretary was not sure about reaching him. I explained the urgency and said I was setting up a call with both attorneys to help them decide whether to postpone. Forty-five minutes later, he had not called. I called again. His secretary said he left me a message: "The mediation has been cancelled. Neither my client nor I will be coming to the courthouse tomorrow." I was shocked that he left a message with his secretary rather than calling me. Court rules require attorneys to cooperate with the mediator in scheduling. Also, calling me was common professional courtesy. I emphasized my urgency, adding that he was placing me in a difficult situation with Ms. Waters. I now knew he was manipulating us and insisted upon speaking with him. My insistence was strong—too strong. In hindsight, I had lost all aspects of mindfulness described earlier: of physical sensations, including awareness of my breath and my body (my somatic intelligence), of the feeling tone of those physical sensations (my somatic and emotional), of my mental state (my somatic, emotional, and cognitive intelligences), and of the fundamental laws that govern human behavior and life as it unfolds (my cognitive and spiritual intelligences).

Another hour passed with no call. In a stressed, unmindful state, I called a third time. Reaching the office manager, I demanded to know why Mr. James was not calling. Urgency and anger at being manipulated altered my voice tone. He repeated the message: "The mediation has been cancelled," adding that Mr. James was unavailable. I asserted,

"A mediation is not cancelled until both sides agree. I must speak with him. Otherwise, I have no choice but to go forward with mediation and report him to the judge supervising the court ADR program, if he and his client fail to appear." The conversation was unpleasant. I was forceful and insistent, without any mindfulness.

At that moment, the ADR program director walked into the office, saying, "Come listen to a voicemail I just received from Mr. James." His voicemail attacked me for allegedly promising to cancel, then reneging, and being inappropriate with his staff. He said, "I refuse to mediate this case or any case with Mr. Bowling." My heart sank as I listened, with my mindfulness slowly returning. What an embarrassing mess!

I called Ms. Waters. To my surprise, Mr. James had called her, leaving a message that the mediation was cancelled, yet another example of his manipulative, challenging behavior. I summarized my efforts to get in touch with him to arrange our conference call. Recognizing the problem, she graciously agreed to postpone, if Mr. James would respond within a week to a request she would send him for additional financial information on his client. Relieved, I promised to convey that message and get back to her about rescheduling.

Six Roots of Conflict

In the *At Samagama Sutta,* the monk Cunda rushed to tell Ananda, the Buddha's cousin and personal attendant, of the death of Nataputta, a famous Jain teacher. Together, they informed the Buddha. Cunda described hearing Nataputta's disciples arguing, stabbing each other with verbal daggers—a powerful image of how conflict manifests— saying: "Your way is wrong. My way is right. I am consistent. You are inconsistent. What should have been said first you said last. What should have been said last you said first. . . . Go and learn better . . . if you can!" (Nanamoli and Bodhi 1995, Number 104. 2).

Ananda expressed concern about a similar conflict arising in the *sangha* after the Buddha's death. In response, the Buddha described the Six Roots of Conflict:

1. Anger
2. Contempt
3. Greed
4. Deceit
5. Wrong view
6. Clinging to our views (Nanamoli and Bodhi 1995, Number 104.6)

Mr. James and I were both angry and believed the other was treating us with contempt. I believed his underlying greed drove him to be deceitful in manipulating the scheduling, and he resented me for not fully respecting him as a civil rights attorney. We both had the classic *wrong view*—each believing what the other did was all about us. I believed that Mr. James did something to the individual limited sense of self, known as "Daniel," and so what he did had a powerful impact on that sense of self that I call "me." And we were clinging to our views. He demanded a postponement. I demanded normal, professional courteous treatment—all six roots in a few calls. We failed to heed the Buddha's warning that anger has a "poisoned root and honeyed tip" (Bodhi 2000, Number 2.3), which clearly embroiled both of us in a tricky conflict. Yet again, I was faced with the humbling reminder that even thousands of hours of mindfulness meditation does not guarantee mindfulness, because my mind is literally grooved with thousands of unskillful neuronal pathways developed over years of unmindful behavior. Given my human condition, what antidotes did the Buddha offer when we experience the roots of conflict?

Four Noble Truths

The answer begins with the Buddha's very first teachings: the Four Noble Truths, a classic, scientific analysis of the underlying dysfunction of the human mind, reworded here into a conflict resolution formula.

Know Conflict as Dukkha

In this first truth, the Buddha presented our daily reality: the challenge of *dukkha*, our familiar lifelong mental suffering, experienced as stress, anxiety, miscommunication, conflict, dissatisfaction, and more (Moffitt 2008). The etymology of *dukkha* is an unbalanced axle wheel, resulting in a rough ride. Whenever conflict is present, the first step is mindful recognition of conflict as *dukkha*. Mindfulness enables us to see the *dukkha* of conflict as part of life's ebb and flow, rather than believing *dukkha* is wrong. Mindfulness enables us to recognize when the Six Roots of Conflict are present. As mindfulness deepens, we learn to shift our view that conflict is wrong, therefore avoiding conflict is good. The Buddha never taught *dukkha* was wrong or we could or should resist it; rather, he taught us to train our minds to "know" *dukkha* mindfully as it actually is (Nanamoli and Bodhi 1995, Number 10.44). Practicing mindfulness generates this *knowing*, including awareness of internal doubts or resistance (Number 10). For example, we train our minds to note silently when experiencing conflict: "The experience of conflict is like this," enabling us to be present and observe mindfully that moment's experience. I forgot this basic practice during my phone calls. Rather than mindfully *knowing* the events by silently noting, "Anger is arising; Conflict feels like this," I lost myself in the events, became identified with my anger, and had no mindful awareness of my behavior. I literally became my behavior.

Know that Clinging Is the Source of the Dukkha of Conflict

In the Second Noble Truth, the Buddha presented the underlying cause of mental suffering: we experience *dukkha* because our untrained minds react to the ever-changing nature of life—such as the conflicts and miscommunications we frequently encounter—by clinging to what we like and resisting what we do not like. He never taught that clinging to what we want is sinful, an important distinction from other teachers. Since we can only experience life through our senses, and our untrained minds cling to sense pleasures, if such pleasures are wrong, then much of life would be wrong. Rather, he taught that *tanha*, thirst—our uncontrolled desires for what we want—is the source of *dukkha*, of "all the troubles and strife in the world, from little personal quarrels in families to great wars between nations and countries" (Rahula 1974).

Desire, according to the Buddha, includes its opposite, aversion. Aversion to any sense experience is the manifestation of thirst for its opposite. We cling to futile efforts to avoid conflicts and control life, thereby producing the conflicts, violence, and wars plaguing humanity on all levels from the personal, family, community, country, to the world. We also cling to *becoming,* which the Buddha defined as our existence, status, or self-identity and to *non-becoming,* meaning wanting something to disappear, not to be seen.

I want to be respected as a mediator and believe returning my phone calls is a sign of respect. When people respect me, I feel good. When they do not, I feel bad, experiencing aversion. Anger arises in me. Early in my interaction with Mr. James, I was unmindful of my attachment to *becoming,* to being seen and respected, or of my aversion to *nonbecoming*, not being seen and disrespected. My unmindful clinging allowed the Six Roots of Conflict to arise in me. The ensuing conflict trapped me.

Know the Cessation of the Dukkha of Conflict

The Buddha's Third Noble Truth promises a solution to this ancient human dilemma—the possibility of cessation of mental suffering, ending our dysfunctional relationship with life. Often we avoid or resist conflict, because we do not believe we can deal with it skillfully or it will ever actually end. As mediators we work with parties lacking faith in the possibility the suffering of their conflict will ever end. They are consumed with anger, fear, projection, and blame. The source of conflict, parties assert, is not *their* clinging, attachment, or aversion; rather, it is the behavior of *others*. To assist parties to resolve conflict, it is essential that we embody this mindful *knowing* of the cessation of the *dukkha* of conflict in our own lives, not just as an intellectual understanding. Without mindfulness, we miss the moments of peace and connection in the midst of conflict. We fail to recognize moments when the conflict ceases and connection arises, because we remain blinded by our attachment to the conflict. Through dedicated mindfulness practice, we experience cessation of conflict moment by moment, especially recognizing moments when our internal experience of conflict ceases, even if the external reality has not changed. We train our minds to awaken, silently repeating when conflict arises: "Conflict is like this," and when a moment of connection arises, "The cessation of conflict is like this."

Blaming Mr. James for our conflict trapped me, given my past experiences with him. I struggled to *know* that conflict with him could cease, leaving me without faith in the possibility that our conflict could cease. With this mindset, how could I possibly offer assistance to the defendants? As mediators, we must learn to live the possibility of conflict ceasing in our own lives, in order to bring that awareness into our work. Only by mindfully recognizing the possibility of my internal conflict with Mr. James ceasing, and practicing to create conditions for it to cease, could I remember how to release my clinging and recognize when the roots of conflict are *not* present in me, moment by moment.

Know the Path Leading to Cessation of the Dukkha of Conflict

The Fourth Noble Truth describes the Eightfold Path to cessation of *dukkha*. This path is usually divided into three sections: wisdom practices: wise view and wise intention; virtue practices: wise speech, action, and livelihood; and concentration practices: wise effort, mindfulness, and concentration (Moffitt 2008). Wise view develops cognitive intelligence by training our mind to see the distortion of making events be about "me," when in fact they are actually arising from causes and conditions. Wise intention trains our cognitive intelligence to focus on the subtle intent before every action. Wise speech develops cognitive, emotional, and somatic intelligences by increasing awareness of the impact of our speech on our thoughts, our body, and on others. Wise action and livelihood develop somatic and emotional intelligences by increasing awareness of the impact of our actions on our body, others, and the Earth. Wise effort, mindfulness, and concentration develop cognitive, emotional, somatic, and spiritual intelligences through precise training in awareness of the subtle aspects of every experience.

Each practice is designed to train our unruly minds to work skillfully with life and with conflict, creating conditions to release clinging, rather than continuing futile efforts to control our experience. These practices do not describe how to become a good person, rather they train us to develop mindfulness of our intentions, mental habits, and reactive thoughts and to abandon unskillful actions while cultivating skillful approaches to life, including the resolution of conflicts.

Like a physician, the Buddha described our illness, diagnosed its underlying cause, clarified the cure, and recommended the medicine to achieve that cure (Moffitt 2008). This same analysis is applicable to resolving conflict. As mediators, we initially help parties understand their conflict. Then, we guide them to recognize the positions and interests underlying that conflict and encourage recognition that resolving their conflict is possible. Finally, we help design and structure a resolution process.

Examples of the Buddha's Teachings for Dealing with Conflict

Attaining mindfulness and skillful behavior regarding the Six Roots of Conflict requires years of diligent practice, but, based on personal experience, worthwhile and partial results arise quickly and build slowly but consistently over time, so long as practice continues. The Four Noble Truths, remember, are not beliefs, but a framework for training our minds. When the Buddha presented the Six Roots of Conflict in the *At Samagama Sutta* (Nanamoli and Bodhi 1995, Number 104.11), he also taught two challenging mindfulness practices. First, if we perceive any of those roots either in ourselves or externally, we practice mindfulness to abandon them; secondly, if we do not perceive any of the roots in ourselves or externally, we practice mindfulness to prevent their future arising (Number 104.6). How then, could I have practiced to perceive these roots as they arose in me with Mr. James and how could I practice to prevent them from arising the next time I feel disrespected? How can I prevent getting hooked, as I did with Mr. James? Fortunately, the Buddha gave numerous teachings regarding specific conflicts that arose within his community of practitioners. Here are four to sharpen our mindfulness regarding the roots of conflict, within the framework of the Four Noble Truths.

The Entanglement of "I'm Right/You're Wrong"

In the *With Canki Sutta,* the Buddha conversed with Brahmins, discussing the distinctions between his teachings and their studies of the Vedas, ancient Hindu scriptures. Kapathika, a Brahmin student who was only sixteen but already known as a master, asked a pointed question: "Master Gotama, in regard to the ancient Brahmanic hymns that have come down . . . in the scriptural collections, the Brahmins have come to the definite conclusion: 'Only this is true, anything else is wrong.' What does Master Gotama say about this?'" (Nanamoli and Bodhi 1995, Number 95.12).

The Buddha asked several questions regarding whether any living Brahmin, any teacher going back seven generations, or any ancient seer who authored the Vedas could affirm their truth from personal experience. To each question, Kapathika answered no. The Buddha then compared the Brahmins' belief in the absolute truth of the Vedas to a line of blind men leading each other, all failing to see where they were going, underscoring the fundamental distinction between accepting teachings on belief, rather than by verification through personal practice—the approach the Buddha encouraged.

Each of us has experienced conflict when we firmly believed, "Only this is true, anything else is wrong" about some issue, forgetting that clinging to a view is the source of *dukkha* according to the Second Noble Truth. I certainly felt that way about my conflict with Mr. James. The Buddha taught Kapathika and the Brahmins there are only five ways to reach any belief-based conclusion that cannot be verified by direct personal experience:

1. Faith
2. Approval from those we respect
3. Tradition
4. Reasoning
5. Reflective practice

Regardless on which of these five we base any belief, the Buddha affirmed the reality that our belief can only be true or false.

I may believe Toyotas are the best automobiles, on faith. I could believe the opposite, on faith. Upon investigation, either belief only turns out to be either true or false. Alternatively, I could believe in Toyotas because people I respect agree. Upon investigation, my belief can only be true or false. I could believe in Toyotas because my parents did. Same result. I could thoroughly investigate their repair history, reliability, and engineering. Same result. Finally, I could reflect on my experience gained from driving Toyotas. Still the same result.

Regardless of my faith, others' approval, tradition, reasoning, or reflection, my belief can only be true or false, again, unless I am able to verify my belief by direct experience, which I could not do in the situation with Mr. James. Following this examination process, a wise person, the Buddha said, desiring to honor the truth, realizes she cannot conclude definitely about anything, "Only this is true, anything else is wrong." Why? Any such conclusion is based on reasons that cannot yield certainty. Thus, a wise person, who desires to honor the truth, only says, "My faith is thus . . . , but I cannot come to the definite conclusion: 'Only this is true, anything else is wrong'" (Nanamoli and Bodhi 1995, Number 95.15).

Thus, any of the "I'm Right/You're Wrong" views that drive so much conflict must shift, for a wise person, to "This is my view, my perspective. I cannot definitively conclude that what I believe to be true is true and anything else is wrong, unless I have personally ascertained the truth of my conviction." The practices of the Eightfold Path described in the Fourth Noble Truth develop the realization that many belief-based issues causing intense religious, political, and social conflict cannot be verified.

The Buddha taught that lack of mindfulness regarding impermanence is one of three fundamental traps for our untrained minds. We easily see that everything we experience—every material form, feeling, or mental understanding—is impermanent, conditioned by other material forms, feelings, or mental understandings, all of which are "subject to destruction, vanishing, fading away, and ceasing" (Nanamoli and Bodhi 1995, Number 74.11). Unfortunately, understanding impermanence only through cognitive intelligence does not yield deep *knowing* of this truth. My anger at Mr. James arose because I resisted the momentary experience of being disrespected, losing my somatic, emotional, and spiritual intelligences during those phone calls, forgetting impermanence and awareness that the pain would cease as described in the Third Noble Truth.

Through mindfulness practice, we see experiences arising and passing away. We *know* impermanence somatically, emotionally, and spiritually, not just cognitively. We *know* the futility of attempting to hold onto anything—particularly a belief or position in conflict. We gain insight into our behavior patterns of attempting to hold onto beliefs and positions. Insight frees our minds from believing, "Only this is true, anything else is wrong." One whose mind is thus liberated "sides with none and disputes with none; he employs the speech currently used in the world without adhering to it" (Nanamoli and Bodhi 1995, Number 74.13), meaning that, though our speech may imply certainty and permanence, we *know* the truth of uncertainty and impermanence. Mindfulness of the "I'm Right/You're Wrong" entanglement supports our spaciousness and flexibility whenever any roots of conflict arise.

The more I practice mindfulness, the more I see my internal and external experiences arise, remain for a while, and then disappear. Many, of course, return, but always again disappear. When my mindfulness is strong, I am able to note the arising of difficult experiences with a silent, "Here's X again. X is like this. I know this suffering. May this suffering cease." Repeating such phrases allows me to maintain an essential separation from any experience. The experience is present; however, I am not lost in it, nor is it me. With mindfulness, I see X disappear and repeat silently, "The cessation of X is like this." The cessation of X is not me either. Practice frees me from X, moment by moment, regardless of whether X is present or absent.

Reflecting on Truthfulness

In the *Advice to Rahula at Ambalatthika Sutta,* the Buddha taught his son, Rahula, the immense importance of truthfulness: "When one is not ashamed to tell a deliberate lie, there is no evil . . . (that person) would not do. Therefore, Rahula, you should train thus: 'I will not utter a falsehood even as a joke'" (Nanamoli and Bodhi 1995, Number 61.7). He asked Rahula the purpose of a mirror. Rahula replied for reflection. So, said the Buddha, we should reflect repeatedly, practicing mindfulness, before acting with the body, speech, or the mind, by asking, "Would this action that I wish to do with the body, with speech, or with the mind lead to my own affliction, or to the affliction of others, or to the affliction of both?" (Number 61.9). If the action is an unwholesome physical, speech, or mental action with potentially painful consequences, we should abstain, by releasing the clinging the Second Noble Truth describes. If the action is a wholesome physical, speech, or mental action, then we act with confidence, knowing we are practicing aspects of the Eightfold Path.

The Buddha powerfully distinguished truthfulness from our ordinary understanding of speaking truthfully, reminding us that truth involves more than words. It manifests through actions, mental habits, perceptions, and thoughts. The saying "actions speak louder than words" only partly reflects this teaching. A complete reflection would include awareness of the harmful impact of unskillful actions and internal dialogue. By reflecting on both, we develop mindfulness regarding the entire scope and power of truthfulness, while developing our somatic, cognitive, emotional, and spiritual intelligences.

The Buddha also taught Rahula that if a physical, verbal, or mental action is unwholesome, we should confess to someone we deeply respect to encourage future restraint (Nanamoli and Bodhi 1995, Number 61.11). When I reflected alone and with my director about my actions and internal dialogue regarding Mr. James, I recognized an old behavior pattern. When I engage with someone, particularly over the telephone, I unconsciously cling to an expectation of respectful treatment. When I perceive lack of respect, then anger, one of the Six Roots of Conflict, is likely to arise in me, wiping out whatever mindfulness and awareness I have. I am hooked.

Recognizing Being Hooked

In *The Kosambians Sutta,* a quarrel arose among the monks at Kosambi, beginning, as conflicts often do, with a casual misunderstanding. It flared quickly, dividing a large part of the Kosambi *sangha,* including monks and lay people, into two hostile factions that were stabbing each other with verbal daggers. As with most conflicts, "They could neither convince each other nor be convinced by others; they could neither persuade each other nor be persuaded by others" (Nanamoli and Bodhi 1995, Number 48.2).

Being hooked obscures our minds so we cannot *know* things as they actually are. The Buddha identified eight specific obsessions corresponding to ways are become hooked:

1. Desire
2. Aversion
3. Sloth and torpor
4. Restlessness and remorse
5. Doubt
6. Speculation about what happened
7. Speculation about what might happen
8. Quarreling and stabbing others with verbal daggers (Nanamoli and Bodhi 1995, Number 48.8)

He taught us to practice mindfulness of these obsessions, thereby *knowing* whether an obsession is present—whether we are hooked. We mindfully ask, "Is desire (or any of the other obsessions) present in me?" If an obsession is present, we do not resist it; rather, we repeat mindfully, "Desire (or any of the others) is like this." Mindfulness allows us to recognize that, when obsessed, we do not see things as they actually are. Instead, we see through the filter of whichever obsession has hooked us, blocking our clarity. More subtly, when we reflect mindfully and see that we are not obsessed, we acknowledge our awareness of the way things actually are by repeating, "Freedom from desire (or any of the others) is like this."

Such clarity is helpful at all times, but especially in conflict. The morning after my interaction with Mr. James, I awoke with clear *knowing* that I was, for the moment, free of obsessing, ruminating over and over about the event, speculating about what happened and might happen. I saw I had been caught in anger and I was now free. I noted, "Freedom from obsession about what happened with Mr. James is like this." In that freedom, I could see my contributions as being entangled in "I'm right" and lacking complete truthfulness in my words, thoughts, mental habits, and actions, all of which combined to hook me.

Developing Loving Kindness

Having seen my contributions to the conflict with Mr. James, I faced the challenge of having to continue mediating his cases, including the case in which our telephone exchange occurred. After that telephone exchange, he had written the judge who supervised the ADR program to complain about me. Fortunately, that judge understood the challenges Mr. James presented. Because judges referred so many of his cases to our program, the ADR program director and I decided to invite Mr. James to meet with us, hopefully to clear the air and restore our working relationship. The mindfulness practice I used to prepare for that crucial meeting is one that I use before every mediation—*metta*, or lovingkindness meditation.

We have all met people who seem to radiate kindness, who see us whole, such as the great teachers in our lives or our grandparents, who do not love us because we are special, because of our attainments, looks, or intelligence, but rather because of the loving quality of their hearts. This quality is *metta*—the simple wish that we will be happy and free of suffering. *Metta* translates as friendly, "moist," or "sticky," a central quality of friendship. We all have a sense of cohesion with our close friends, of sticking together (Salzburg 2002). *Metta* practice requires the silent repetition, over and over, of certain set phrases:

1. May _____ be safe.
2. May _____ be happy and peaceful.
3. May _____ be healthy.
4. May _____ live with ease.

The categories of people to whom the practice is directed are: oneself, a benefactor, a good friend, a neutral person, a difficult person, and groups of people from various geographic regions, such as one's neighborhood or community. Prior to my mediations, I practice *metta* for myself, a benefactor, and then all the lawyers and parties involved in the case.

Metta practice is quite different from prayer, although it may initially feel like prayer. The distinctions of context and intention are important. Prayer is asking for something from, or seeking a connection with, a higher being. By contrast, *metta* practice is designed to develop the quality of loving kindness in ourselves, with no intent to get anything for ourselves. Also, *metta* is absolutely not positive affirmations; rather, it is training our mind to open to wishing others well. The practice first reveals the hidden attitudes we have toward others and gradually shifts and purifies those feelings. I use the practice before each mediation in order to reveal my actual, unconscious attitudes toward the people who will attend the mediation and develop the quality of loving kindness in me toward them.

Prior to the meeting with Mr. James, I did *metta* for him for countless hours. It was quite challenging. I saw all my judgmental attitudes about him and felt justified because of his behavior, but I also saw how those attitudes got in the way of my working with him and ultimately led to the disastrous series of phone calls. Slowly, I released my negativity and began to see some good qualities.

Conclusion

The Buddha's Four Noble Truths provide a clear framework for his many teachings for developing our awareness of and skill with the Six Roots of Conflict. Practicing mindfulness will significantly enhance our personal qualities as conflict resolvers, particularly if we practice the four teachings highlighted in this chapter:

1. The entanglement of right and wrong that arises whenever we forget the fundamental truth that everything is impermanent
2. The importance of expanding our understanding of truthfulness to include our actions, mental habits, perceptions, and thoughts
3. How to recognize when we are hooked by any of the eight obsessions
4. The practice of *metta* meditation to prepare for conflict resolution

By the time I walked into the meeting with Mr. James and the program director, my *metta* practice had enabled me to release a sense of being right about my actions and to gain insight into my own contributions by not being fully truthful with his staff because of my anger at his disrespect. I entered the conversation with a clear, calm, and focused mind. I began with an apology, acknowledging my anger and inappropriate behavior with his staff. Mr. James did not reciprocate. He was all bluster and denial, which challenged my ability to avoid getting hooked again by taking his attitude and behavior personally.

We were able to reach an understanding about working together; however, I knew for me to be effective at mediating with him, I had to honor fully the Buddha's teachings on truthfulness, although doing so risked undoing our progress. I calmly asked, "Why didn't you simply return my phone call?" He exploded, stood, and slammed both hands forcefully on the table, rattling everything in the room. Instead of reacting with anger and self-righteousness, as I had in the past, I stayed anchored in awareness of my body, following my breath, silently repeating, "Inhale, exhale," and focusing on my loving-kindness feelings for his suffering. Because I did not react, he eventually calmed down. We found our way to a constructive working relationship that has continued for many years, including a successful mediation of this case that gave rise to our angry communications. For example, in a recent mediation, he repeated his behavior in the meeting with the program director and me, standing and slamming both hands forcefully on the table, while shouting at the defendants and defense attorney. I calmly said, "Mr. James, please sit down." He did. Later in a private caucus, he said, "I'm very impressed with how you do not react when I get so upset. I've tried that meditation stuff, but I just cannot seem to do it." I smiled and said, "Well, keep trying."

May these powerful teachings allow you to enhance your personal qualities for resolving conflict, and may many beings find peace through our practice.

Notes

1. The Pali word *dhamma* and the Sanskrit word *dharma* generally mean the collective teachings of the Buddha, or the "way" or "path," which those teachings describe.

2. The dozens of mindfulness practices the Buddha taught are not discussed in this chapter. For an excellent introduction to the topic see Goldstein and Kornfield (1987).

4

Christians as Conflict Engagement Practitioners

M. Brandon Sipes

DURING MY TIME AS A CONFLICT ENGAGEMENT FACILITATOR AND trainer, I have often heard the Arabic phrase *Insha'Allah*, or "If God wills it." The phrase is not used in a cavalier way, as though it could also mean "If we are lucky." Rather, its deep cultural and religious significance draws to mind the idea that the speaker should be so aligned with the mind of God that one's own endeavors would be seen in a favorable light, that God would will them to be successful. Viewing the history of the field of conflict engagement, I see it as unfortunate (though not surprising) that practitioners have often shied away from directly engaging the religious beliefs of their participants. Looking at the brief and hopeful utterance of *Insha'Allah*, as it reveals the deep religious dimensions of many intractable conflicts, we should recognize the importance of engaging religious belief and practice in our work.

My career in conflict engagement began as a graduate theology student at a Jesuit university. While studying a breadth of Christian theology (and in particular Catholic social teaching, liberation theology, and social justice themes), I focused on researching violent conflicts that had religious associations. I traveled to Northern Ireland and the Balkans to gain a better grasp of the way religious belonging contributed to conflict and also its contribution to peacebuilding. Much of my conflict engagement work has been within the context of the Israeli-Palestinian conflict, exploring how the parties might contribute to transforming their long-standing conflict in a just way. During my time there, I have had the good fortune to work alongside incredibly gifted

and seasoned activists, organizers, and conflict engagement practitioners. This group has worked hard to develop a new methodology called
the Kumi method (Brashear et al. 2012), which means "rise up" in both
Hebrew and Arabic. It is a process within which individuals and groups
who are working for social and political change are able to reflect upon
the root causes of the conflicts in which they are involved and collectively mobilize toward creative alternative solutions. It is guided by the
idea that conflicts exist within broader contexts in which deeply rooted
identities are bound together with entrenched social structures. Put simply, the approach holds that meaningful change in situations of protracted and deep-seated conflict is tied together with larger social
change, so that sustainable conflict resolution involves social transformation. Throughout this chapter, I will more fully describe Kumi and
use examples from our workshops to illuminate the ways in which I, as
a practitioner, have accessed resources from my own religious tradition
to improve my work.

Religion in the Workplace

In 2009, during one of our workshops in the West Bank, I found myself
pondering our work that week and our conflict engagement field in general. I had to leave the workshop early but left the following quotes on
one of our ubiquitous flip charts for my colleagues to read:

> It is the task of the prophet to bring to expression the new realities
> against the more visible ones of the old order. Energizing is closely
> linked with hope. We are energized not by that which we already pos-
> sess but by that which is promised and about to begin. (Brueggemann
> 1978, 23)

> We are discerners of newness, people who fashion images for hopes
> that have not yet become visible. We sense the deep undertow of life
> and welcome it. We present images of reality which are expectant and
> expansive. (Brueggemann 1976, 132)

Leaving these quotes was an attempt to remind my colleagues and
myself what the core of our work is: presenting the possibility of a different future arranged around just solutions to conflict and providing an
opportunity to explore how to get there. I doubt very much that anyone
who read these quotes knew who the author was, or that he was a Christian theologian specializing in the Hebrew scriptures. Brueggemann's
language mapping out a new and hopeful future is what he calls the

prophetic imagination, and it is through this religious lens that I often see my work. When I encourage participants to engage their conflicts together, particularly those that are deeply seated in the participant's values, needs, and identities, I am asking them to imagine a different future and to have the courage to hope for it. As other authors in this volume have stated, this is not simply an intellectual exercise. Rather, it will require work in all areas of intelligence: cognitive, spiritual, emotional, and somatic.

As should also be evident from the chapters in this book, religion and spirituality are increasingly receiving positive attention from a variety of academic disciplines and practitioners within the field of conflict engagement.[1] For many years, the trend has been to minimize or ignore the role that religion can play in engaging conflict. There are many reasons for this, but there is now a growing recognition that relegating religious belief and practice to a sphere separate from the work of engaging conflict has been both damaging to religious individuals and to the conflicts that they experience. But why has there been so much resistance?

Is religion the problem? This is a question all scholars of religiously motivated violence must ask. Certainly secularist thinkers like Hector Avalos (2005), Sam Harris (2004), and Christopher Hitchens (2007), who regard religion with skepticism or outright hostility, have all made their cases for the damage religion can cause in the world. However, a more nuanced understanding is that religions have the capacity to become harmful institutions adrift from their traditional, or maybe their ideal, moorings (Kimball 2002). This perspective affirms that religion can play a role in healing violence, but is still very aware of the dangers it can possess. Mark Juergensmeyer, a professor at the University of California well known for his writings on this topic, makes it clear:

> In many of the cases . . . not only have religion's characteristics led spiritual persons into violence, but also the other way around: violent situations have reached out for religious justification. The two approaches are not contradictory: extremism in religion has led to violence at the same time that violent conflicts have cried out for religious validation. (Juergensmeyer 2003, 161)

So it is somewhat understandable that our field has demurred from involving religion actively in healing that violence and conflict. However, this is a relatively myopic view of both conflict and religion. It not only diminishes the identity of the disputants and the complexity of their conflict, it concentrates on the degenerative elements of religion. A person's religious faith is often the most important identity marker for them, and those with deep faith commitments will likely filter the view of their experiences primarily through this lens.

Given this fundamental role of religion in the lives of many, we should then recognize its role in the complex and dynamic elements of conflict as well as the fullness of its capacity to provide exactly the conciliatory elements we strive to re-create as conflict engagement practitioners. There are a host of scholars and practitioners who are now calling for religion to be more actively engaged in the course of conflict engagement and peacebuilding (Gopin 2000, 2009; Appleby 2000; Daly and Sarkin 2007; Volf 2006). It is with this more balanced approach, which avoids "throwing out the baby with the bathwater," that we find the place where both practitioners and participants of conflict engagement processes can be honest about their faith: the way it can divide and the way it can provide a bridge to the other.

If religion can and ought to be utilized in conflict engagement processes, how can we go about it? This chapter will give some answers from my perspective as a Christian theologian and conflict practitioner.

I first will show the resources available within Christianity to heal conflict and division. Christianity is rich with theology supporting this task, and many Christians may find it illuminating that their faith has much to say when it comes to the development of peaceful societies. The resources to which I will draw our attention are the concepts of repentance, forgiveness, and new creation. For each of these resources, I will provide a list of ways I would encourage Christian practitioners to utilize them in their work.

Next, I will take these Christian resources and generalize them to some extent for the wider field of practice. Conflict practitioners who also happen to be religious individuals must, as with much of their identity, learn how and when to access these elements. It would not do, for example, to use Christian theological concepts with a group entirely unfamiliar or even hostile to them. I will discuss in what manner to utilize these religious resources and will relate them to the framework introduced in Chapter 2: separation, transition, and incorporation.

Throughout this chapter, I will transition from the perspective of an academic and theologian to that of a practitioner engaged in conflict work. I will use examples of my work facilitating Kumi with Israelis and Palestinians and others to illuminate how a practitioner can rely on his or her spiritual resources to enrich the work of conflict engagement. The question we should ask of ourselves is: How and when am I able to bring to bear the religious resources available to me from my tradition in order to generatively contribute to this conflict? I hope that by the end of this chapter, we will have fuller answers to this.

Resources for Peacebuilding Within Christianity

What do we believe about reconciliation between people in our world? Are we to believe violence will cease if all Christians live out the most radical notions of peacebuilding found in the Bible? The answer is probably not. However, there is a tension to be kept alive. The Christian religion is about hope. Hope for a future reality where this will occur, and we will be able to answer yes. Miroslav Volf encourages us to ask " . . . the right kind of question, which is not how to achieve the final reconciliation, but *what resources we need to live in peace in the absence of the final reconciliation*" (1996, 109). This "final reconciliation" is a vision of what our world may look like when the kingdom of God has come fully. This vision of the final reconciliation does not come easily, however, and it does not come all on its own. It should be, in the very best sense of the Christian experience, accompanied by spiritually transformative moments in the lives of individuals and in the community called "the church." These experiences I detail here are repentance, forgiveness, and the new creation. For the practice of peacebuilding, I hypothesize that these spiritual experiences become ways in which Christians can both tell their stories and begin to reconcile with their enemies.

I must mention here the point of view with which I approach my Christian faith and my work as a conflict mediator. Christianity, like every other religion, is incredibly diverse in the ways its adherents express their beliefs and act out their faith. And so it is not only helpful, but necessary, to contextualize my comments.

As a teenager, I began my faith life in a very small midwestern town at an Evangelical church and then attended an Evangelical university of the same denomination for my undergraduate work. The church and university were, for the most part, what you would associate with "the Midwest" and "Evangelical." The politics and theology were conservative, and the acceptance of belief and practice outside those boundaries was narrow. There were exceptions of course, including two professors who encouraged exploration, and my home pastor who always exhibited compassion and kindness for others. It was with this theological lens that I began my faith life. After leaving my undergraduate studies, and while still attending an Evangelical church, I began looking for alternatives. I became very involved in a faith community in Columbus, Ohio, that focused on simple, organic community as a way to live out God's call in our lives. Rather than weekly services in a communal building, they were held in several house churches that met throughout the week. These services were characterized by an appreciation for the arts, social justice, and a commitment to the urban neighborhoods in which they were established. Later, I attended a Jesuit Catholic university for my master's degree, where in addition to being exposed to a more liberal and inclusive theology, I began to study and spend time with persons of other religions. My worldview quickly expanded due to my research, travels, and interaction with others very much unlike myself.

It would have been very easy for me at any given time to leave the Evangelical denomination that I had always been a part of. After all, my perspective on so many things had shifted considerably from my time as a young Christian. I no longer shared much with them in terms of theology, politics, or Christian practice. Individuals in the United States tend to gather among others who are very similar to them, and this is especially true of Christians (Bishop 2008, 39).

However, I have stayed committed to this denomination and, in particular, to my local congregation. The reasons are many, but the results have been incredibly formative for my life and my work. Constantly being dedicated to a community with those who are different from me has pushed me to rigorously reflect upon and question my own assumptions. The choice has made me break down the stereotypes of others with whom I might not normally spend time. And most importantly, it has taught me how to lovingly embrace others with whom I have deep and significant disagreements.

This spiritual and emotional intelligence is not something I could have or would have ever learned in a seminar or training opportunity. And yet, it has so deepened my faith and my work. I am able to both describe the experience of and model the behavior that can lead from disagreement to understanding, to showing care and concern for each other. I believe, strongly, that my spiritual life and commitment to be in relationship with those who are different from me has made me a better facilitator, a better mediator, and a better human being.

Repentance

For most Christian believers, their faith life began with a moment of repentance. Whether they are led to this moment because they have wronged another or feel they have sinned against God, there is contrition and a wrong that must be rectified. We should understand repentance in terms of a real change in behavior and direction, not simply a verbal statement. When Jesus asked people to "repent and believe," it was not a simple request to apologize and believe in the reality of Jesus:

> Consider, for example, the Jewish aristocrat and historian Josephus, who was born a few years after Jesus' crucifixion and who was sent in

A.D. 66 as a young army commander to sort out some rebel movements in Galilee. His task, as he describes it in his autobiography, was to persuade the hot-headed Galileans to stop their mad rush into revolt against Rome and to trust him and the other Jerusalem aristocrats to work out a better *modus vivendi*. So when he confronted the rebel leader, he says that he told him to give up his own agenda and to trust him, Josephus, instead. And the word he uses is remarkably familiar to readers of the Gospels: he told the brigand leader to "repent and believe in me," *metanoesein pistos emoi genesesthai*. (Wright 1999, 43)

Assuming this understanding of repentance is more accurate to Jesus's intentions, and that repentance is the beginning of the Christian life whereby the individual expresses a desire to turn away from their past harmful behavior, then perhaps it can also be seen as the beginning of the reconciliation process between individuals.

In March 2009, our Kumi team held a workshop just inside the West Bank in Beit Jala, a few kilometers from Jerusalem and within eyesight of an Israeli settlement, Gilo. Early in the workshop, we had already gone through several exercises designed to form the group, most of which were either cognitive or somatic in nature, without a great deal of work focusing on the emotions. We were then moving into the emotional arenas to look closely at conflicts with each other and, conversely, our connections to each other. Up until now, the "separation" process of moving from the existing reality into this pseudo reality of the workshop had not sufficiently engaged all the areas of intelligence.

It was at this point that one of our Israeli participants became irritated with the dialogue. A woman I will call "Ofra" was responding to a question from a Palestinian woman about why young Israelis were so keen to join the army, serve at checkpoints, and cause so much hardship for Palestinians. Ofra said that the Palestinians had created a reality in which Israelis feared them and saw them as irrationally violent. She argued that their behavior had often proven them to be an aggressive people and that Israelis were only reacting against that aggression. She went on to talk about her mother, who over the course of her life grew increasingly afraid of the possibility of being attacked by Palestinians or some other menacing, unknown assailant. Whether they were walking through the streets of Jerusalem or traveling abroad, her mother always felt the same fear for her life.

From listening to Ofra, I could tell that her way of being in relationship to the Palestinians had been defined by fear and it became clear to me as she spoke that she had inherited this from her mother. It was crucial for her now to recognize this and to consider another way of looking at the Palestinians, to turn away from blame and turn to understanding. It was up to us as facilitators to help Ofra (and others in the room stuck on blame) to begin looking at her own role in the conflict. This is how repentance begins, with a nudge from a trusted source to take a better look at your own responsibility.

In Kumi, this process begins in a seemingly paradoxical way when we ask disputant groups to list how they believe the *other* conflict party escalates the conflict, and to listen to the blame that the other has for them. It is a difficult process, akin to being accused in public. In the best of our workshops, it allows participants to both be clear about how they see the other and hear how the other sees them. It is a process designed, at its core, to bring to light the pains of the past and the damaging perspective they have of their "enemies" and help them bring this into the present.

In Kumi, we take our time, ensuring that the emotional process that participants are experiencing is not prematurely cut off. But, as much as possible, we also attempt to move people along so they do not become mired in the same mind-set with which they arrived. After we have given carefully monitored equal time for the disputant groups to focus their blame on the other, we ask their permission (and in that way gain the ability to hold them to their decision) to begin looking at their own role. And so we make a shift from participants blaming others to participants asking themselves why they care so deeply about the issues and what needs they feel are at stake in the conflict. Here, we spare no expense with time, ensuring that everyone who wants to speak is able to. We encourage them to share stories that illuminate why they have felt so bitterly about the other, and why they felt their needs were so threatened by the others. Here it was that Ofra began to pull back from her earlier statements. You could see the recognition in her eyes as she began to hear and understand the Palestinians more deeply:

> I grew up with the fear of being exterminated. This big sentence is repeated in Israel at every ceremony: "Remember, don't forget. If you forget for a minute, it will happen again." We convince ourselves in stories, textbooks and the media that we are good, moral—it's a mechanism that I don't understand but I know that it exists. We, as soldiers, believe that what we're doing is moral, even at checkpoints. It is possible to kill someone and to think it is moral. In order to fight, to be a soldier, you have to lose something—an innocent child [inside of you] must be killed.

From that moment on in our workshop, Ofra began to shift her focus from blaming the Palestinians in the room for their perceived aggression and violence to the fact that she and her mother were afraid and the reasons for being so. It was as though she had turned in another direction with this recognition and was, at least for our time together, seeking a new relationship with those whom she formerly feared. This is what we hope for: that the "transition" the participants experience allows them to engage each other deeply, to discover their shared needs and concerns, and to deeply explore the reality of the conflict they are experiencing. This occurs most easily when participants have developed the capacity to admit their role in the conflict and acknowledge a new approach is needed.

This is the repentance that can be encouraged in our conflict work, and which for me is rooted in my Christian experience. In both my spiritual life and in my conflict work, I cannot be pleased with any arrangement other than the one that eschews verbal-only apologies and instead makes the building of relationships the priority. Repentance may just allow us to see the perspective of the other whom we so eagerly vilified. This then is the beginning of the reconciliation process: the realization of our guilt and our decision to turn away from our former actions in order to heal the relationship with our enemies. For practitioners, some actions that can support this include:

- Encourage participants to consider how their actions and attitudes have escalated or prolonged the conflict.
- As the facilitator, remember how difficult it can be to admit responsibility. Look for moments when individuals seem ready to do this and encourage those notions.
- Allow lots of time for this back and forth process of considering their own roles and the roles of others.
- Solidify repentance by acknowledging it in the group, recording it, and using those admissions to provide the foundation for next steps (see "Forgiveness," below).

Forgiveness

The magnificent novel *Les Miserables* (1943) by Victor Hugo is among the most poignant and beautiful stories written about the power of forgiveness and the new life it can engender. The story describes the life of Jean Valjean, a man sent to prison for stealing bread for his starving family. He spends nineteen years in a hard labor prison and is finally released on parole, where he eventually finds himself staying at the home of a bishop. Valjean became a hard-hearted man in prison and he received no human grace following his release. And so, feeling desperate and as if nobody is on his side, he decides the only way to start a new life is to steal some of the man's silver. Valjean is caught shortly afterward by the gendarmes and returned to the bishop's house. Instead of handing him over to the authorities, the bishop tells them that he gave the silver to Valjean and that he forgot the candlesticks, the most valuable of his silver. After the gendarmes leave, the bishop exhorts Valjean to use the silver to make himself an honest man. He tells Valjean that he belongs "no longer to evil, but to good. It is your soul that I am buying for you. I withdraw it from dark thoughts and from the spirit of perdition, and I give it to God!" (Hugo 1943, 39).

The magnanimous grace of the bishop is in my mind one of the most accurate reflections of the grace of God rendered in fiction. Valjean accepts the gift and repents of his former life. He tears up his parole ticket and literally becomes a new man, taking on a new name. The power of forgiveness offered and accepted, the understanding that you are forgiven by someone who has no reason to do so, is an incredibly powerful and transformative experience. Volf addresses what the bishop's response might have been, if only he were more concerned with his security and possessions than he was with the redemption of men:

> Revenge multiplies evil. Retributive justice contains evil—and threatens the world with destruction. Forgiveness overcomes evil with good. Forgiveness mirrors the generosity of God whose ultimate goal is neither to satisfy injured pride nor to justly apportion reward and punishment, but to free sinful humanity from evil and thereby reestablish communication with us. (Volf 2005, 161)

Eschewing revenge, overcoming evil with good, and reestablishing communication are all hopes of the conflict practitioner, and to draw on these themes in appropriate ways could benefit our work greatly.

During one of our very first Kumi workshops, I remember vividly a moment when forgiveness was requested and given, which changed the outcome for at least a few of our participants. This workshop was the first in which we implemented Kumi, and so the participants (Israeli and Palestinian activists, international conflict experts, and, because we were holding the event at the University of Hamburg, German students) were invited to give us input on the method.

We were at the section of the workshop where the participants were in small mixed groups attempting to develop plans to implement when returning to their various homes. A group of mostly young activists and students were discussing the trips arranged for Israeli students to visit Holocaust sights across Eastern Europe. Their discussion was centered on how many of these trips promote a narrative of victimhood of Israelis and shaming of Germans and how this narrative needed to be challenged. As they worked together, one of the German participants made an offhand comment that she could not understand why she should feel blame or even responsibility for what had happened so many years before. She further went on to ask how Israelis could possibly still feel like victims after so many years. This question may have provoked an interesting conversation, but because it so quickly followed a statement that seemed to exempt her from any ties to the history of the Holocaust, it was not taken well among the Israelis in the group. The group was self-facilitated, and we only discovered their dialogue had deteriorated several minutes later when we saw each of them with their arms crossed and chairs pushed back from the table. I and another facilitator noticed this together and sat down on the outskirts of their group. After some questions about how things were going, and why they were "stuck," as they described it, we asked the participants what upset them about what was said (the possibility that Germans now should feel no shame over history) and recorded it for them. Then we placed that aside, stating we would return to it in just a moment. We then introduced a conversation around the German student's second question (why do Israelis still feel like victims?). The Israelis described the precariousness of their existence for decades even after the Holocaust, the stories they still hear from relatives who experienced it firsthand, and the ongoing anti-Semitism around the world that is a constant reminder of their trauma. At the end of this conversation, we returned to the statement we had set aside previously and asked the German student if, given what the Israelis had shared, she better understood why her statement was received so poorly. She said she did, and described how she saw parallels between the ongoing Israeli trauma and the ongoing culture of self-blaming in Germany. She was, however, very quiet as the group moved back to work, pushing their chairs back to the table and leaning into their conversation. My colleague and I wandered away to allow the group to form back on its own, but we noticed the German student was reluctant to engage. At a break, I asked her how things were going. She said she felt a little worried she might say something else "wrong." I assured her she would! I also assured her that we were here to learn how to handle those moments better and to hopefully reduce their frequency. She still did not seem satisfied, so I asked if she felt like she had damaged her relationship with the Israeli participant. She responded, "I said something I'm not sure I actually believe, and I'm afraid that I both hurt him and gave him a bad view of myself." I encouraged her to simply talk to him and see if he actually felt that way. Above all, I encouraged her to be honest about how she felt, and that if he was hurt, to ask for forgiveness. The participant walked away immediately to find the Israeli participant. I found this to be an incredibly *reflexive* moment on her part. That is, she moved beyond simple reflection (This is what happened and how I reacted) to reflexive practice (This is what happened and I am examining why I reacted in that way). Later at dinner, the two of them sat together, laughing and in conversation. She had asked for forgiveness and he had responded positively, thanking her for her honesty and letting her know he appreciated her coming to him. Now they were enjoying downtime, talking excitedly about their plans from the day and looking ahead at how they might make them a reality.

I do believe it is possible that their plans might have been made otherwise, and that once they returned to dialogue together, the workshop could have gone on as normal. But the participant in this case who would have missed out was the German student, who felt like she could not enter the conversation any longer because of the damage she had already done. In this case, the damage was minimal, and not lasting. There will be more difficult cases, where we are not simply inviting participants to mend their damaged relationship by asking for forgiveness, but cases where we are asking enemies with deep enmity to see each other as human again, and to ask forgiveness for ever viewing them otherwise. This, profoundly, is the beauty of forgiveness: the invitation to be fully human again, in the eyes of God and in the eyes of the other.

This is a key area of a movement when attempting to resolve conflicts: the kind of shift that happens when disputants speak with each other about their essential concerns and resonance is fostered between them. In Christian language, we could see this occurring through the offering of repentance and the possibility of forgiveness. The power of "I'm sorry" or "I have wronged you" is enough to shift the entire perspective of those in conflict. It is often unexpected, works contrary to the normal dynamics of conflict escalation, and centers the interaction of the participants on each other and their humanity rather than the conflict they experience. It would be reductionist to imagine that this is all it would take for successful conflict engagement, but participants who have a deep sense of grace and forgiveness can often move forward more quickly and more intentionally than those without this same sense.

These movements have become part of our larger Kumi method that we have been developing for the past several years. Our goal, in many ways, is to move participants (and the conflict) from a degenerative space (in which the conflict only escalates) to a generative one (in which needs are met and the conflict de-escalates). That is, instead of seeing only that things are getting worse, and that the *other* specifically is making them worse, we hope that they may reach a point where they move through this process of reframing, which will enable to them to look more deeply and generatively at the conflict in order to develop sustainable solutions. Some practioner tips are

- Do not allow hurtful comments to fester. While many difficult things can be said in conflict engagement, it is up to the practitioner to provide a framework that allows for the healing of those comments.
- Acknowledge the power of healthy relationships. Point out the deterioration of communication when a participant feels hurt or slighted. Link it to the capacity to develop solutions and working relationships to implement them.
- If a person is hurt, encourage him or her to express why, so that the offender can better understand these feelings and needs. Understanding the needs of the other is key to being able to forgive.
- In complex intractable conflicts, especially those that are violent, it is often too difficult to ask traumatized people to forgive even if the offender has repented. Do not force this question on those who are obviously dealing with deep trauma and need time to process it.

New Creation: The Reconciliation of All Things

I believe the greatest hope found in the Christian faith is the idea of *new creation*, when God reconciles all to himself. There are glimpses of this newly re-created world found in scripture, one of which provides the most insight to our current topic:

> Then the angel showed me the river of the water of life, bright as crystal, flowing from the throne of God and of the Lamb through the middle of the street of the city. On either side of the river is the tree of life with its twelve kinds of fruit, producing its fruit each month; and the leaves of the tree are for the healing of the nations. (Revelation 22:1–2, New Revised Standard Version [NRSV])

This passage describes, in metaphorical terms, this new creation. The image is designed to represent how God's rule will spread throughout the earth, bringing healing. There are other passages that help color the picture of that time: the wolf will dwell with the lamb; nation will not rise up against nation; and the amazing announcements of good news to the poor, the mourning, the meek, and others listed in the Beatitudes. (Isaiah 11:6; Isaiah 2:4; Matthew 5:1–11, NRSV)

How are we to live with this hope of the future now? If our world is to be re-created in the image of God, as are his people, what should our world look like *now*? Is the hope of the Christian only for the future, or are there already signs of the things to come? It seems that Jesus's understanding was that it is both present and not yet fully realized: "The Kingdom of God is a dynamic conception . . . It is not completed but always becoming; not present, neither immanently nor transcendently, but always 'at hand'" (Tillich 1990, 35).

So we ask the question roiling in the minds of those affected by war and strife. Can we hope for something better in the future? The answer lies in the fact that this world will not always be ordered in the manner it is now: by men who are pursuing power and violence. And those men, with their systems of dominance and corruption, coercion and violence, desperately want to stay in control. Ultimately, however, that type of control will be superseded by the daily actions of those living out the kingdom of God and by the new creation inaugurated by God (Brueggemann, 1978). Our hope for that reality is what sustains.

Sometimes, I believe, in our work we get distracted by all-or-nothing thinking: "I want to go to the West Bank, collect as many people as possible, and define the solutions to the conflict so that all can start contributing to them." So we develop this vision for what the perfect set of solutions will look like, immediately recognize how hard it is to create, and then despair. Instead of moving forward, we simply wait for someone else to create the future for us. "Camp David Accords, we cry out to thee!" "Oslo, come save us!"

And so my encouragement to participants is always that they are contributing to something . . . that they need not wait around for perfection to come crashing down around them. Each and every little act they do that counters the conflict, that breaks down division, and that humanizes the other is a significant contribution to the resolution of the conflict. This is not an encouragement to work at the lowest common denominator, but it is a way for us to encourage participants to overcome the perception that reality is too complex to deal with. We ask them to throw reality out the window when it comes to developing their vision. When we get to looking at what they can do to reach their new vision—their new creation—then we begin to look closely at the barriers in front of them as well as the resources they have at their disposal. In this way, the visions they develop really do look brand new: they have energy and dynamism because they were not limited by the current negative, complex reality. But their plans are also realistic because they have taken the time to ground them within their areas of influence.

After completing one of these visioning and planning sessions with a binational group in Israel and Palestine, we found out that the Palestinians among the group had planned a trip to the Yad Vashem museum in Israel, dedicated to memorializing victims of the Holocaust. This excursion, at that time and still today, is not a regular occurrence. The participants also invited along media and politicians to be a part of this trip. For them, the trip signified a reaching out to hear the narrative of the Israelis, to better understand who they are. It was deeply personal for their own growth. They did not imagine, however, that this act was only for themselves. Rather, they saw it also as an act designed to show others what the newly created Israeli-Palestinian relationship could look like. In some ways, this was a small act that did not contribute significantly to the resolution of the conflict. However, in other ways, the act is a signifier of right relationships and a marker of new ways of being now possible in a land of division.

The role of all of this in the reconciliation of broken and conflicted societies is clear. No longer are we bound by images of war, oppression, and coercion. We can see the world "as it will be," rather than how it is. We refuse to see the world only in terms of the current reality, but live life according to a vision of how the world "could" be.

This requires, of course, the commitment to walk alongside conflict parties and support them as they work toward that future vision. *Incorporation* in our design means a long engagement with workshop participants after the workshop ends. If incorporation is to be successful, that is, if the decisions that were agreed upon during the time the participants spent together (in the separation and transition phases) are to become concrete, there will need to be follow-up on behalf of the workshop organizer/intervener and of the participants themselves. However, keeping in mind the thrust of this book, it is not enough simply to have a detailed action plan and follow-up meetings. What sorts of practices can we put into place that will take seriously the emotional weight of the end of this type of intervention? How might the facilitators and participants together explore the depth of their commitments to each other by viewing them through their spirituality? What we find at the end of many workshops is an energy and a willingness among the participants to make something real and concrete out of their time together, even if things have progressed poorly. How can we make sense of this in ways less analytical than an action plan, as necessary as that is? The group that visited Yad Vashem maintained contact and support from us as they continued to think about ways in which they could take their conversations into action.

And finally, through each stage of the process, from *separation* through *transition* and into *incorporation*, there needs to be increased focus on the wisdom elements within the human experience. While some conflict engagement practices exclusively focus on these elements (and end up underdeveloped as well), the majority of conflict engagement methods are highly analytical, highly cognitive, and rather unconcerned with the emotional and spiritual factors at play. We would do well as a field to begin incorporating tools, methods, and theory that reflect these missing dimensions by:

- Not allowing participants to be constrained by their current reality. Yes, there is a place for recognizing the obstacles they face, but as you work on envisioning a different future with the participants, allow their creativity and hope to reign supreme.
- Acknowledging that the way things are now is not the way we are intended to live, nor is it likely that anyone in the room prefers it to be that way in the future. So, how can we change it?
- Affirming that *new creation* requires creation. Participants have a responsibility to act on their vision if they have the courage to develop one. It will not become reality if they do not act.
- Advising that new creation takes time. Participants should know that their actions will take time to have significant impacts on their conflict. They should also feel supported by the facilitators to enact those changes.

Some Final Thoughts on the Religious Practitioner

There are serious questions to be asked about both the role of the religious practitioner and the role of religion in any given conflict engagement. As I alluded to, there are a great many times when it would be inappropriate for a practitioner to overtly draw on his or her religious views to affect an outcome or steer disputants in a certain direction. There are also times when unearthing and discussing the participants' religious identities could cause more harm than good. I continue to affirm that conflict engagement is as much an art as a science, and it would do practitioners a lot of good to approach these topics with humility and caution.

However, there are times when it makes sense for practitioners to explore them. I will briefly discuss the question of when this is appropriate and then how to do what I call *disciplining our own bias* as a practitioner.

As both a Christian and a practitioner, I can say that I have had very few instances where I have explicitly used the theological frames I described above. This has everything to do with the context in which I am working, the makeup of the disputants, and the relationship I have with them. These three things are part of what I use to help me determine to what extent to explicitly use Christian themes.

For example, many of the workshops I facilitated were held near Beit Jala, between Jerusalem and the West Bank city of Bethlehem. These sessions have included very diverse participants: from binational organizations looking to improve their work by engaging internal conflicts to antagonistic disputants from their respective communities meeting the other for the first time and dubious about the outcome of their time together. In almost all of these, my theological framework was kept to myself. I could not discern that the concrete theological ideas would be grasped or prove helpful in formulating new energy to move forward together. This is not to say that internally I did not access these resources. While facilitating, I can recall moments where spiritual language crept in and I encouraged participants to grasp onto hope and believe in change despite their reality. I believe I spoke these things with some spiritual authority because of my own belief. However, there was never a moment where it made sense to me to share an explicit formulation of belief or to encourage the participants to "accept Jesus," as much as my Evangelical friends might have wanted me to!

In other cases, it may make sense to develop and utilize this framework explicitly. Clearly, when working with a Christian community and participants, it makes sense to draw on these themes. They are understandable to the participants, and it is likely that these are the concepts that are most motivating for them. A congregational conflict where participants are likely very committed to each other and the health of their community would be a prime opportunity for this type of intervention.

In 2010, I was contacted by a young woman, "Sarah," who had been asked by her Unitarian congregation to plan a bicentennial anniversary event. Previously in the congregation's history, there had been a lot of division and many people had left. One of the men on the panel for the celebration was insistent on addressing that period of time, as he had been personally involved (and hurt). Sarah was concerned that this man might both dominate the presentation and conversation as well as reopen old wounds the church had moved beyond. After much conversation about the backstory, I asked Sarah a leading question: "What would you say is the major strength of the Unitarian church, and of your congregation?"

"Inclusion," she replied. "Being welcoming. That's what makes this such a hard topic. I don't want to bring up an issue that might again cause division and hurt." We talked about this for some time and I urged her first to talk with the man about what he planned to share and in what way. I told her I did not think it would be wise to have me come in and speak with anyone, as it might actually escalate the issue more than needed ("It must be bad! They brought in a mediator!"). I encouraged her to ask the man to reflect deeply about the conflict and the time that had passed since then. Why had he remained committed to the congregation throughout? Why had he not left? In essence, I encouraged Sarah to have the man access the spiritual resources I spoke of earlier in this chapter. After Sarah talked to the man, and after he had taken some time to ponder her questions, they both felt comfortable with him sharing the history in the form of his spiritual narrative throughout that period rather than an objective, cognitive history lesson on the facts. Afterward, she told me this spiritual engagement of the issues opened quite a beautiful dialogue in the midst of their celebration and reminded them of their spiritual commitment to God and to each other.

Finally, the relationship you have with your participants can determine the extent to which you can discuss, and make useful, your Christian resources. During one of our workshops, I was facilitating a small group of Palestinian participants. They were in the process of listing all the blame they had for the other participants, both Israelis and internationals. When they came to the internationals, they listed the American Christian community's financial support of settlements throughout the West Bank. Because I had developed a close relationship with several of the participants both inside and outside of the workshop, I was able to jokingly bring up that I belonged to the Evangelical American community. It opened a conversation that would not have been previously held about the diverse nature of the Christian communities in the United States (since I did not seem to fit their perception of Evangelical), and furthermore, about how diverse any group is (e.g., Israelis). This moved the conversation along nicely and allowed the participants in the later stages of the workshop to more easily acknowledge that their stereotypes and attributions of others were not nearly as accurate as they had supposed.

All in all, there is a great amount of discernment involved in our use of religion in conflict. An important characteristic of a skilled practitioner is the ability to discipline our bias. There has been much discussion in our field about the necessary neutrality of mediators and conflict workers. I think this is an unhelpful approach. Neutrality simply does not exist, particularly among those charged to work toward the end of conflict. We all have our assumptions, our beliefs about the conflicts in which we work—even our approaches and methods have their own bias. What is more helpful is to talk about disciplining our bias. We make the recognition that we are human, that we have bias, and that we work toward disciplining ourselves in order to help facilitate healthy conversations. The participants then see a model of a person recognizing and affirming their own identity in a healthy way without letting it overpower the task of resolving conflict.

It is always helpful for a facilitator to be knowledgeable, but that knowledge will almost always lead to opinions and perspectives on the issues at hand in the workshop. So my continuously growing understanding of the Israeli-Palestinian conflict has left me with a set of opinions on what is just, what solutions should be considered, and what escalates the conflict. But my role as a facilitator is not to inject those opinions and steer participants toward my own assumptions. So I must discipline that bias in order to preserve the self-determination of the individuals in the room. In order to do that, I keep the following things in mind:

- Humble yourself. You do not know as much as you think you know, and there truly is always someone in the room more knowledgeable than you.
- Learning does not always equal experience. The research you have done does not equate to the experience of growing up and living within this conflict.
- Different opinions equal different solutions. Someone in the room is going to come up with something you would never think of.
- Solutions are not the only goal. By assuming you know the answers, you steer them in the direction of your solutions and rob them of the opportunity to learn new ways of speaking and being together.

Conflict engagement practitioners who also happen to be Christians have a great deal to add to our field. We understand hope for a new reality, we practice forgiveness of others (and receive it too), and we acknowledge our failures. A skilled practitioner who embodies these traits both understands their power and can translate these experiences into questions, processes, and conversations that allow participants to explore them as well. The question of whether to explicitly share these resources rests on the nature of the engagement, as described earlier.

But not in question is the practitioner's increased capacity to encourage these traits in others given his or her own experience with them.

Conclusion

It has been a pleasure to take part in this writing project. As a person who had explored religion and theology, it was somewhat disconcerting to enter a field that had so much resistance to utilizing religion in positive ways. I knew the resources were there, and that a great many disputants in conflict had accessed those resources in myriad ways throughout the twentieth century. So why was our field not supporting them, encouraging them, developing approaches from them?

It seems now that the momentum is shifting. One beneficial by-product of the emphasis on religious violence has been that a great many scholars and practitioners have discovered the alternative narratives in the religions that provide resources for conflict engagement and peacebuilding. It is up to us, the religious practitioners, to more fully develop ways in which religion, in all its forms and at all levels, can be positively and productively included in our processes.

In the case of Christianity, there are already many communities with long-standing traditions of peace and justice work. My task (and the task of my fellow Christians committed to peace) is then to continue building on these narratives, to continue supporting and developing this work. The vision of the kingdom of God is one of reconciled peoples, of a violent world turned upside down by the people of God who are committed to be people of peace. So let us work diligently toward that end.

Note

1. For this chapter, I use the term *conflict engagement,* as it can refer to the many purposes of conflict work: conflict management, resolution, transformation, etc.

5

Developing Embodied Awareness and Action in Conflict Resolution

Julia Morelli and Christopher Fitz

SOMETIMES THE SMALLEST, SEEMINGLY INSIGNIFICANT INTER-
action can open a window to much deeper observations about how we
react and interact in conflict:

> I was mediating with two participants[1] about fifteen years ago. Even
> though I had seven years of experience as a mediator, it was neverthe-
> less a memorable session. I noticed one participant was writing
> tensely with her pencil, her notes scrawled in dark print. The sight of
> her distressed writing suddenly made me aware of tightness in my
> own body. I realized that my tension and hers were probably con-
> nected. So I continued sitting up straight, and took several slow, deep
> breaths until I had relaxed, while listening to the account given by the
> other participant. When he finished talking, I paraphrased what I heard
> calmly and quietly.
>
> Without obvious reason, the feeling of tension in the room began
> to dissipate. The two began working together, and the session shifted
> toward them finding resolution. I still can't be sure that calming
> myself prompted the change, but I knew then and I know now that
> managing my own body's responses to stressful situations makes me a
> more effective mediator. (Morelli 2014)[2]

Mainstream training in conflict resolution, using a classic North American model of mediation or an interest-based theoretical approach to
conflict interaction, is rooted in a relatively linear, rational model of
human interaction. This system also tends to focus on the attitudes and
behaviors of the participants, assuming that the third party is a disinter-

ested guiding force, not an integral part of the conflict dynamic. In this model, third parties are famously told to separate the person from the problem and are encouraged to work through a process that intellectualizes conflict while attempting to remove emotions from the conflict resolution equation (Fisher and Ury 1981). Many in the conflict resolution field have already pointed out how multifaceted this work is—even messy. This chapter seeks to build on existing conflict resolution literature about the wisdom of the body (Cloke 2013; LeBaron et al. 2013; LeBaron 2002; Nan 2011; Noble 2014; Shank and Schirch 2008) in arguing for expanding conflict resolution beyond its rational and disembodied roots.

This chapter is based on two observations about the current state of the field of conflict resolution and one argument about where the field should be headed. The observations are, first, that there are an increasing number of theorists and practitioners who understand that emotional/physical reactions, rooted in the body, are a natural part of the conflict process. Second, that there are an increasing number of theorists and practitioners who see the third party as an active element of the conflict dynamic whose emotional and physical reactions need to be managed every bit as much as those of the primary parties.

The argument is that although embodied awareness and approaches have gained popularity outside and, to some extent, in the conflict resolution field, bringing them fully into the mainstream of the field can greatly enhance the discipline and its effectiveness in a wide range of conflicts.

To pursue this argument, we will examine two ways to conceive of the body's role in conflict, and we will present a theoretical and practical view of three broad fields of study that have contributed to our knowledge about body-based practices. The two primary conceptions of the body's place in conflict are as *bellwether* and as an *instrument of change*.[3] As a bellwether, the body can reveal hidden dynamics in conflict situations, a reference to the bell carried by the lead sheep in a herd.[4] As an instrument of change, the body can be used to positively alter the conflict environment and the interactions among participants and the third party. We focus on three fields that exhibit the body's potential in conflict resolution: mind-body practices, somatics, and embodied creative arts. All three fields will be defined and explored in detail in the sections to follow, while the term *embody* is used in various forms to describe approaches emphasizing physical presence, awareness, or technique as distinct from traditional verbal or rational approaches.

To contextualize these three areas, we present examples of their use in conflict situations and suggest related embodied techniques that could enhance conflict resolution practices. These come largely from interviews conducted with practitioners using embodied practices in conflict situations.[5] An in-depth exploration of practice is found in the case study of a particular approach using Playback Theatre. It applies the Multidimensional Practice Framework (discussed in Chapter 2) to suggest the potential diversity of creative embodied approaches to conflict resolution. This is followed by one of the authors' experience integrating mind-body practices personally and professionally using Playback Theatre. As this and the case following it represent the experience of the authors, these accounts are written in the first person.

Some of the knowledge and techniques presented herein translate readily for practitioners at any level. Others require specialized training to minimize risks for the parties involved. First, however, we will consider the traditional conceptions of the body's place in conflict, and some of the work that has been done to bring nontraditional concepts of the body into the theory and practice of conflict resolution.

The Body in Conflict: An Evolving Debate

The classic reference to conflict and the body in popularized conflict resolution discourse harkens back to the work of Walter Cannon and his study of *fight-or-flight* responses to stress during World War I (Cannon 1929; Goleman and Gurin1993, 8). The insight is useful in acknowledging the limitations of conscious decision making in situations of high emotion or stress. Cannon's opening story also suggests how unconsciously expressed stress can influence a mediator, participants, and mediation. But the dominant fight-or-flight rhetoric also reinforces a cultural association with the body as an obstacle to rational discourse and thus, to resolving conflict. We also note that references to fight-or-flight are often used in analyses of conflict participants, not the mediator, as if the mediator's emotions and stress are peripheral at best.

Conflict resolution as an area of study has largely grown out of existing academic fields. As Rainey and Wing argue, "Notwithstanding significant development on its own, conflict theory has been drawn largely from scholars and practitioners in 'traditional' disciplines. . . . " (2012, 36). This orientation and affiliation with established fields has brought legitimacy but hindered the development of emotive, spiritual, and embodied perspectives in conflict resolution. Contributions like *Bringing Peace into the Room* (Bowling and Hoffman 2003) and *The Moral Imagination* (Lederach 2005) have suggested that the potential of mediation is greater than the sum of its techniques—that personal and even aesthetic qualities are important for a mediator's effectiveness. From the perspective of anthropology, some in-depth accounts have addressed mediation structure or ritual and how it can enable a shift in participant patterns (Schirch 2005; Davidheiser 2006). Nonetheless, while their work circles around the body, from the personal to the collective, it falls short of directly exploring the embodied quality of participants, mediators, or their conflict practices.

Substantial arguments have already been made for considering all aspects of the practitioner in conflict resolution practice (Cloke 2004; Cloke 2013; Donlon 2001; Goldberg and Blancke 2012; Gopin 2004; LeBaron 2002; Nan 2011). Adding to the existing literature about the body's wisdom in conflict (LeBaron 2002; LeBaron et al. 2013; Nan 2011; Shank and Schirch 2008; Siegel 2010), we provide an overview of the trends that support the proposition that the body's innate intelligence should be incorporated into all levels of conflict resolution training and practice.

In 2002, Julia Morelli presented a workshop, "The Mind, Body and Conflict," at the annual conference of the Association for Conflict Resolution (ACR). At the time it was an unusual topic, but the room was packed. The topic is still uncommon, but body awareness in conflict resolution has nonetheless expanded beyond the traditional observation of nonverbal cues and footnotes about fight-or-flight responses.[6] Indeed, newer work addressing conflict resolution through movement and dance (Eddy 2009a; LeBaron 2002, 83, 94; LeBaron et al. 2013; Alexander and LeBaron 2013), theater (Cohen et al. 2011), and aikido (Linden 2007) begins to tap the enormous potential for more embodied approaches to conflict resolution than is the Western norm.

Research in neuroscience and psychology demonstrates the relevance of our physiology to conflict and stress, and points to a need for a more integrative and holistic approach to conflict resolution. The first challenge to incorporating the body in conflict resolution is recognizing the fight-or-flight response in oneself. On the personal level, how effectively can one work with conflict when the rational mind is under siege? On the theoretical level, how can the body be an instrument of change in conflict resolution when it creates the stress response in the first place? Daniel Goleman, author of *Emotional Intelligence*,[7] characterizes the fight-or-flight physiological response as a *neural hijacking* that triggers a response before the *thinking brain* can react (1995, 14). Davis, Eshelman, and McKay describe the fight-or-flight response and the corresponding *relaxation response*. For the former, when someone is threatened or experiences high anxiety, adrenaline prompts the body into physical responses that act as an early warning system or bellwether (1995, 1–2). This state is associated with knee-jerk responses and reduced rationality and creativity. The relaxation response is a natural restorative reaction that enables the body to reduce heart rate and blood pressure, slow breathing, release muscle tension, and allow reflection. Through increased awareness, training, and practice, one can learn to detect and even anticipate the fight-or-flight response and insert a pause that allows the body and mind to become calm. This enables a person in conflict to consider a wider range of options. The significance of the relaxation response is evidenced by research conducted by the National Institutes of Health's National Center for Complementary and Integrative Health.[8] Although there is a third response to stress that has received less attention—freeze—we will not address it since it is most often associated with trauma and a sense of extreme helplessness.

Another lesser-known and potentially important stress response is known as *tend and befriend* (Taylor et al. 2000). This response has been linked to the hormone oxytocin, which sometimes also is released in conflict situations. It provides an impulse to draw closer to or befriend the other. It is most often associated with females and caregiving, although it does occur in males (Taylor et al. 2000). Conflict resolution practitioner Kenneth Cloke, noting the important connections to this response with conflict and the mediation process, finds, "The physical basis for collaboration, altruism, trust, forgiveness, and interest-based conflict resolution techniques, has been clearly identified with the 'tend and befriend' hormone oxytocin" (2009). At a minimum, it is worth exploring the roles regulating adrenaline (fight or flight) and oxytocin (tend and befriend) responses and how they could maximize positive outcomes from conflict.

Further insight into and support for embodied conflict approaches comes from the discovery of *mirror neurons* and the role they play in interpreting action and emotion. Mirror neuron networks can produce *emotional contagion*, which is a process that describes individuals' impact on each other's brain states in unconscious, perhaps contagious, ways, whether in pairs or groups (Cloke 2013, 89–101; De Gelder et al. 2004; Goleman 2011, 82–83, 106–109). While the primacy of mirror neurons and emotional contagion is the subject of debate and further study, mounting research makes it increasingly hard to ignore the central role played by unconscious physical and emotional dynamics in a conflict situation.

The study of adrenalin, oxytocin, and mirror neurons reminds us that conflict is essentially an embodied event. Moreover, the research suggests that accessing innate mechanisms that have the potential to *befriend* and spread *contagious* collaboration may play an important role in conflict resolution. This implies that the rational techniques we consider essential to conflict management may play a smaller role than is generally assumed when placed alongside neurophysiologic factors.

Mind-Body Practices and Conflict Resolution

One important field to examine to understand how the body can be an asset to conflict resolvers includes mind-body practices. Mind-body and stress reduction techniques include mindfulness practices such as meditation, yoga, tai chi and qigong,[9] and the Japanese martial art of aikido.[10]
     One practitioner explains:

> I sit in a very specific way so I can stay integrated. I sit near the edge of the chair, both feet on the floor, sitting upright with a relaxed and open body, breathing from my belly. These somatic techniques help me stay present in the moment and actively aware of my emotions, thoughts and physiology. Because of this awareness, I am much more sensitive to when I become tense or stressed. This awareness also warns me of when I feel threatened and provides me with an opportunity to choose another response, instead of instinctually lashing out at a perceived threat.
>
> During a particularly challenging mediation it was revealed that one of the participants had, or may have contracted, AIDS. The impact of the message was like an atomic bomb had gone off in the room; I sank back into my chair stunned and visibly shaken. Feelings of rage and fear filled the room.
>
> There is a Japanese saying, "fall down six times, get up seven." I thought, "What am I here to do?" Then, I hit my metaphoric "reset" button and was able to re-establish my focus by consciously returning to an upright, relaxed open body posture and breathing from my belly.
>
> These changes in my physiology allowed me to calm my mind, come back into the moment, and reconnect with the participants. I would not have been able to do that without my training in somatic skills. When it really mattered, I was able to help those who needed it. (S. Kotev, pers. comm.)

Stephen Kotev uses somatic skills derived from the Japanese martial art of aikido, taught to him by Dr. Paul Linden (Linden 2003), because they allow him to "not get in [his] own way when it matters the most" (S. Kotev, pers. comm.). Kotev teaches novice and experienced conflict resolvers how to embody calm in the midst of challenge using techniques focused on breath and posture. He teaches students how to use their body both as a bellwether and an instrument of change, enabling them to respond effectively to challenging circumstances.

Like Kotev's approach, mindfulness practices often include observing the body in terms of comfort, and releasing physical tension. While the practices can vary widely, mindfulness is generally about developing an awareness of what happens moment-to-moment—physically and mentally. It is characterized by openness, curiosity, and awareness without judgment (Ciarrochi et al. 2013, 10–11). A review of the literature on mindfulness-based stress reduction practices shows they allow practitioners to act more reflectively rather than habitually, and they also enhance one's spiritual values (Chiesa and Serretti 2009, 593). Mindfulness practices can reduce stress by creating opportunity for *positive reappraisal*.[11] This physiological, psychological, and behavioral process enables fluidity in the stress response through conscious *feedback* when stressful events are evaluated as potentially beneficial or meaningful (Garland and Fredrickson 2013, 42–49).

The last twenty years have seen both increasing interest and mounting scientific evidence about how and why mind-body techniques work. However, as the conflict resolution field moves toward a more holistic perspective and approach, questions remain about how to incorporate this knowledge about some of the less tangible factors in conflict resolution.

Bowling and Hoffman began an integration of mindfulness-related practices in their articulation of *presence* (2003, 21–24), which they describe as the qualities that a mediator brings that influence and enhance the mediator's impact. These practitioners recognize both a physical presence and the dynamic relationships that are affected by these qualities. They suggest that mediators develop self-awareness and a reflective practice that includes understanding how they resolve their own conflicts. In essence, Bowling and Hoffman suggest a more holistic approach to professional development that includes personal growth (2003, 21–45). Practices that include physical self-awareness are important in accurately reading and interpreting embodied signals as they allow a mediator to make use of the body as an indicator of conflict dynamics.

Mind-body practices can enable the body as an instrument of change, albeit in subtle ways. One optimal quality often is referred to as the state of being *centered* or *grounded*. Jonathan Reitman portrays it as *being the eye of the storm* from his experience as a group mediator in war-torn Bosnia-Herzegovina. He describes feeling his breath shorten and a short-circuiting of his brain. After becoming aware of his own embodied reactions, he noticed his comediator having a different experience. "She was breathing slowly and rhythmically, with a half smile on her face, sitting with her feet on the floor, her arms at her sides, in a vulnerable and open posture" (Reitman 2003b, 238). Her centered physical and mental presence became an instrument allowing him and eventually the participants to become calm. Feeling centered is a quality already valued by conflict resolution practitioners, a sense of awareness and connection. It inspires trust, provides greater clarity, and encourages new perspectives (Gold 1993, 56; 2003, 192). In short, practices that cultivate a feeling of being centered present obvious benefits in even the most conservative mediation environments.

Mind-Body Techniques and Suggestions for Practice

Here we list some specific practices that can be used both for the practitioner and for participants. During an interview, Tracey Cairnie described something that is easy to forget: "As a practitioner, I bring my day with me, too." Before mediating or facilitating, she centers herself by heightening her body's awareness. If it is possible, she takes a brisk walk, notices nature, feels the wind, soaks in the sun, or simply looks at a tree or plant. This embodied practice helps her let go of her ego, mental distractions, and stress, so she can create a safe and calm space for her clients (T. Cairnie, pers. comm.).

We suggest that developing body awareness is a basic foundation for novice and advanced conflict resolution practitioners. The simplest tools include noticing how the body feels at various times and focusing on one's own breathing. To release tension or tightness, let the breath flow downward allowing the abdomen to expand. Then, slow down the breathing by counting to four while inhaling, and count to five while exhaling. Visualize sending out tension on the exhale, and let the body relax. This process automatically slows the heart rate and has the potential of reducing stress, fear, and anger, which often manifest as holding the breath and muscular tension. We find that mind-body practices have the added benefit of being excellent forms of self-care and can promote resilience in the practitioner.

Meditation is a common mindfulness practice. It can be characterized as either *formal* or *informal* (Goleman and Gurin 1993, 263–265). Seated meditation is considered formal and usually involves a single point of focus, such as slowly and systematically scanning the body for areas of tightness or noticing the qualities of the breath (for example, shallowness or fullness, or coolness while inhaling and warmth while exhaling). Formal meditation can be very challenging because the mind tends to wander and physical sensations such as discomfort become distracting. Movement can make it easier to practice formal meditation (for example, slowly practicing yoga or tai chi while observing the breath, and perceiving the effects of the stretches.) For those learning to meditate, Kenneth Cloke offers the following advice: "Don't panic, don't worry, don't beat yourself up, don't give up, but keep trying. Progress is slow at first, but it accumulates, and over the course of years, your body and mind will gradually learn, in spite of all your lapses and distractions, how to find their own natural resting state" (2013, 157). Additionally, learning to meditate is easier when someone guides you through the practice and there are few distractions.[12] Practicing formal meditation can support the ability to be more mindful in daily life (ibid. 265). Informal meditation can be as simple as a quick self-check to observe whether there is tension in the body and consciously releasing it. Shifting the focus from the external to the internal helps quiet the mind, and this is a precursor to the body becoming an instrument of change.

It takes time, experience, and additional training to determine which mind-body techniques may be appropriate to share with participants and under what circumstances. A simple breathing exercise such as asking participants to pause and take a few deep breaths requires less skill than that of using guided imagery, which can be focused on progressive relaxation, problem solving, and healing. The practitioner should know how to safely and effectively lead an embodied practice and effectively explain the purpose of the exercise.

In the following section we move from the practitioner's embodied awareness to similar principles and methods in somatic psychology and conflict coaching, especially as they relate to an interpersonal application of embodied approaches.

Somatics in Conflict Resolution

> As a therapist, I don't do formal mediation, but I deal with conflict all the time, especially with couples. If you're not present with yourself and your body, how can you deal with conflict, either for the parties or me? I just saw a couple. He doesn't like conflict so he checks out. He just goes blank, his eyes, his facial expression, like he's somewhere else. So I said, 'Look, you're not here. Are you willing to come back here, be with your wife and do this work?' If they can get themselves back in their bodies, they can take care of themselves. Then they can make good choices. (P. Freeman, pers. comm.)

Pamela Freeman is a Gestalt therapist also trained in several forms of group facilitation. Her comment describes one way she uses the body as a bellwether, assessing ownership of a shared process. Gestalt therapy stems from the psychotherapeutic work of Fritz and Laura Pearls begun in the 1940s. Gestalt practitioners are trained to focus on the "I and thou in the here and now," in other words, the presence of the other and oneself. The approach emphasizes present physical sensations, feelings and thoughts, rather than focusing on personal history like traditional psychoanalysis. Gestalt was among the most prominent modalities preceding a movement of contemporary somatic psychology that began in the 1960s, seeking to heal both body and mind (Yontef and Jacobs 2007). These approaches to psychotherapy have also been strengthened by more recent research suggesting their effectiveness in treating trauma and stress disorders over traditional talk therapies (Levine 1997; Malchiodi 2005, 11–12).

Somatics is a word used to describe a range of practices that refine awareness of body and mind, with emphasis on the personal awareness of embodied experience (Strozzi-Heckler 2007, 93–96). Thomas Hanna coined the term *somatics* in the 1970s (Eddy 2009b; 7–8; Hanna 1970), using it to characterize a trend in thought and therapeutic approach. Disciplines like somatic psychology are unique among traditional therapeutic practices in articulating both the nuanced physical mechanics (the "what") and the inherent wisdom of the body's messages (the "how" and "why") (Hanson and Grand 1998, 8–10). These disciplines offer technical and theoretical tools for not just personal analysis but also interpersonal situations and interventions like mediation. While mind-body approaches can enhance the personal effectiveness of the mediator, somatic approaches to psychology and coaching show how similar embodied principles of awareness and presence can operate in formal interpersonal interventions. This is exemplified in the burgeoning field of conflict coaching as illustrated below.

Conflict Coaching

The role of a coach in interpersonal and professional conflict coaching is to improve the client's understanding of conflict-related interactions. The goal is generally to develop strategies and skills to improve interactions. Although there are similarities between conflict coaching and somatic psychology, Tracey Cairnie, a coach, mediator, and facilitator, explains that coaching is not about diagnosing and treating (T. Cairnie, pers. comm.). Like Gestalt and somatic psychology, coaching uses one-on-one practitioner-client interactions. All three focus on self-awareness and the present moment more than on clarifying past stories, as in traditional talk therapies or mediation. Unlike the healing orientation of related therapies, however, coaching is focused on action, often through setting and meeting personal goals, and it may focus on changing responses or behaviors. Coaching is a growing subfield in conflict resolution. Tricia Jones and Ross Brinkert describe this trend as unfolding over twenty years from two simultaneous developments: (1) executive coaching for professional development, which includes conflict management, and (2) coaching one-on-one in a conflict resolution process to promote skill development and conflict competence (2008, 4–12).

Conflict coaching is an area that demonstrates a keen interest in somatics (Strozzi-Heckler 2014). Some coaching training programs focus on mind-body awareness related to leadership and conflict engagement, and these approaches are moving into the mainstream. For example, the Strozzi Institute offers somatic coaching courses and the Newfield Foundation coaching program includes a focus on the body and movement.[13] Jones and Brinkert assert that conflict coaching can support the advancement of conflict resolution (2008, 18). We see the use of embodied training in both conflict coaching and conflict resolution as a development that will both strengthen their connection and effectiveness.

Cinnie Noble specializes in conflict management coaching, a process that helps people gain increased competence to engage in interpersonal disputes (2014). It is common in this coaching specialty for clients to concentrate on how to shift physical reactions that contribute to the discord. In the initial contracting phase, Noble obtains permission from clients to provide observations about when they demonstrate the behaviors they want to change as they occur during the coaching conversation. Using the clients' descriptions of how they experience a specific situation and/or other person (for example, "my stomach churns"), she helps them gain increased awareness about how they manifest their somatic responses to the conflict and why. This type of discussion serves to distance clients from the situation, giving them a different perspective, which facilitates a shift from being reactive to being reflective. With time and practice, clients ultimately become more able to change their somatic habits and interact in more effective ways.

As an example, one of Noble's clients, "Tim," fidgeted whenever he was questioned about his decisions. His staff experienced this as a way of shutting them down. Noble shared her observations when she saw Tim fidgeting as he discussed certain situations. Through her questioning and feedback, he was able to identify a fear of losing control when he perceived he was being criticized. Tim explained that he started to fidget many years before as a way of controlling a bad temper. He gained insights about the impact of his fidgeting and the assumptions he made about others' intentions. He focused on how to reframe his thinking and to respond differently to stimuli that usually triggered fidgeting

(C. Noble, pers. comm.). In essence, through somatic conflict management coaching, Tim experienced a positive reappraisal as a previously stressful event became more meaningful.

The somatic practices highlighted demonstrate how practitioners access the body as a bellwether for otherwise hidden dynamics. In Pamela Freeman's case, one participant was visibly "checked out," in how he presented his body language. In Cinnie Noble's case, habitual fidgeting drew attention to the client's discomfort with criticism. In both cases, the body showed a deeper reality than the words expressed and led to unlocking and shifting negative patterns. Once embodied dimensions become conscious, the body can be more fully accessed as an instrument for conflict resolution.

Somatic Techniques and Suggestions for Practice

As suggested above, there are many somatic techniques available to a practitioner. When a mediator, coach, or therapist has the knowledge and experience to explain fully an embodied approach and the rationale behind it, participants are more likely to feel a sense of trust and comfort. The explanation can be shared prior to the session(s), during caucus or joint session, or right after using an embodied technique. Sharing information, especially about something as potentially foreign as body awareness, can increase someone's willingness to participate in an embodied practice.

As knowledge increases and skills develop, students and practitioners may consider working with the innate intelligence of the body, judiciously using more advanced intervention techniques. For example, one might observe a participant's physical response and say, "I just noticed a shift in your expression, how did you experience that change in your body?" More advanced training can help the practitioner know how to develop the rapport needed to have the participant feel comfortable with this kind of work, and to know how to follow up with an appropriate and effective response.

As they advance, practitioners will also address ethical questions that arise—such as, "If I want to use an embodied approach, is it appropriate and how can I make it feel safe?" or "Is it better to bring up an observation related to the body in joint session or in caucus?" or "Is incorporating qigong as part of the process going to alienate some participants and create a sense of connection for others?" We suggest that as the field progresses in using these techniques, we will also need to further explore these kinds of ethical questions.

Next we examine embodied approaches to conflict resolution in the creative arts. There may be fewer opportunities to incorporate the creative arts into traditional conflict resolution practices, but we believe that knowledge and experience in the arts will greatly deepen a practitioner's work, as Lederach persuasively argues (2005). In the case of embodied creative arts, practitioners can also benefit from an expanded repertoire of conflict resolution process designs and from enhanced techniques to involve the body in resolving and transforming conflict.

Creative Arts Approaches:
The Body as Pedagogical and Aesthetic Instrument

Practitioners who work with young people around conflict have found creative techniques that go beyond verbal dialogue particularly useful, even indispensable. One practitioner, Martha Eddy, recounted:

> I was working in a tough high school in Manhattan, teaching conflict resolution skills for teachers, helping them train the students to use the skills. I was thrilled to work with a disciplinary dean who was also the physical education teacher. She was a tough woman but she wanted to try another way to intervene during "incidents" versus resorting to disciplining of students after the fact. In her Physical Education classes she taught up to forty girls at a time on a theatre stage. The day I visited the only equipment they had was four basketballs. I was invited to lead a session on Conflict Resolution and saw this as an opportunity to share some of my embodied approaches using techniques I've developed from martial arts, dance, and body awareness. I began the class with simple movement warm-up exercises to build trust. Next we did problem-solving about what they could do with just four balls. They came up with great ideas. For closure we stood in a circle and did some "kiai," a battle cry–like vocalization from martial arts that comes from the belly. There were many timid girls who had probably never raised their voices in their life. I felt that I was taking a risk as I demonstrated it, but I also felt they were ready. We did a few as a whole group, and then I took the time to have each girl make the loud sound on her own in the circle. They were respectful and engaged. Indeed, at the end of the lesson as students were leaving, a few of the girls pulled me aside, an unusual occurrence in and of itself. They shared excitedly how the exercise affected them. "That was really deep," communicating an appreciation with what seemed like a new sense of personal power. (M. Eddy, pers. comm.)

An educator with a background in dance and somatics, Martha Eddy's professional career has focused on bringing embodiment techniques to conflict resolution and conflict prevention work.[14] The story illustrates how her experience enabled her to quickly grasp the needs in the group and offer an exercise to fit them, in this case, empowerment. Additionally, it shows how such approaches rapidly move beyond the body as a bellwether in conflict. Here the body was the vehicle for change. The *kiai* exercise, combined with the problem-solving activity, shifted the tenor of the group and appeared to elicit a new kind of self-confidence. Rather than focusing on calmness as many of the practitioners interviewed for this chapter do, Eddy often sees opportunities to "go for strength."[15] The illustration shows how that deeply felt empowerment can be achieved in a creative, embodied approach to skills training and problem solving.

As in therapeutic work, somatics and related methods of embodied awareness have gained prominence within dance, theater, and other expressive arts since the 1970s (Wozny 2006; Amory 2010). They are part of a trend toward balancing an artist's performative appearance with their inner experience. This is akin to what Augusto Boal argued in his seminal book *Theatre of the Oppressed*, that a liberating art form must shift the locus of creativity and decision making from the artistic director, playwright, or choreographer to all participants (1985, 154–155). Increasingly in performing arts, the director is becoming a facilitator and audiences are invited to become active participants. It is a trend similar to the direction of conflict transformation, empowering participants to become creating actors on their own life's stage (Benjamin 2003, 120–123).

The converging trends in somatics, creative arts, and conflict resolution are an immense opportunity for mutual learning. We focus on theater and dance owing to their obvious body-centered performative structures. In dance, several practitioners have already documented work in somatic approaches to creative movement in conflict resolution, and interest is growing (LeBaron et al. 2013; Eddy 2009a, 97–98; LeBaron and MacLeod 2012). In theater, there is also increasing interest, especially from education-focused techniques (Sternberg 1998) and variants of applied theater such as *Theatre for Development* (Arendshorst 2005).[16] These approaches have already enriched conflict resolution practice and expanded its domain. And the opportunity for more cross-pollination is vast. We have chosen to focus on two types of theater that articulate distinct ways that the body can be an instrument of conflict transformation—a pedagogical instrument and an aesthetic instrument. Later we demonstrate this potential through a case study of an embodied experience in conflict resolution using Playback Theatre and the Multidimensional Practice Framework (Goldberg and Blancke, Chapter 2).

In *Acting Together*, Cohen, Varea, and Walker (2011) thoughtfully assemble a unique range of performance initiatives primarily aimed at large-scale social conflict transformation in different parts of the world. The two-part anthology is instructive as its contributors engaged with principles of conflict transformation and moral imagination as articulated by Lederach (2005), connecting them to three categories of approaches: (1) traditional ritual, (2) community-based performance, and (3) artist-based performance. Their work highlights theater initiatives that vary greatly in structure and form. Only two address specific theater practices that have consistent structures: Augusto Boal's Theatre of the Oppressed (Cohen et al. 2011, 1:112–114) and Playback Theatre by Jo Salas (Cohen et al. 2011, 2:93–123). Both Theatre of the Oppressed and Playback Theatre are specific improvisational forms that contain consistent, repeated practices in which audience members participate in some aspect of the theatrical event. We chose to highlight these two forms because of their consistency, which may offer transferability to other kinds of processes, like large-group facilitation. The two theatrical forms also offer complementary insight into the different ways that embodiment, ritual, and conflict resolution can manifest artistically.

The Body as a Pedagogical Instrument: Theatre of the Oppressed

Augusto Boal is the most famous pioneer in social intervention theater. In *Theatre of the Oppressed* he theorized, experimented with, and articulated a series of theatrical forms that facilitate group discussion and problem solving. Boal's system calls for participants ("spect-actors" or audience members) to engage in a period of lively physical warm-up prior to serious work on issues. The activities create a shared atmosphere of lightness, joy, and "artistic communion," preparing participants for the issues to follow (Boal 2002, 23). His steps in developing this group process are instructive: "(1) *knowing the body* through exercises and games, (2) *making the body expressive* with exercises that explore emotion and abandon habitual expressions, (3) practicing *theatre as a language* by acting inside of initial situational vignettes," and finally, "(4) using *theatre as a discourse* by interacting with multiple dimensions of a common and challenging scene or story" (Boal 1985, 126; italics added).

This system employs the body as an instrument of change by shifting its physical and mental patterns through warm-up, then accessing the newly embodied faculty of each participant to elicit new solutions.

Boal's four-stage social theater progression bears notable resemblance to the Multidimensional Practice Framework. In the first two parts of a typical Boal workshop,[17] participants experience a liminal *separation* from their previous realities in a series of warm-up activities or games that invite them to play, devising creative responses to new rules. In one exercise, for instance, participants run as slowly as possible across a short distance, creating new movement patterns and reversing typical conventions of winner and loser. The techniques emphasize new patterns of embodiment, as Boal understood "ideas, emotions, and sensations are all indissolubly interwoven" (2002, 49). In the third step, participants enter a *transition* phase when they share stories from their own experience and experiment with depicting, or *sculpting*, these vignettes. They do this by composing an image or symbolic representation of a conflict through the configuration of fellow participants whose bodies serve as sculpting material. The sculpting cultivates embodied and creative thought process, clarifies the conflict and allows participants to step into or out of various roles in the conflict. When people organize themselves to sculpt the conflict, unexpected insights emerge. For instance, who is below and above, what ways are people intertwined, what does this show about their relationships in the conflict? The final step moves to *incorporation*, in which participants are invited to reenact and experiment with multiple scenarios of their own conflict, reflecting on how different outcomes feel.

Boal's methodology provides a collaborative framework for imagining creative solutions to conflict. The fourth step embodies those solutions through the participants' enactments, using the body as a tool for learning new ways to see and interact with a conflict. Because of the conscious use of embodied interactions for problem solving, much like role-plays, Boal's system is especially adept in its pedagogical function, helping a participant "train himself for real action" (Boal 1985, 122) as the parties work together to literally enact solutions to challenges faced in their society.

The Body as an Aesthetic Instrument: Playback Theatre

The collection of conflict-focused theater projects assembled by Cohen, Varea, and Walker features projects that give "attention to aesthetic values" as well as educational and social outcomes (2011, 1:8–9). Here "aesthetic" refers to the quality of senses in a given experience—appearance, sound, smell, and the visceral, kinesthetic, and tactile feel. The next case using Playback Theatre demonstrates how an aesthetic aspect of the body can also play a key role in transforming conflict. Combined with intentional and contextualized use of ritual, embodied aesthetics in Playback Theatre, and perhaps in arts and conflict resolution work generally, may indeed elevate its transformative potential.

Multidimensional Practice Framework Applied to Playback Theatre: A Practitioner's Case Study by Christopher Fitz

In 2008, I was involved in a community-wide initiative addressing tense race relations in a small northeastern US city. Responding to high-profile incidents, the mayor formed a multiracial working group of active community members, city representatives, and an adviser from the Department of Justice. The working group began to hold discussions and implement symbolic reconciliatory gestures to inspire wider, harmonious race relations. They also sought community dialogue opportunities with a broader segment of residents so I suggested Playback Theatre. Working group members voiced support for this approach because they worried that "talk dialogue" would attract the usual vocal activists to make familiar statements and essentially reenact dysfunctional conflict dynamics. We believed that Playback Theatre could attract a more diverse group of participants in a forum likely to shift the expected conversation.

Playback Theatre was developed in the United States in 1975 primarily by Jonathan Fox and Jo Salas. It elicits audience feelings and stories in an improvised and ritualized theatrical performance by an ensemble of trained actors and musicians. Now practiced in more than thirty countries, Playback Theatre performances and workshops take place in educational, therapeutic, community, or corporate contexts. With a background in both conflict resolution and theater, I trained in Playback Theatre over several years at the Centre for Playback Theatre.[18]

For this community initiative, I prepared for twelve months, training a special ensemble of four actors and a musician. The ensemble trained in the ritualized forms of Playback Theatre and explored personal and transpersonal stories of racism and community. With support from the working group, we produced a series of performances that culminated in a final event with fifty audience members of mixed race, age, and socioeconomic background. The publicity and personal outreach for this event was exceptional and vital in generating its audience and impact. It also set the stage for a powerful Playback Theatre event.

The public Playback Theatre performance was set in the city high school's *black box* theater, a small, intimate theatrical space, which was deemed friendly across a wide racial and geographic spectrum. The publicity and preshow aesthetic experience communicated that this would be both a theatrical event and a community dialogue. Attention was given to the entrance to the theater, which included special lighting, program bulletins, a comments wall, and news clippings. Similarly, the performance was introduced by the theater program's director and then by two facilitators from the working group. By the time our ensemble took the stage, there was already significant anticipation in the audience.

Our Playback Theatre ensemble entered through the aisles singing a South African chant with both powerful rhythm and harmonies. On its completion, each of us introduced ourselves by name and a feeling that we carried. The other actors embodied the feeling in an artistic, ritualized offering of sound and motion called a *fluid sculpture*. Using the Multidimensional Practice Framework, the ensemble's song and introductions completed an initial *separation* phase in our event, establishing a new sense of reality with different rules, a ritualized rhythm of tell-and-playback and an aesthetic quality that would characterize the performance (Salas 1993, 104–107). It also modeled a personal vulnerability that would encourage the audience to express their own stories.

In the next phase of the performance, I stepped into the role of *conductor*, a facilitator tasked with maintaining group process, personal safety, and artistic sensibility (Salas 1993, 65–78). "How was your day?" is a typical first question, and each answer given by a participant from the audience was played back by our acting ensemble. As the interplay continued, I asked incrementally more poignant questions like, "What was the mood here in 1968?" (the year the city was engulfed in racial violence). The responses and enactments began to create a common audience story. In Playback Theatre, a brief spell of ritual silence precedes each enactment, and the form ends with our ensemble acknowledging with eye contact the *teller*, or audience member who shared. Throughout, multiple dimensions of the tellers' emotions and stories are publicly embodied, recognized, and legitimized. Paradoxically perhaps, tellers who watch their story embodied often gain detachment from it, allowing them flexibility to reconstruct it in relation to the collective audience narrative (Park-Fuller 2005, 9–10). This period forms the first half of the *transition* stage from the Multidimensional Practice Framework by bringing everyday experiences from the participants, in this case around the theme of local racial division, into the newly created ritual space.

The second part of *transition* stage in Playback Theatre happens in three to five longer personal stories told by participants, embodied by long-form enactments lasting roughly four to eight minutes each. Stories emerge spontaneously from the audience so it becomes difficult to guarantee particular outcomes or learning goals in this phase. Training and experience in the discipline have taught me, however, that stories emerging in this process are often just what the audience needs to tell and hear in that moment. Training also equips facilitators to guard against people hijacking the process. In this performance, the authentic cascade of stories allowed us a deep discussion of local racism without the judgment and shame that normally accompanies such processes.

Indeed, we would have been hard-pressed to plan a better and more authentic progression of stories for a community theater performance on this theme than what organically evolved: (1) an African immigrant's new uneasy experience in the community, (2) a black mother's frustration with her neighbors' unwillingness to name her nephew's killer to the police, (3) a white mother's equality-minded grandmother, and (4) a black mother's struggle with institutional racism in her daughter's school. As it generally happens when Playback Theatre is performed skillfully, the tellers in this performance showed increasing trust by telling personal stories that showed their willingness to be vulnerable. In effect, the transition from suspicion to trust escalated.

In the portrayal of the performance's fourth and final story, the actor playing the mother enacted her struggle to protect her daughter and challenge officials in a biased school system. As if coordinated, her voice faded and another actor walked across the stage behind her singing softly, "the wheels on the bus go round and round . . . all through the town." The actors came to stillness. The audience and the teller (who was sitting beside me) murmured in recognition of the power of this metaphor of institutions and the impersonal momentum they carry. After a long pause, the audience broke into applause, actors silently acknowledged the teller with their eye contact, and both teller and audience digested the experience. Numerous participants later reported a profound awe in response to the enacted stories recounted that evening. The woman who was the teller later shared how she had a new perspective on her adversary and his racist actions. "When I first told the story, I was just into the incident . . . how it shouldn't have happened. Playback just opened that up for me. We didn't just listen to a story. It called for a response."

The response, perhaps closest to *incorporation* in the Multidimensional Practice Framework, may be where Playback Theatre differs from more traditional conflict resolution and from Theatre of the Oppressed. In our community performance, as in many Playback Theatre events, the stories effectively played out a kind of dialogue, responding to each other both by affirmation ("yeah, that kind of happened to me, too") or by contrast ("actually, it was like *this* for me") (Salas 2011, 97–98). The continued embodied enactment of individual stories essentially became the third shared story of the community that evening. As audience members become viscerally invested in each other's stories and their common story, they begin an invisible *incorporation* of the ritualized reality with the former reality. Embodied enactment encourages participants to experience *incorporation* viscerally and form a new reality that draws out a desire to respond, perhaps very differently from their original response.

After the stories concluded in our community performance, I asked for reflections about the common threads in the stories. As audience members responded, the actors again enacted the feelings and insights that had been evoked, for example, "gratitude," "amazement," and "curiosity." This began a more traditional form of *incorporation*, eliciting conscious integrative reflection. The ensemble concluded the performance by saying a few words of gratitude, then singing the South African chant used in the opening, after which the audience joined in familiar ritual applause. Thereafter, two facilitators led a postshow debriefing in small groups and in the full group, with questions about their vision for the community and next steps they could take. The facilitators completed the *incorporation* phase of our event by disseminating their recorded notes of participant contributions.

Artistic embodiment of these community stories had a lasting impact on participants. One relative confided how she had seen Playback Theatre before but had not grasped its potential until that night. Others mentioned it years later when they asked me to conduct a similar event in their nearby community. I attribute the collective affirmation primarily to its emotional and communal impact on participants, rather than the insights, new ideas, or even potential solutions that came out of it. Neighbors saw their stories as connected and grew closer through empathy, moving beyond stereotype, ideology, and issues. In effect, fifty people sat in the theater as naked, vulnerable human beings. In the words of one participant, "I've heard stories like this on TV, but here we all were in the same place together. It was for real."

The ritualized structure of Playback Theatre created predictability and safety for those who felt vulnerable and an environment in which trust could grow among strangers. Within this container, the embodied theatrical aesthetic of Playback Theatre created a beauty with deep relationship to the stories told, rather than a sensational exhibit. The emotional impact rippled beyond the tellers, and the entire audience was moved. In effect, the combination of embodied ritual and aesthetic was fundamental to the transformation experienced at our event.

We did not solve race relations in this community that evening. But we did create a powerful experience of respect, empathy, and trust for those who came. For this project, in which high emotions hampered discussion and a charged community atmosphere challenged trust, the ritualized embodiment provided an essential expression where traditional sit-down dialogue would have been severely constrained. It also went one great step beyond: it created something beautiful, a work of art from everyday lives, both painful and glorious.[19]

Interactive Theater as Embodied Conflict Resolution

Can conflict resolution be a process of beauty and catharsis? The Playback Theatre case answers a resounding yes, even suggesting that sometimes beauty and catharsis may be essential elements in resolving conflict. Augusto Boal expresses another view, arguing against being swept up in the emotion of a story and sympathy for its characters (1985, 106). Playback Theatre founder Jonathan Fox, on the other hand, challenges this suspicion as a "modernist attachment" inherently uneasy with emotion. He asserts that pre-literary cultures often viewed theater and ritual as an immersive ordeal that entailed significant emotional involvement and challenge (Fox 2004, 69–73). The cultural comfort zone of current conflict resolution practice falls within the modern rationalist school of thought. But this debate makes explicit the choice that practitioners face. Are we, as Joy Meeker wonders in Chapter 6, to be a curiously dispassionate Mr. Spock? Or, faced with high emotions and traumas like the racial division in our case study, can we embrace deeply embodied feelings in creative and transformative ways?

Embodied creative arts like somatic-based dance, Theatre of the Oppressed, and Playback Theatre provide multidimensional insight into how the body could be fully engaged as an instrument for transforming conflict. Though the approaches here are just a slice of what has been developed, they amply hint at the diversity of situations conducive to such approaches and the range of techniques that they might include. The articulation of expressive qualities in Eddy's *kiai* story, the attention to embodied learning in Theatre of the Oppressed, and the refinement of aesthetic and ritual skill in the case study of Playback Theatre suggest exciting frontiers for a postrationalist orientation to conflict resolution that recognizes the embodied, emotional, thoughtful, and creative potential of everyone in conflict.

How One Practitioner Integrates Embodied Techniques: A Journey of Mindful Self-Awareness by Julia Morelli

A sign on the studio wall where I took yoga teacher training says, "Right here. Right now. Just this." It is a visual reminder to be mindful, to notice what happens in each moment. In the opening story I became aware that it takes time, practice, and a willingness to observe the effects of an interaction on my mind and body. While writing this chapter, again I came to the realization that being fully present is difficult, and is becoming increasingly so in our fast-paced, technologically "enhanced" world. So, I challenged myself to turn off the radio, to resist the impulse to check e-mail at stoplights, and to consider ways in which my yoga, qigong, and meditation practices heighten my ability to work with conflict—personally and professionally. While sitting in silence, I reflected on a phrase I sometimes use in mediation, "We'll explore the past so we can focus on the future," and noted that it could imply that we should not focus on the present moment. The juxtaposition of that phrase and the yoga studio sign, "Right here. Right now. Just this," reminded me that mediation is a dynamic art. Conflict resolution is about finding a balance between the past, present, and future. For me that means balancing my mind, body, emotions, and spirit.

A number of years ago in a particularly challenging situation I was able to find that balance through conflict coaching. I decided that I would benefit from working with a coach to help me examine my role in a relationship that I characterized as periodically tense. My coach asked what I wanted most. My reply, "I want a better relationship." It became my mantra, and I still use it to help guide my actions and reactions because I know how easy it is to slip into old patterns of behavior. I needed a way to make the change and realized that my training in mind-body skills could make that possible.

I started by deciding to make a conscious effort to pause before every interaction and relax my body by deepening my breath. It would work until I let another hot button get pushed; when that happened I went back to my mantra using slow conscious breathing. This practice, and focusing on my desire to improve the relationship, helped me have more constructive conversations with this person. Although by choice we do not interact often, when we do talk, I manage my responses more effectively, and over time, the relationship has improved. That experience gives me hope and strengthens the empathy and compassion I feel for others working through their conflict. It encourages me to check in with my body whenever I interact with conflict or feel negative emotions—mine or someone else's.

I admit freely that the most difficult conflict to deal with is my own. Some may see this as a weakness, but for me it is a form of strength. After being trained in conflict coaching and after being coached, I feel that recognizing my own challenges with conflict and understanding my own responses help me as a conflict resolution practitioner. To me it seems self-evident that the field of conflict resolution could benefit from incorporating self-awareness and mind-body skills into mainstream theory and practice.

When I am scheduled to mediate, facilitate, or present training, I meditate in addition to doing my daily yoga practice. On days when my time is limited, I still practice yoga, albeit for a few minutes. I like to start my day with yoga or qigong because it wakes up my body, and the moving meditation clears and enlivens my mind. These mindfulness practices help me feel more centered and instill a quiet and resilient confidence. I use them any time I face a challenging situation.

A couple of years ago I worked with a group that became dysfunctional because of conflict. The original request was for mediation between two people, but it became clear that the issues were broader and affected the whole group. I interviewed all of the team members. One individual's outlook was particularly negative; he blamed others. Toward the end of our interview he seemed more optimistic. On the morning the whole group was scheduled to meet, he arrived to help me set up and complained vehemently about his coworkers. When he left the room I felt frustrated and noticed my body was tense. There were just a few minutes left before the group was to arrive, and I decided that I needed to get centered. I stood tall with my weight evenly distributed on both feet, half closed my eyes, deepened my breath, and began to practice a qigong movement. This practice combines arm movement with the breath, and I visualize gathering cleansing energy from the universe that descends into my body. Within a few moments I gained a sense of profound peace, going into the session feeling focused with a renewed optimism.

My mindfulness practice provides me with solace because, as a practitioner, it enables me to be present, listen fully, and respond without distraction. It helps me to act and react in personal and professional situations with more equanimity, clarity, and poise. When I engage in mind-body practices regularly, it is easier for me to find a state of balance and peace. For me it begins with a pause, a pause that allows me to become aware of my body and breath—to recognize that they are my partners in conflict resolution and in life.

Conclusion

There are many paths to accessing the innate peacemaking potential of the body. The varied examples of practitioners in this chapter show how richly conflict resolution practice can be enhanced by embodied practices in at least three distinct ways. First, the field will benefit from improving articulation and interpretation of the body as a bellwether, as in the accounts by Morelli and Freeman. Second, it will benefit by cultivating embodied skills that practitioners or participants can access to shift conflict situations, as in the accounts of Linden, Reitman, and Noble. Finally, it will benefit from a more knowledgeable, skillful, and creative design of conflict resolution processes that include embodied pedagogical, aesthetic, and ritual elements, as in the accounts of Eddy, Boal, and Fitz. In each case, accessing the body was at least helpful and often indispensable for the quality of positive outcomes achieved. Collectively, the cases demonstrate how skillful use of different embodied techniques can expand the reach of conflict resolution practices well beyond the mediation table.

More conversation is warranted. This chapter is an overview rather than a full exploration of the range of embodied practices in conflict resolution. Much is happening on this frontier. Increasing numbers of mediators, therapists, coaches, and artists are exploring embodied approaches to conflict resolution. Given the growing interest, an extended conversation within conflict resolution discourse can help ensure responsible, appropriate, and effective application of these approaches.

In the realm of practice, some approaches present low-hanging fruit that can be picked by any practitioner and used in most any situation. Conflict is already an embodied event. Breath, posture, and movement are universal qualities regardless of our culture or demographic orientations. Techniques involving the bellwether functions of embodied practice, such as mindfulness, can be integrated into conflict resolution training and practiced at all levels.

At the same time, as Eddy's story shows in introducing *kiai* to high school girls, appropriate embodied approaches that access the body as an instrument of change will vary greatly in different contexts. This may reveal a tension between the available techniques and the limiting personal discomforts or cultural norms in a particular situation or venue. Such a tension can be brought into balance and more skillfully navigated when it has been more thoroughly explored in both theory and practice.

As this volume demonstrates, a multidimensional approach can enhance the range and effectiveness of conflict resolution and our understanding of it. The body, in addition to housing our cognitive, emotional, and spiritual faculties, has its own intelligence. The convergence of discoveries related to neuroscience, mindfulness, somatic psychology, and the creative arts now compels us to welcome the wisdom of this all-too-overlooked member of the conflict resolution team. As embodied practices are more fully explored and developed, they can be more seamlessly integrated with thought, emotion, and spirit in a reconstructed and unified practice. Such integration can serve as the foundation for a reinvigorated and more holistic approach to conflict resolution that can more fully humanize us as practitioners and participants.

Conflict resolution, especially in transformative approaches, is based on the assumption that conflict is an opportunity for positive change. We concur and go a step further. As Lederach suggests, conflict resolution is necessarily creative work—or play. As such, it can be a thing of beauty (2005, 70–74). Reitman's serenely smiling comediator, Eddy's circle of empowered girls, and Fitz's evening of enacted empathy all paint vivid pictures of the power of embodied peacemaking. In addition to rationale, we hope this chapter has provided inspiration to continue deepening and integrating truly holistic approaches to conflict resolution.

Notes

1. We use the term *participant* because *party* is associated with legal processes.

2. Recounted by Julia Morelli (2014). Morelli is a mediator, trainer, coach, and facilitator in Virginia. She practices and teaches yoga, qigong, and meditation. She received training from the Center for Mind-Body Medicine in 1999 and the Strozzi Institute in 2014. For more information see http://cmbm.org and http://strozziinstitute.com (accessed March 30, 2015).

3. Michelle LeBaron and Carrie MacLeod (2012) identified bodies as "instruments of awareness," in "Dancing at the Crossroads: Body-based Ways of Transforming Conflict Across Cultures" (Handout for the preconference workshop presented at the Association for Conflict Resolution [ACR] 2012 annual conference, New Orleans, LA).

4. See http://oxforddictionaries.com/definition/english/bellwether (accessed March 28, 2015).

5. Unless otherwise noted, practitioner comments in the rest of this chapter come from the authors' interviews.

6. At the ACR Annual Conference in 2011, no sessions specifically addressed body awareness and practices. In more recent years, the number of such sessions offered at the conference has ranged from zero to three. In 2014, Stephen Kotev of George Mason University's School for Conflict Analysis and Resolution offered a semester-long course on somatics skills and conflict resolution for the first time. Daniel Rainey also incorporates body awareness in the 40-hour basic mediation training offered through Dominican University.

7. Goleman (1995, 37–47) for references to Howard Gardener, Peter Salovey, and others whose work contributed to the concept of emotional intelligence.

8. National Institutes of Health National Center for Complementary and Integrative Health, https://nccih.nih.gov/ (accessed March 28, 2015).

9. The word *qi* has several transliterations include ch'i, chi, and ki (Japanese). The meaning is akin to the Hindu yogic word *prana*, and both mean life force, breath, or vital energy. The practice of qigong includes moving and non-moving forms of meditation, and incorporates breathing practices with movement in a way that is similar to aikido and yoga.

10. Aikido is a defensive or soft martial art developed in the 1920s in Japan, characterized by using an opponent's momentum to resolve an aggressive encounter. One translation of *aikido* is "the Way of Harmonious Spirit" (Westbrook and Ratti 1970, 16–96). Also see Judy Ringer, "Hidden gifts: What aikido can teach us about conflict." Available online at http://www.judyringer.com /resources/articles (accessed March 28, 2015).

11. This principle is based on extensive research from positive psychology and much of it is summarized in Kashdan and Ciarrochi (eds.), which asserts, "The working assumption of positive psychology is that the positive healthy aspects of life are not simply the bipolar opposite of distress and disorder" (2013, 4).

12. Resources for guided meditations include Health Journeys, http://www .healthjourneys.com/; UCLA Mindful Awareness Research Center, http://marc .ucla.edu/body.cfm?id=22; and University of Virginia School of Medicine Wellness Programs Mindfulness Center, http://www.medicine.virginia.edu/clinical /departments/medicine/divisions/general-med/wellness/the-mindfulness -center/resources/audio-recordings (accessed March 28, 2015).

13. For more information, see http://www.strozziinstitute.com and http://www .newfieldnetwork.com (accessed March 28, 2015).

14. Martha Eddy draws on somatic training in a number of modalities including Laban Movement Analysis, Bartenieff Technique, and Body-Mind Centering. For more on her work and background, see http://www.wellnesscke .net/cr.htm (accessed March 28, 2015).

15. Ibid.

16. As an example, see Search for Common Ground's Participatory Theatre for Conflict Transformation, http://www.sfcg.org/programmes/drcongo/pdf /Participatory-Theatre-Manual-EN.pdf (accessed March 30, 2015). For an excellent overview of applied theater approaches, see Applied and Interactive Theatre Guide, http://www.tonisant.com/aitg/ (accessed March 30, 2015).

17. Boal's techniques, which he first called *Theatre of the Oppressed*, have been adapted and renamed in different contexts, for example, *Theatre for Development* and *Drama in Conflict Transformation* (Arendshorst 2005).

18. The Centre for Playback Theatre houses the training programs begun by the founders of Playback Theatre, Jonathan Fox and Jo Salas. See http://playback centre.org (accessed March 28, 2015).

19. Recounted by Christopher Fitz in 2014. Fitz has more than 15 years of experience in mediation, facilitation, and numerous forms of improvisational theater and dance. He received training from the Centre for Playback Theatre 2004–2014.

6

Staying With Emotions in Conflict Practice: Opening a Space In-Between

Joy Meeker

ABOUT TWENTY YEARS AGO, I ATTENDED A MEDIATION TRAINING in central New York that sparked my long-term interest in the relationship between emotions and conflict. The trainer asked us to imagine who would make the ideal mediator, and she listened patiently as we suggested popular figures from that cultural moment. The trainer kept looking at us with anticipation; clearly she had someone in mind. To my surprise and slight amusement, when someone suggested Spock from *Star Trek,* she wrote his name on the top of a flip chart and then asked us to name the characteristics that made him an ideal mediator, which included objective, neutral, rational, and unemotional.

I was not fully surprised by the suggestion of Spock, nor was I fully amused. My social justice sensibilities were troubled by the not-so-subtle suggestion that conflicts and their accompanying emotions should be quickly resolved and calmed down. Invoking the spirit of Spock was an attempt to teach us that conflict interveners should remain rational and detached as we sift through the human, emotional mess of conflict. Reflecting now on this incident, I recognize the stubborn persistence of a familiar Western story that suggests conflicts are best efficiently ended through rational problem solving. Yet what is lost when we accept this default story and always seek efficient, calm solutions to the differences that matter to us?

I am not suggesting this training incident is indicative of the priorities of conflict interveners then or now. Instead, I remember this story here because it personifies an inheritance embedded in the conflict field, which I seek to destabilize—the related bias against conflict and emotion. In the last several decades, the critical edge of the conflict resolution field has reworked the field's foundational focus on ending conflict by emphasizing that conflict can catalyze personal and social change (Curle 1971; Galtung 2004; Lederach 1995; Trujillo et al. 2008). Relatedly, the field has also distanced itself from the anchoring logic of neutrality—arguing that taking a neutral stance when intervening in conflict is impossible (Goldberg 2009; Mayer 2004), and suggesting that when practitioners attempt to enact neutrality, they are likely to inadvertently affirm the status quo (Cobb 2001; Gunning 2004; Wing 2008).

While the conflict field has argued persuasively that conflict can catalyze productive change—and it has also challenged notions of neutral, value-free practice—it has much less to say about the foundational assumptions that the field carries about emotions. As a result, commonsense interpretations of emotions prevail. Emotions are most often considered natural, internal, private forces that are dichotomous and inferior to rationality. I am convinced that a more complex attention to emotions is necessary for practitioners to respond to the full complexity of conflict. In particular, as a conflict practitioner who navigates by the values of social justice, I join those who have begun to consider how emotions can move us to contribute to *personal-social* change (Chené 2008; LeBaron 2002; Roy 2002).

To set the stage for my exploration of emotion in conflict work, I suggest three reasons why emotions are significant to a conflict practice that aims toward transformation. First, emotions accompany conflict. As Jones and Bodtker (2001) argue, emotions are foundational to all conflict. Second, emotions are crucial to social-justice efforts. Emotions provide useful guides to "what we care about and why" (Boler 1999, xviii), and the fullness of human capacities is necessary for interpersonal and social change—including emotions (Ahmed 2004; LeBaron 2002). Third, as I will explore in more detail subsequently, how we interpret the meaning of emotions impacts how we respond to conflict.

In this chapter, I suggest that the emotions that accompany conflict help create a gap between our current realities and more just realities—which is an invaluable space for conflict practitioners. Next, I situate emotions within the conflict literature by reviewing four orientations to conflict practice to demonstrate how distinct interpretations of emotions matter. I then suggest several guiding strategies on emotions for conflict practitioners who seek to align their practice with social justice, concluding with a story from my mediation practice to illustrate how creatively engaging with emotions can enrich conflict praxis.

On Spirit, Emotions, and Social Justice

I appreciate the invitation by the editor to consider "how to access multiple dimensions of knowledge, or wisdom, in a way that uses our whole selves and seeks to engage the four dimensions, somatic, emotional, cognitive and spiritual understandings" in our conflict practice. My commitment to honor the dimension of spirit in my conflict work centers on two principles. First, I seek to be fully present and to welcome the wholeness of each person, and second, I acknowledge our fundamental interconnection. This connectedness is communicated evocatively in the South African term *ubuntu*, which Mab Segrest (2002) translates as "born to belonging" (see also Bowland 2008). Segrest seeks to practice *ubuntu*, describing her life work as a "praxis of belonging" that is guided by a commitment to social justice (2002, 5). This resonates with me. I translate a *praxis of belonging* into my conflict work by aiming toward change that does not only occur inside ourselves, but that is also fundamentally linked to social transformation.

To welcome personal-social transformation in conflict work, I have found emotional sensibilities, or "embodied thoughts," invaluable guides (Rosaldo 1985). In this sense I reject the Western assumptions that emotions are dichotomous and inferior to cognition and instead consider emotions as having a mutual relationship to thought and as indispensable for interpretation (Demasio 1994). I also join Sara Ahmed (2004), who is less interested in what emotions are than in what they do—particularly how emotions signal an engagement with oneself, with one's relationship with others, and with one's relationship to the social world.

After reflecting on my own conflict praxis and after gathering insights from conflict educators through my qualitative research on emotions and social justice (Meeker 2012), I have come to consider the emotions that accompany conflict as catalysts that can open a space of transformation. This space holds rich potential for our conflict practice—akin to a ritual space where we are invited to imagine how we may feel, think, and act otherwise.

Emotions and a Space In-Between: A Place of Transformation

The space in-between the present world and the world we desire is unsettled and unsettling. Emotions can signal the presence of this space—bringing our attention to the gap between current realities and a more just world. I am convinced that conflict interveners can be signif-icant guardians of these spaces in-between, these liminal sites where those in conflict navigate the distance between their present reality and the reality they hope for as they contest, reinterpret, and imagine alter-natives to their conflicts.

Davidheiser (2006) builds on Victor Turner's (1969) work to sug-gest that the space of conflict practice is not unlike a ritual space, a "special social space in which the conventions and scripts of everyday life are loosened, enabling personal and social transformation."[1] Fem-inist writers such as Gloria Anzaldúa also speak of liminal or border-line spaces where transformation can occur. She suggests transforma-tion occurs in a vulnerable space—a "liminal zone": "Transformations occur in this in-between space, an unstable, unpredictable, precarious, always in transition space lacking clear boundaries . . . and living in liminal zones means being in a constant state of displacement—an uncomfortable, even alarming feeling" (Anzaldúa 2002, 1). Anzaldúa considers the discomfort accompanying this space as necessary for nourishing consciousness. I agree that this place in-between extends beyond comfort zones, and that conflict workers should anticipate this dissonance and support those in conflict to stay with these discomfort-ing emotions long enough for new interpretations to become available. For practitioners who seek to create spaces for transformation—to invite both changes of selves and heightened consciousness of inter-connection—how might bringing creative attention to emotions open new possibilities?

Four Stories of Conflict Practice and Their Orientation to Emotions

As I suggested above, the complexity of emotions is typically side-stepped in conflict resolution. Indeed, emotions hold an *absent presence* in much of the conflict literature (Boler 1999, xv). In other words, emo-tions mark the presence of conflict while their meaning is most often assumed. Since emotions consistently accompany conflict, it is no sur-prise that particular orientations to conflict tend to align with corre-sponding orientations to emotions. To demonstrate this, I offer the following sketch of four common stories of conflict practice.

Four broad stories or orientations of conflict that are relevant for interpersonal conflict practices include (1) conflict settlement, (2) per-sonal empowerment, (3) conflict transformation, and (4) narrative. The distinctions between these four orientations certainly do not withstand the complexity of lived practice, which is further complicated by the fact that the terminology in the conflict field is strikingly nonuniform. My intention is not to reinforce these categories but to use these stories to illustrate how divergent assumptions and discourses about conflict and emotion within the conflict field matter. Specifically, in each orientation I illustrate how distinct interpretations of emotions signal divergent priorities to settle conflict, personally empower individuals, or to engage conflict for personal-systemic change.

Conflict Settlement

The initial orientation of *conflict settlement* remains the dominant conception of conflict theory and practice—while its assumptions are increasingly contested. In part based on its resonance with dominant paradigms in the West (Wing 2009), this school achieved early dominance and often assumes the general name of *conflict resolution*—collapsing the conflict field as a whole into its own version of theory and practice. Conflict settlement seeks to create integrative, mutual solutions to conflicts (Fisher et al. 1991). Its goals closely align with an ideology of management, and the model assumes the humanist subject as autonomous and rational (Adler et al. 1998).

An orientation of settlement does not address the structural issues of conflict, and instead "starts with an acceptance of a given political and socioeconomic status quo, which may need some adjustment but is fundamentally sound" (Mitchell 2002, 20). Conflicts thus become moments to help people more successfully and efficiently navigate the expectations of the status quo. The role of the particular intervener is not problematized, and instead is likely to be understood as an extension of an accepted logic and practice—commonly named *neutrality* (Cobb and Rifkin 1991; Mayer 2004; Wing 2008).

The settlement orientation can be understood as holding a negative bias against both conflicts and emotions (Bodtker and Jameson 2001). The value of conflicts is found in conflict endings, and emotions are seen as moments of destabilization that must be removed or calmed down by rational narratives. This strand of praxis relies heavily on the absence of emotions to distinguish what it means to "talk rationally," or to negotiate (Bazerman 1991). When emotions are discussed in the conflict settlement literature, the emphasis is on diffusing or rechanneling emotions for more productive means of communication, i.e., calming emotions down in order to rationally problem solve.

More recently, after a prolonged period of neglect, there has been an awakened attention to emotions in the settlement strand of conflict resolution (Fisher and Shapiro 2005; Ladd 2005; Ryan 2006). However, those holding a settlement lens tend to add and stir emotions into intact models—reconsidering neither the meaning of emotions nor the rationalist assumptions of the models themselves. For example, while acknowledging the importance of emotions in responding to conflicts, Fisher and Shapiro largely flatten the power of emotions by providing prescriptive suggestions of how to "use emotions as levers" to "help get what you want" (2005, 107). Thus, these authors largely retain a narrow value of emotions as instrumental cues that can enhance the prioritized activity—rational problem solving in hopes of meeting individual interests.

Personal Empowerment

A second orientation in conflict resolution I refer to as the *personal empowerment* story, whose assumptions challenge the negative bias against both conflicts and emotions. Those who advocate this praxis "move beyond the settlement ethos" (Cobb 2004, 1) and instead seek to transform people by changing the interactions of those who are directly involved in conflict. They further critique the orientation of settlement for holding an individualistic ideology, instead arguing that humans are essentially social and formed through interaction with others (Della Noce 1999). In this orientation, the unit of change moves from changing the conflict to changing the interaction of the parties—independent of the outcome of the dispute and of structural, institutional constraints (Bush and Folger 1994, 2012).

Bush and Folger's (1994) model of mediation is a particularly influential example of the personal empowerment orientation. Their model, which they name "transformative mediation," challenges the dominant rational problem-solving orientation by advocating the dual goals of empowerment and recognition. Following this model, conflicts are considered moments to capture opportunities of moral growth by moving parties from weakness to empowerment and from self-absorption to a recognition of the other by utilizing skills including dialogue, listening, storytelling, recognition, and emotional management (Bush and Folger 1994; Della Noce 1999).

This story of conflict praxis initiated a fruitful dialogue and self-reflection of the field regarding the purpose of conflict practice (Cobb 2004). But in relationship to social justice concerns, personal empowerment practitioners adhere to a micro focus on disputing individuals (intraparty empowerment) and on their direct relationship (interparty recognition) (Bush and Folger 2012),and explicitly bracket a macro analysis (Gunning 2004). While advocates of personal empowerment suggest that their praxis can have a "spillover effect" by transforming individuals who later enter into the larger macro world with an increased capacity to engage social change (Bush and Folger 2012), this additive model of change holds troubling assumptions. For instance, attempting to narrow and simplify conflicts into micro dimensions assumes people can somehow step outside of their already situated and structurally embedded reality. First, this shields practitioners and parties from self-reflexivity regarding their biases related to structural positions (such as gender, race, class). It also assumes that a "bias through silence" on social forces is preferable to considering the impact of social structures (Gunning 2004, 92), but this silence on structures is not a neutral absence. Instead, the silence quietly bolsters the credibility of those who are empowered by current power arrangements while discrediting those with less power.

In contrast to the settlement story, which considers emotions to be obstacles, instead emotions are acknowledged as deeply significant to personal empowerment models (Della Noce 1999). The expression of emotions is seen as an opportunity to understand, to deepen, and to meet individual and relational needs. Significantly, in this orientation, emotions are constructed as "intrapsychic phenomenon" (Cobb 2004, 2) emerging from within the individuals experiencing conflict and signaling a rupture in the parties' relationship. Thus the personal empowerment orientation values emotions, but they interpret them on a therapeutic level, calling up conceptions of emotions as natural, individual possessions that can be expressed—not as culturally and socially informed forces shaped by beliefs and perceptions from the start.

Conflict Transformation

A third story of conflict resolution is *conflict transformation,* which resonates with my conflict practice. The term *conflict transformation* is unevenly used, and it is commonly used to mark a departure from the dominant model of conflict settlement. I use conflict transformation here to refer to "a search for processes that can make possible myriad transformations of self, self-in-relationships, self-in-society, as well as transformations in the structural realms" (Fetherston and Kelly 2007, 263).

Conflict transformation departs from settlement or empowerment models by widening their goals beyond achieving better resolutions (settlement) or transforming interactions (personal empowerment). In contrast, conflict transformation understands transformation as linked to broader elements of social change, including asymmetries of power and the historical, social, and cultural contexts of conflicts. The unit of analysis is thus complicated and includes the personal aspect as fundamentally linked to wider communities and society (Lederach 1995). Conflict transformation practitioners thus see conflict as a site of practice where structural violence and relationships of domination can be made visible, and potentially where more just relationships on personal and social levels can be enacted (Curle 1971; Lederach 2003).

When emotions are discussed through a conflict transformation lens, they are understood as socially and culturally negotiated and connected to the potential of change (Chené 2008; LeBaron 2002; Schirch 2005). This lens suggests that emotions can signal an awareness of contradictions, which can mobilize the questioning of the ideas, assumptions, and discourses that inform the common sense of society (Fetherston and Kelly 2007). Thus emotions are understood as both powerful clues to our internal investments as well as signals that something is amiss with the outside world.

Roberto Chené (2008) provides an example of how staying with the emotions that accompany conflict can create opportunities for personal-social transformation. He suggests that *creative discomfort* is an essential component in refiguring more open, pluralistic, and creative responses to conflict, particularly conflicts with intercultural dimensions. According to Chené, acknowledging the intercultural dimensions of conflict in the United States will inevitably invite discomfort, because we are socialized to treat meaningful differences as problems to solve: "According to our differences, we are already institutionalized into conflicted, unhealthy . . . human relationships. The conflicts between us are already set up in the dysfunctional paradigm that we have constructed for relating to each other. What we are mediating are the frequent flare-ups of an unworkable system" (2008, 33). Chené argues that the emotionally charged flare-ups of conflict are powerful opportunities to recognize and to challenge the consequences of unjust asymmetries of power. Creative discomfort can thus awaken us from a thin comfort in the familiar—from habits of interpretations that ignore the structural dimensions of our lives. When we settle for surface comfort, we actively submerge an awareness of inequitable patterns of power, including unearned privilege, internalized oppression, and nonreciprocal relationships. Chené advocates that practitioners anticipate and support those who are experiencing the discomfort that accompanies conflict, giving parties support to stay in a space in-between. In this liminal place, parties can use the energy of their discomfort to develop a deeper consciousness of the structured dimensions of their relationships, which is a necessary step to create more expansive alternatives.

Narrative

A fourth and most recent story in the conflict field is the *narrative* framework, which also resonates with my conflict practice. Similar to the conflict transformation lens, the narrative orientation relies on social constructionist interpretations and understands conflicts as situated in cultural, historical contexts and embedded in relationships of power. Further, a narrative orientation joins conflict transformation by being dissatisfied with approaches to conflict that narrow their goals to ending the dispute (as in the settlement story) or changing the interaction (as in the personal empowerment story). Instead, both conflict transformation and narrative orientations seek to catalyze personal and social change.

Distinct from the conflict transformation orientation, the narrative orientation understands narrative as "the location for analysis, intervention, and evaluation of conflict and its evolution" (Cobb 2003, 296). Narrative practitioners and educators build on the analysis of discourse theory—in particular the work of Michel Foucault (1980)—to bring attention to how discourse, understood as a social practice, is implicated in the politics of meaning making and in the production of knowledge. In the narrative orientation, the unit of change becomes the story itself, and the goal becomes to create richer, less polarized stories of conflict (Winslade and Monk 2008).

A prominent example of the narrative approach to conflict is *narrative mediation* introduced by John Winslade and Gerald Monk (2008). Particularly significant for this chapter, these practitioners destabilize the taken-for-granted meaning of emotions. From the lens of narrative, emotions are complicated beyond either-or formulations—beyond either a contaminating force (as in the settlement frame) or a potentially empowering force (as in the personal empowerment frame). Instead, as Winslade and Monk articulate, emotions are understood as a "narrative in which the person is situated" (2008, 7). In this orientation, it no longer makes sense to divide emotions into positive or negative categories. Those in conflict are "encouraged to experience their own feelings about the disputes embedded in a wider context" (2008, 15). In this way, pain, exhilaration, or any emotion is understood as attached to the story itself: if one shifts the story, emotions will shift as well.

Winslade and Monk also emphasize how the expressions of emotions are embedded in the wider webs of cultural stories. For example, they discuss a conflict in which a person suggests that he was just trying to "speak nicely" to the other, but she "wouldn't listen" (2008, 22–23). The authors unpack this seemingly simple claim to suggest how background discourses are being called upon to link "speaking nicely" with being reasonable, and to thus position the person who rejects the nice talk as an unreasonable person. Winslade and Monk state (2008, 23): "There is a long history in the discourse of Western cultures of privileging rational control over emotional expression, and that history lies in the background" of this comment. They further suggest how gendered and racialized histories of domination are entangled with discourses of rationality, delegitimizing speakers who are positioned as emotional, including the historically marginalized, such as women and people of color, as well as those committed to engaging conflict for social change. Because members of these groups are positioned as emotional, their identity can be used to make their claims appear unreasonable, particularly if their claims threaten to disrupt the status quo—such as when challenging structural inequities. The narrative orientation suggests that bringing these kinds of background assumptions into view can reveal assumptions that would otherwise remain hidden, thus opening space for new stories that rely less on discourses of delegitimization.

A careful look at each orientation above suggests that emotions play a central yet underexplored role in conflict practice. Indeed, the distinct responses to emotions in the conflict field provide a key indicator of whether conflicts are used to help parties better adapt to the status quo, to promote more productive interactions on micro levels, or to aim toward relational and social change. Given the powerful and complex influence of emotions in conflict, practitioners who are interested in inviting both personal and social change must bring creative attention to emotions in their conflict practice.

Creative Engagement with Emotions in Conflict Practice

While a full conversation of how to respond to the emotions that accompany conflict is beyond the scope of this chapter, I will suggest several guiding strategies for practitioners who seek to engage emotions in ways that invite personal-social change. The following three strategies emerge from reflecting on my own practice and from my qualitative research with conflict educators: (1) destabilize commonsense assumptions about emotions; (2) support parties to stay with emotions; and (3) aim toward creative discomfort.

Destabilize Commonsense Assumptions About Emotions

To make room for more fruitful responses to emotions, practitioners need to destabilize normative assumptions about emotions. As discussed earlier in the chapter, the conflict field's dominant orientation of settlement assumes that emotions are obstacles and in hierarchal relationship to rationality. This bias can disappear as common sense, camouflaged by normative cultural beliefs. Yet enacting a Spock-like rational stance is not neutral—instead, it suppresses enlivened senses, actively affirms current power relationships, and disperses the parties' energy for deeper change.

An alternative assumption circulating in the conflict field assumes that emotions are natural forces emerging from individuals and thus can be interpreted outside of context and power relationships. Revaluing emotions in this way falsely imagines a discrete division between the personal and social—privatizing the force of emotions and blocking parties from connecting their inner and outer worlds. Because inherited habits of interpreting emotions inform habits of practice, practitioners should bring critical awareness to their assumptions about emotions in preparation to engage emotions in more self-reflexive, creative ways.

Follow and Stay with Emotions

Akin to the concept of "staying with conflict" to respond to the ongoing aspects of disputes (Mayer 2009), I suggest practitioners follow and *stay with emotions* to give parties the chance to make deeper sense of their embodied thoughts. To be clear, the strategy of staying with emotions is not based on the intrinsic value of emotions—like all sources of interpretation, emotions can inhibit or open change, and people are often emotionally invested in interpretations that delegitimize others and themselves (Boler 1999). Yet, acknowledging emotions, while risky, is pivotal to transformation (Jameson et al. 2010) and is necessary to nourish changes in relationships to oneself, to each other, and to one's social world (Ahmed 2004).

Staying with the emotions that accompany conflict can inspire moments of learning or turning points in conflict—such as when parties become newly attuned to how structures are woven into their differences. Indeed, conflict intervention provides a rare, supportive space where the tangible implications of patterns of power can be unearthed and contested; yet doing so is emotionally demanding, messy work. As a seasoned conflict educator who I interviewed suggests, many are unprepared for this challenge: "People feel comfortable with the structural analysis at a societal level, realizing that there is a lot of oppression or injustice [that] has occurred. When this happens in a real personal and direct way, how should it be handled, that's a real hard jump for people" (Meeker 2012, 162). Practitioners can anticipate and support those who make this "hard jump" that lands parties in ambiguous, often unfamiliar territory. Without support to stay in this emotionally charged space, parties are likely to settle its energy, thus turning away from more complex understandings. In light of this challenge, practitioners can select from a diverse set of strategies to assist parties to stay with emotions long enough for new interpretations to be available, such as asking elicitive questions to identify and reappraise emotional experiences (Jones and Bodtker 2001), supporting "difficult listening" to explore links between emotion and personal-social contexts (Roy 2002), inviting ritual (Schirch 2005), using humor (Maise 2006), and playing with metaphor (LeBaron 2002).

Aim Toward Creative Discomfort

Third, I suggest practitioners aim for *creative discomfort* (Chené 2008) in their conflict practice so that parties are uncomfortable enough to want change yet are still able to access their creativity. There is a delicate balance between calming conflict and overwhelming parties; the first encourages parties to settle for a thin peace, and the latter can polarize parties and inhibit new perspectives.

To keep conflict creative, practitioners can support those experiencing discomfort, particularly as parties consider the structured dimensions of their conflicts. This support is crucial in cultural contexts where individualism thrives—where people have been socialized to screen out structural constraints and contradictions so that the status quo *feels right* or at least feels inevitable (Jaggar 1989). Further complicating this challenge, the parties' level of discomfort and their needs for assistance are rarely evenly divided. For example, interpretations that reveal or disrupt current power relationships may evoke more dissonance for parties whose identities or roles align with those dynamics. Practitioners may need to provide these parties extra time, space, and support, thereby helping create alternatives to accepting the field's default norms of calm expression or narrowing conflict analysis into micro dimensions.

Next I tell a mediation story that illustrates my efforts to enact an emotionally thick conflict praxis that is guided by the hope of inviting more just relationships—but first a few caveats. While all conflicts are embedded in structures and discourse, not all conflicts have structural elements that are salient to address. Further, creatively responding to emotions does not mean that disputants will *choose* to take on the challenging work of unearthing and responding to the structural elements of their conflict—regardless of how germane structures are to their presenting conflict. Respecting the right of disputants to author their own futures suggests that interveners *invite* consciousness of structural elements and the possibilities of deeper change, while refraining from imposition.

Praxis Story:
Hard Listening and Learning How to Be an Ally

I was recently hired to mediate a conflict between a supervisor "Matt" and a high-level information technology technician "Janet," who both worked for a federal agency. During the first hour of the mediation, their interactions were strained, but they negotiated through their list of concerns easily enough. When I asked if there was anything else about their communication that they would like to discuss, Janet added a crucial detail: "He can never call me at home again, ever." Her tone was angry, sharp. Matt quickly agreed, but dismissively.

I soon learned that not long before the mediation, Janet was ill at work and was taken to the hospital. That same evening, Matt called Janet at home to confirm that she was all right. Exploring this incident, I noticed that Janet appeared to hold a controlled anger, which mystified Matt. He remembered she had requested never to be contacted at her home, but he insisted this case was exceptional: "We're a family; of course I needed to make sure you were ok."

"This is a workplace," Janet stated coolly, "not a family." Matt quickly retorted that if he was ever worried about Janet again, he would make sure to ignore his concerns and stick to business. I remember feeling a mixture of trepidation and attentiveness as I recognized their charged exchange suggested something deeper was at stake. I chose to explore their divergent metaphors, asking Matt to say more about how he understood their office as a "family," at one point asking him which member of the family he might be.

"Well." He paused, and gave it some thought. "I guess I'm the parent, in a sense."

"The father." Janet quickly inserted. "He thinks he's the father."

When I suggested that the two of them might make sense of this difference, they both stated they were done with the mediation and would like to leave. I felt my heartbeat quicken, feeling a mixture of vulnerability and attentiveness—vulnerable because I was not quite sure how to respond, and attentive because I sensed that we were close to the heart of their conflict. I also noted that their body language and tone was tight and alert. Matt seemed both baffled and annoyed, while Janet appeared exasperated. Further, while they both stated they wanted to leave, neither showed any signs of leaving. This contradiction fueled my sense that both held an unarticulated hope that deeper understanding was possible. I asked if each would meet separately with me, and they both agreed.

Meeting first with Janet, I took some time developing more trust between us and then asked her to make sense of how strongly she felt about the separation between work and home. Janet spoke of her previous job where her partner was constrained by the military under the policy of "Don't Ask, Don't Tell" to keep their relationship strictly private.[2] I recognized Janet's dilemma. She had adapted her life to a policy that asked her and her partner to hold the structural violence of homophobia by dividing their lives and denying their family. The results did not neatly end when the policy changed. While Janet did not want to discuss her private life with Matt, she agreed it might be useful for me to explain why she felt so strongly.

In my subsequent caucus with Matt, we worked to make sense of Janet's anger after he called her at home, and he particularly struggled to make sense of Janet's wishes to not speak with him directly about the deeper cause of her anger. I felt my role shifting from mediator to a facilitator of learning, or conflict coach, as we spoke of how people who hold marginalized identities are often asked to explain themselves—giving them the burden of educating those more aligned with privilege, and also using their painful stories of marginalization as learning moments for the privileged. I also asked questions to open an exploration of the difference between "parent" and "father," particularly its gendered dimensions in relationship to power, and we discussed how both metaphors position Janet and her coworkers as children, which Matt had not considered nor intended. Since Matt stated he wanted to support Janet, I asked him to consider what alternative role he might take that Janet might welcome.

Meeting back together, Matt expressed his genuine sadness for the homophobia Janet had shouldered, confirming that he would respect her decision to not talk further about matters she considers personal. He also told her that he would like to be an ally if she welcomed this. Janet told him, "Thank you, you just were." In the following silence, I felt their relational tone open and shift. I sat back as they spoke on a deeper level about the climate in their office. When Janet spoke about a subtext of homophobia in the office, Matt leaned forward and stated emphatically that he would make sure this stopped. Janet exhaled loudly, crossed her arms and sat back. This time, Matt was attuned to the dynamics enough to read her frustration, caught himself positioning himself as a "father," and smiled. He asked Janet for some patience, saying that he could be a slow learner, but he was trying. She smiled back and shook her head, and they shared a very quiet laugh.

Not long after the above exchange, they began speaking collaboratively about ideas for change in their office, which signaled to me that they felt they had sufficiently located their conflict and were ready to articulate and reintegrate what they had learned together. I tried one more intervention. I asked Matt and Janet to imagine what they hoped a workplace like theirs would look like long after they retired. After they both suggested, among other things, a future workplace that would welcome everyone in equity, they considered if there were any steps they might take now that might make their desired future more likely. In the end, one thing they added to their agreement was to request a diversity workshop.

Reflections on the Mediation

I will first use the mediation story above to illustrate the significance of destabilizing commonsense notions of emotions, reviewing how divergent responses to emotions matter in conflict practice. Next, I will suggest how staying with emotions and aiming toward a creative discomfort helped create a space in-between that nourished transformation.

Previous to the mediation, I was already practiced in destabilizing commonsense notions of emotions, which prepared me to be curious about the personal-social meaning connected to Janet's and Matt's emotions. In contrast, if I had used a settlement lens to guide my practice, I likely would have considered Janet's emotion as nonrational and as an obstacle to creating a reasonable solution. Based on this assumption, I may have diffused Janet's anger via reflective listening so that Janet might present her individual interests in a way that Matt could hear.

If I had used a lens of personal empowerment, I would likely have interpreted Janet's anger as a "negative emotion" that should be reworked to promote a more productive interaction. Toward this aim, I might have supported the disputants to listen to each other and to acknowledge the respective divergent worldviews as expressed in the metaphors of "family" and "workplace." But I would have stopped short of inviting the disputants to consider how these metaphors are informed by a wider context, or how the expression of anger is embedded in structural asymmetries and unjust policies—in this case, homophobia and the policy of "Don't Ask, Don't Tell."

In contrast, I have learned to *stay with emotions* long enough for new meanings, feelings, and options of response to emerge. Trusting my embodied senses informed me that Janet's anger signaled that something powerful was at stake for her. Based on my awareness that exploring metaphors is a rich way to interpret emotions and patterns of power, I used their divergent metaphors of family/work and parent/father as points of entry to consider what was beneath Janet's anger. As I subsequently heard the structured backdrop of Janet's conflict story, I began to consider Janet's anger as an *outlaw emotion*—the kind of emotion that can unearth the contradictions between marginalized people's lives and the status quo—and one that is notoriously challenging to hear (Jaggar 1989).

In relation to finding a balance of creative discomfort, I struggled. As their divergent emotions became more vivid, they both expressed a desire to leave. To regain a sense of balance and to honor the spirit of their request, I invited both into separate caucus spaces. I also recognized that their needs for assistance were not evenly divided. Matt needed compassionate support to do the *hard listening* necessary for him to understand the complex sources of Janet's anger and to avoid narrowing the anger into a strictly personal level (Janet is an angry/unreasonable person) or into an interpersonal realm (Matt made Janet angry). This support helped prepare Matt for the pleasure of being an ally. Later when we met back together, in hopes of harnessing their creative prefigurative power, I invited both to imagine and begin to author a different future. After Matt and Janet fleshed out what a preferable future might look and feel like, they considered what steps they could take to move toward this more inviting, inclusive reality.

Conclusion

Creating a space for Janet and Matt to learn through their conflict involved *holding a space in-between*—an uncomfortable place full of the potential of personal and social transformation. Janet's anger helped open this space, which was taken up by Matt's caring curiosity about the source of her anger. To be clear, both Matt and Janet initially sought to avoid this space by settling for a thin solution—effectively turning away from the possibility of transformation. Because entering a space in-between goes against commonsense approaches to conflict and to emotions, interveners need supportive and creative strategies to assist parties in entering and finding their footing in this uncomfortable, transitional zone.

My intention in this chapter is not to solve the "problem" of emotions by offering prescriptions of how best to respond to emotions in conflict practice. Instead, I hope my discussion informs a search for conflict processes that are more emotionally fluent and more likely to inspire meaningful change. Our field has invested more energy in practices that stop or narrow the energy of emotion than in practices that harness our enlivened senses to advance fuller, more just relationships. I encourage practitioners to move beyond this inheritance by cultivating more emotionally self-reflexive approaches and by attending to the personal as well as social meaning of emotions. Doing so makes it more likely that we honor the complex lives of those in conflict, and also that we provide alternatives to turning away from opportunities to create more just, inclusive futures in which every one of us belongs.

Notes

1. As cited in Goldberg and Blancke (2012); see also Schirch (2005).

2. Don't Ask, Don't Tell is the US policy (1993–2011) that barred openly gay, lesbian, or bisexual persons from military service.

7

Supporting Creative, Whole Peacebuilders: An Apprenticeship Program

John Paul Lederach, Rachel M. Goldberg,
Yago Abeledo, Kathryn Mansfield, Laura Taylor,
María Lucía Zapata, and Myla Leguro

IN 2008 THE KROC INSTITUTE AT THE UNIVERSITY OF NOTRE DAME, supported by a grant from the Fetzer Institute, launched a pilot apprenticeship program. This pilot program was designed to meet an educational need that Lederach and others felt was not being met. In his words:

> The field of peacebuilding has grown immensely over the past decades. Greater numbers of academic degree programs, professional training, and organizations dedicated to the preparation of people and their capacities now exist. Nonetheless, the training and education strengths tend to focus heavily on analytical and technical skill capacity. In the wider field, we have not equally evolved creative and robust ways to provide the deepening of vocation, presence, character, and spiritual sustenance for the rising generation of leaders. In a word, with our rising peacebuilders we have tended to focus more on the development of the outer journey than on nurturing the inner strength, clarity and fortitude so necessary for the quality of presence needed in this work. . . . Our primary purpose [for this program] is to nurture the rise of peacebuilders with sustaining, transformative presence capable of making a constructive difference in violence habituated systems. (Lederach 2008, unpublished data)

What he and Kroc are trying to foster is an ability to work with what Lederach calls

> the *"below and the beyond"* . . . something that goes deeper and penetrates under the surface of the technical layer [of our expertise]. Rather

131

> consistently I have found that when you have a real connection with people, when you get to *the below,* you touch something deeply connected to . . . a basic and shared sense of humanity. Simultaneously I experience this as connected to something transcendent.[1]

Lederach feels that if practitioners avoid or lose the ability to work with this deeper, more complex, and transcendent part of themselves and the work, the practice can become entirely cognitive, structural, contractual, divided—and thus sterile, barren, incapable of growing what we want and need to grow:

> That for me was a powerful insight because a lot of peacebuilding can move very strongly towards the structural side. You can have a ministry of peace, you can have peace processes and the thing [you are developing] is going to be defined with structures, and roles and functions, and all of a sudden everything that was creative about it dies. So how we retain a sense of purpose but in an ever-evolving creativity, is really a big challenge.[2]

The apprenticeship program was designed to engage these goals with several different components. There were *"experienced reflective practitioners* (anchor-mentors) with vocational commitment . . . who [were] continuously involved in ongoing peacebuilding initiatives on the ground" working with "small cohorts of *fellows* (apprentices) in order to work together on real-life initiatives" (Lederach 2008, unpublished data):[3]

> The purpose . . . was to have students engage much more deeply in what I would refer to as the vocational work, vocation here used [as] in the origin of the word, to reach and touch something of your voice. . . . I am using the term much more in reference to how you come into a sense of who you are and a sense of purpose and how you live with that purpose across a lifetime . . . [to be] able to touch in a deeper level your sense of voice.[4]

This project was intentionally designed to be different from classic academic endeavors. It was designed to engender the engagement necessary to support the development of real vocation through three levels of deepening: an expanded time frame (working together for three years), three creative teams in direct experience with each other to foster "spaces for wider shared reflection," and

> spaces for deepening the sense of vocation, voice, spiritual sustenance and practices, along with the building of character and wisdom . . . valued equally with intellectual and skill development. This expansion

requires intentionality to develop diverse modalities for learning as deepening the capacity for transformative presence; cross-fertilizing different ways of knowing and understanding that promote creativity, innovation and integrity of both profession and personhood. (Lederach 2008, unpublished data)

Over three years, the teams worked together on peacebuilding initiatives, supported the professional development of the apprentices, and explicitly focused on long-term vocational concerns. The term *apprentice* was used to underscore a quality of relationship that explored craft and character as much as analytical capacity and skill. Lederach defines it this way:

> The apprenticeship traditionally would have been with a blacksmith, a leather maker, a shoemaker, or paper maker. People that gave a lifetime to a craft would take an apprentice. Usually they were people who were extremely skilled in the technical aspects of their craft, but they had a mysterious, mystical relationship with their craft even though they may not have ever expressed it or written about it. There is a certain level of respect the wood carver or furniture maker will have with the wood, or the paper maker will have with the paper, so I proposed that it would be interesting if in the peacebuilding field, we started thinking more in lines of apprenticeship than in the lines of formal technical preparation for people in the academic programs.[5]

Of particular interest for this book, the pilot initiative intentionally pursued three broad questions: How do we better prepare rising leadership in the field? How do we assure integrity of presence? How do we deepen and understand vocation? These questions translated into an overarching concern: How do we nurture wholeness as part of professional development?

The authors of this chapter represent the team established at the Kroc Institute, as well as Rachel Goldberg and Yago Abeledo. The Kroc team included a practitioner-scholar with thirty years of active practice and teaching (Lederach), two recently graduated master's degree students (Kathryn Mansfield and María Lucía Zapata), one newly arrived master's degree student with extensive field experience (Myla Leguro), and one incoming student pursuing a doctorate (Laura Taylor). Their work carried them to many places on more than four continents, while their origins were in Colombia, the Philippines, and the United States.

While many aspects of this apprenticeship program merit exploration, this chapter will focus on one: the approach to integrating spiritual practices as part of preparing for and engaging in peacebuilding. The Kroc team developed this within an academically based program.

This chapter has two major sections, one by Lederach and the apprentices and one by Goldberg. The introduction above represents an amalgam of Lederach's and Goldberg's writings, which summarize some key information, but loses in fluency what it gains in information. As Goldberg reviewed Lederach's initial chapter, she became deeply interested and asked Lederach for further materials. She conducted two interviews and collected background and supplementary materials, using them to explore some areas that were touched on by Lederach but, if expanded, offered greater richness. In order to preserve the clarity of writing, the material will be presented in two sections. The first will include John Paul Lederach's original chapter with the apprentice narratives. We start with an overview provided by John Paul that describes several practices incorporated into the process over the past three years. Each of the four apprentices will then reflect on how they experienced these practices and the impact, if any, on their lives and professional careers. Each segment written by Lederach and the apprentices is written in the first person, starting with Lederach's practices. Goldberg's work follows after this, deepening the information presented in Lederach's section, and the chapter ends with Lederach's conclusion.

Lederach

I should note that at the time of this writing, the pilot initiative has ended and each person is now located at a different professional stage and geography. Laura is starting a tenure-track position in a Peace and Conflict Studies department; Myla has returned to the Philippines and coordinates peacebuilding efforts in Mindanao for Catholic Relief Services; Katie coordinates peacebuilding programs for Mennonite Central Committee based in Kenya, and Maria Lucia moves between a PhD program in Winnipeg and active peacebuilding through JANO, an organization focused on restorative justice and conflict transformation she has helped establish in her home country of Colombia.

Three Practices

For many years I have experimented with how to bring a deeper level of reflection and an opening of the spiritual imagination to classes and trainings. Academic rigor, practical skill development, and spiritual opening do not have easy or natural bridges. They require different kinds of pedagogies and methods. Practices that best link spirituality and preparation for peacebuilding have three qualities. First, they are best when they are simple, accessible, and provide something anyone can use. Second, they are particularly effective if people do not consider them spiritual, as if they are something religious or apart, or would require special wisdom. Basically, they function best if they are fun. Third, they must invoke and provoke a deeper quality of reflection. In other words, the practices foster an awareness of deeper meaning yet inherently carry a dose of joy that creates a surprise factor. It is not always possible to combine all three, but I keep watching for and experimenting with ideas and approaches that seek this kind of space.

Poetic listening. For many years I have explored and linked the connections between poetry and peacebuilding. I have come to believe that when we experience, when we speak and hear honesty and truth, several things are present. First, the moment and the language shared have a simple and natural quality, so much so that we may not notice its extraordinary depth and value. Second, the beauty of the moment and emergent language has poetic eminence. What I find is that poetry enhances my capacity to both listen for and speak to a deeper truth, within myself and in others. I would call this poetic listening, and I think it can be developed and practiced.

Poetry mostly notices things. Truth lies in this noticing and expressing. I have found a particular gift in approaching everyday conversation as poetry, to listen and soak in unexpected beauty and honest insight. For me, reading and writing poetry, not with the goal of producing poetry but as the practice of noticing and listening, has increased a capacity to perceive in others and myself the gift of touching a deeper meaning and understanding.

Poetic listening reframes our attention away from content and toward the source of voice, the heart speaking. In our field, especially true of conflict resolution approaches, we have been trained to listen to others and primarily for the meaning-content but less for the heart flow seeking to emerge. We are rarely, if ever, encouraged to listen to or notice our own heart speaking. Parker Palmer wrote about this when he noticed how people take notes in seminars and classes. They would often write extensive notes on what he as the lead facilitator had just said. They took some but fewer notes on what their fellow participants would contribute. But they never took notes on what they themselves said (Palmer 1999). Among our challenges is how to begin and sustain a practice that pays attention to our heart speaking.

How might we increase poetic listening while engaged with an academic course or training on conflict resolution?

In our apprenticeship process we often started our joint seminar with fifteen minutes of open but focused writing. One of us would provide a short poem or, more often, a single line from a poem or essay. Rainer Maria Rilke's advice to a younger poet provides an illustration I have often used: "Ripen like a tree." Together, in silence or with background music playing lightly, we would write for fifteen minutes "without lifting the pen from the paper." At later points in the semester we would revisit what was written, noting and lifting a few key phrases out, perhaps sharing them, and in some instances developing poetry from the lines that were not originally written with that intention. This combination has five qualities I believe may invoke poetic listening, and these have some intriguing connections to peacebuilding:

• We are alone together—each person in their own internal world but in the presence of others, a physical reminder of the simultaneity of the inner and outer journey.

• We begin by soaking in and circling around a provocative insight, a twist of words that requires a second look and creates a catalyst.

• We write without stopping. Without noticing, we bypass the demanding perfection so much a part of academic expectation and obligation. Embedded within the writing, the deeper heart may speak in unexpected ways.

• We take notice of what we wrote, at times surprised that a theme unnoticed in its first iteration begins to emerge. On other occasions we find a gem of Truth we ourselves had not known we penned or even felt.

• Over time we notice the hidden heart flow, increasing a capacity to observe and appreciate poetry present in everyday life and conversation.

Walking and talking. Over the past number of years, I have included Henry David Thoreau's essay titled "Walking" as a required reading in the peacebuilding course focused on the *Moral Imagination* (Lederach 2005). I describe the rationale behind the reading to students with an anecdote from when I was director of a new program on conflict transformation at Eastern Mennonite University. To achieve certification, we needed to prove that our courses had sufficient *seat hours* to meet master's level standards. By seat hours, they meant how long students were in class. I found the metaphor provocative and disturbing. If we look back to the preeminent masters of education—from Buddha to Jesus, from the Greeks to Gandhi—we find rather consistently that their preferred pedagogical method involved teaching while walking. Ironically, we seemed to have come to the conclusion in our formal education that we learn best while seated.

I believe that walking can be a spiritual practice. And walking together has a profoundly different effect on insight, learning, and understanding than do the formal discussions that take place in class or offices. I have introduced walking into many of my training sessions and also into university classes. It is not uncommon to find one of my classes walking together around the campus of Notre Dame (though South Bend winters do not make this easy!). Throughout our apprenticeship process, walking together, at times as a wider group though almost always in pairs, provided a modality of sharing that had an impact on the quality of our conversation. Over time I found that the apprentice-colleagues would ask me for a walk. Walking has a number of qualities that should not be overlooked:

• The physical movement increases circulation, creates a flow of endorphins that research suggests sparks creativity and happiness, and provides a coordinated rhythm that seems to encourage a sense of shared conversation.

• Walking as a pair creates an *alongsideness*, a word my spell check does not like but that I feel describes most accurately the felt sensation of accompaniment—being with another person and sensing their person, support, and connection.

• When we walk and talk, we talk "with" each other rather than "at" each other.

• When we walk, we listen differently. Walking together physically emulates and may encourage "coming alongside" the views and concerns of another.

• When we walk, we speak differently. Walking provides time to circle around ideas, come over them step-by-step, and deepen the grasp of what we may be struggling to know, touch, or fully comprehend. Rather consistently, walking and talking has the effect of "arriving" at a better understanding of what we said.

The vocational pause. Peacebuilding, particularly in settings of deep-rooted conflict, is never easy—hectic, demanding, at times overwhelming, and an enterprise for which we cannot always see concrete results. Sometimes, when I describe to others the nature of this work, the difficulties faced, the risks required, and the few, if any, signs of success, on more than one occasion I have found myself facing a blank stare. And then the inevitable question: "Why do you do this work?" In the midst of the conversation, I pause—even going silent for a moment. In order not to appear out of sorts, recovery may come with a quick explanation, a slight exaggeration of a recent event that went well, or a quick appeal to an idealistic motivation. But inside, the question has stopped me short.

I have come to refer to this moment as the *vocational pause.*

The pause happens because, in the midst of one conversation happening in real time, another conversation, lifelong in nature, has reopened. The question knocked on the door of uncertainty and unleashed, inside, hidden from view, the ongoing conversation with the deeper inner voice. To enter that conversation requires exploration of the ever-circling questions: Who am I? What I am up to? What gifts do I bring to this world? What is my place in the bigger order of things?

When we first proposed the apprenticeship pilot, I envisioned the process as focused centrally on peacebuilding initiatives. While the various initiatives and travel together certainly held a key part of our collaboration, as I look back, I have been surprised to note that perhaps the most significant aspect of the process gravitated toward the moments of vocational pause experienced by the rising leaders, when they struggled with questions about place, identity, worth, and life purpose. We did not set aside a time that we called vocational pause, but this is what I would call some of the most significant and sacred exchanges.

The challenge of the pause is the uncertainty and insecurity we feel when we suddenly realize we do not have an answer to the questions. A final answer does not exist. But that is also the gift of the vocational pause. It reminds us to explore, search, and listen. These are deeply spiritual moments, whether we choose to name them as such or not. They are spiritual because they strip us to our bare selves—we feel vulnerable and recognize our broken humanity. They are spiritual because we learn humility and remember that the fullness of truth has not been attained. They are spiritual because they keep us curious about life, about ourselves, about meaning and purpose.

My sense is that the apprenticeship relationship permitted a more regular accompaniment and open embrace of these deeper inquiries and the search for meaning. At times this search was emotional and intensive as the vocational pause expressed itself in one form or another. But the pause also afforded a space to develop greater capacity to embrace the search as a lifelong series of encounters rather than a once-and-done answer. The practice, if we can call it a practice, was to notice the significance of the moment and insights emerging, and to hold and intentionally enter the deeper space the pause created. Sometimes this came in the middle of class, sometimes on a long walk. It is not something one controls or predicts. It is something we can recognize and embrace.

Apprentice Narratives

Business as Usual . . . or Not?—María Lucía Zapata

During the 1990s, peacebuilding was not a career choice for a young lawyer like myself in Colombia. It was not only that the field of peace and conflict studies was incipient within Colombian academia, but also that there were not many jobs available in the public or private sector. Most of my fellow colleagues interested in social change ended up working as human rights advocates or as public servants. As with many of my colleagues, I first approached peacebuilding through the field of alternative dispute resolution (ADR). After all, mediation, negotiation, and conciliation are important skills every lawyer must know. ADR's theory and practice gave me a good understanding of conflict and its management. Its efficiency and straightforward processes, as well as its promise in providing fast solutions satisfactory to the needs of the parties involved in the conflict, were certainly appealing.[6] However, my work with the presidency of the Republic of Colombia and the mayor's office of Bogotá in the implementation of community mediation programs showed me a different perspective. ADR is undoubtedly an important concept and its tools are invaluable in concrete interventions. But the complexities of social conflict and intractable, internal, armed conflict demand a different set of lenses. In this learning process, the theory of conflict transformation called to my attention (Appleby and Lederach 2010; Curle 1971, 1995; Galtung 1996; Lederach 1997, 2005; Reiman 2004). Its emphasis on relationships, long-term interventions, as well as the inclusion of a broad range of actors and issues, responded to some of the gaps I noticed.

Despite the theoretical and practical developments in peace and conflict studies, and after some years working in peacebuilding, I believe that our field still looks more like an industry than a vocation. Indicators, reports, publications, and conferences are the measures of our success. For many practitioners and professionals, it is easy to get entrenched in this competitive dynamic, losing sight of the purpose, meaning, and impact of our work.

It is in this context that I arrived at the apprenticeship program. I had just finished my master's degree in International Peace Studies and I was doing some consulting. I originally approached the spiritual element of the apprenticeship with some uncertainty. "Who knows?" I thought. "Maybe it will be a useful tool for my toolbox." In this way, I am not different from any other practitioner in the field. However, I was not prepared for the deeper reflections that the apprenticeship inspired, and the vocational pause that came afterwards. As a lawyer, and in a way, also as a peacebuilder, I was trained to believe that "the touchy-feely" word "spirituality" was more appropriate for psychologists, social workers, and religious people. It is a word incompatible with the concrete elements, realities, and responses that are the cornerstone of our discipline. Or so I thought.

The three main practices John Paul explored—poetic listening, walking and talking, and vocational pause—created a safe dynamic for inquiry and reflection, not only with my mentor, but also with my fellow apprentices. I found two main activities particularly valuable for me: focused writing and walking and talking. During my master's program, John Paul advised me to keep a journal and encouraged me to write every day, whatever was in my mind—without considering academic or grammar rules, just thoughts, ideas, reflections, feelings, perceptions, doodles. I found this exercise fruitful not only at a personal level but also from a professional and academic perspective. Writing provided an escape to release the demands and pressures of everyday peacebuilding; but also, the ideas and reflections, once registered without a care, later became the building blocks of future academic papers. Although different from the fifteen minutes of focused writing that John Paul describes at the beginning of the chapter, this activity is one that I try to follow in my daily practice.

During the apprenticeship, walking and talking became one of the favorite practices. At the beginning it was a little intimidating: "What am I supposed to say to my mentor?" "Is this an evaluation?" "I better say something intelligent." Later, it became a safe place for self-reflection, sharing experiences, and wisdom (and yes, evaluation, too, but a friendly one!).

At the end of the apprenticeship, strong communities of support, trust, and care emerged. We were able to create a place for a slow and silent process of self-reflection in which fears, doubts, and reservations, as well as joys and satisfactions—once hidden under deadlines, indicators, and techniques—emerged with full strength. This has not been an easy journey. At one point, I found myself in a multimonth vocational pause that triggered doubts about my place, direction, and identity. Nevertheless, it was also an opportunity for self-exploration and searching, helped by my fellow apprentices who were pivotal in helping me navigate this process of understanding and vocational strengthening.

I am currently pursuing a doctorate in peace and conflict studies at the University of Manitoba in Canada. Although my fellow apprentices are scattered throughout the world, I believe that the most important outcome of the apprenticeship process was the development of this unique community of care. This space of trust allowed me to approach peacebuilding from different angles, to refocus and to reconnect with my chosen profession in different and innovative ways. Although I know certain aspects of my work in peacebuilding will be business as usual, my underlying approach has greater depth and will be more meaningful because I have a community that will encourage me to be curious about life and curious about the meaning and purpose of my contribution to this field.

Learning a New Dance—Kathryn Mansfield

I work for the Mennonite Central Committee with Kenyans trying to prevent violence and heal from past harms and build peace—from within churches, community based organizations, and nongovernmental organizations (NGOs). They seek to repair relationships harmed by historical land theft, marginalization, and ethnic and gender-based violence. They work through economic empowerment or infrastructure building "connecter" projects by promoting dialogue, by strengthening the capacities of local peace actors, by developing early warning–early response mechanisms and networks, by delivering civic education, by promoting strategies to report and reduce sexual and gender-based violence, and by working with students in school peace clubs and even with public-service vehicle operators (in the Kenyan context, a group frequently paid by politicians to create violent chaos, and a group looked down upon by many).

Some peacebuilders here are driven by their Christian or Muslim faith, others by hope and ambition for Kenya. Some are driven by the fact that peacebuilding jobs and meetings pay good money. Some are keeping up appearances, saying the right words to look good in a meeting but carrying on with *negative ethnicity* once they leave. Negative ethnicity is the term most often used in Kenya to convey bias, privilege, discrimination, exclusion and/or violence based along ethnic lines. In other words, rather than ethnic differences being celebrated, they are used as a way of detaching from and excluding one another and of justifying ethnic violence. Other peacebuilders risk their health and sanity running all over the country, driven by a deep vocational commitment to transformation.

As I write this, many people are celebrating the fact that the 2013 elections passed without mass violence, after the 2007–2008 elections and their aftermath wreaked havoc on Kenya, killing more than 1,500 and displacing more than 600,000 people. Many others are questioning whether the elections were legitimate, whether their voices matter in this nation, and whether they are part of the nation at all; they are questioning the value of peace without justice. In other news, politicians are clamoring for higher salaries, although a Member of Parliament makes, astonishingly, fifty-five times as much as a teacher.

Many Kenyans have resigned themselves to hierarchies that only serve the few, to political exclusion and corruption, to deep divisions between ethnic communities, and to limited opportunities for social and economic participation for the majority. Understandably, Kenyans cultivate cynicism and toughness.

I showed up in Kenya extremely idealistic and soft, easily moved to tears (amused when my Swahili teacher sneered, "the *whites*—they even cry at movies!"). By way of background, I had made a massive career shift six years earlier. In 2004, I left my position— after eight years at a major multinational bank in New York and London—searching for something more in tune with my soul and semiconsciously still nursing my wounds from September 11, 2001. On that day, my community lost dozens of loved ones, childhood neighbors and friends; I was there in lower Manhattan, hustling away from the fires and the cloud of debris, smelling the smoke from fires that smoldered for weeks. Soon after my departure from the bank (after a few years of recovering from September 11), I encountered teachers in peace education, who helped me see a role I could play in building peace personally and in the larger structures in the world. I studied conflict transformation. I worked with inspiring practitioners in the United States, Philippines, Colombia, and India. I began to study dance and movement therapy, trauma healing, and restorative justice. I danced in jail with women inmates in the United States. I came to Kenya inspired by East African classmates who were creative, inventive, and courageous peacebuilders. I was your basic privileged, white, thirty-something New Yorker with a big, fat vocation and limited experience living and working within a community that has experienced mass violence (other than for one terrible day).

The realities I encountered in Kenya gave me great pause, as I found so much frustration and cynicism (not least of all in myself). John Paul states above that spiritual moments "strip us to our bare selves— we feel vulnerable and recognize our broken humanity. They are spiritual because we learn humility and remember that the fullness of truth has not been attained."

The notion of vocational pause provided me a source of renewal. The practices of asking those questions, of accepting (however ungraciously) that I do not have answers, of engaging my own brokenness and vulnerability, helped me listen to—and then quiet—my internal noise. I pause by journaling and by talking via Skype with fellow apprentices or with friends and colleagues here in Kenya. Sometimes I cry (the whites!). I engage the practice of asking questions—writing question after question after question—and I encourage other colleagues to have question-based conversations, not trying to arrive at the answers too quickly.

For me, a form of poetic listening—as John Paul says, "the practice of noticing and listening"—has become a mainstay of my peacebuilding work in Kenya, not through the practice of listening and writing, but through listening in talking circles. John Paul has discussed circles elsewhere, making reference to Aboriginal culture in Australia, and in particular the practice of *dadirri* (listening circles) described by Judy Atkinson in *Recreating Song Lines* (Lederach and Lederach 2010; Lederach 2011). Kay Pranis's *Little Book of Circle Processes* also sheds great light on the myriad possibilities of circle processes to assist communities in healing, making decisions, sharing leadership, deepening relationships, and even pursuing justice (2005).

Kenyan cultures are often called oral or storytelling cultures, yet practices of sitting together and listening deeply to each other—to every voice in the room—have been scarce in my experience in (admittedly, mostly urban) Kenya, as modernization, globalization, and the presence of the television, as well as dedication to observing hierarchical protocols, take their toll. Yet when people are invited into the practice, (1) it does seem to call out something that is naturally, deeply within them; (2) I have seen people listen to each other in deeper ways than in the typical meeting setup; (3) I have seen people share stories they typically keep inside and even cry (often a taboo here); (4) I have been told that people feel like their lives have changed after sharing a story of their woundedness in a circle.

Dadirri is a practice that requires patience, time, and presence. I know that I am still working toward patience, and my presence still offers less-than-perfect enlightenment. Even so, just setting up the space for Kenyans to listen deeply to each other—to practice poetic listening—in this "new, old" way (Pranis 2005) has helped me melt some of my own feelings of cynicism and frustration. At least as importantly, it has opened spaces for Kenyans to listen to each other's stories.

An African proverb says, "A story is a bridge that leads to truth." In a place where truth is so contested, the practice I began with the apprenticeship circle has now become a gift I can pass along, providing spaces for Kenyans to share and listen to each other's stories. The economic empowerment, the civic education, the formal dialogues and other initiatives continue; yet somehow it seems important to find a way to make it all more human, less like checking boxes off for a project plan. Poetic listening in circles has been that way for me.

Lastly, the listening I experienced in the apprenticeship and my own vocational pause have together provided me a space to recognize my deepest vocation, which is to use dance and movement as ways of healing from violence.

A colleague recently asked, "Is there any way to drop the baggage of privilege in this work?" Whether it is white privilege, or educational privilege, or male privilege (or freedom privilege in the case of my work in jail), it is there. We are benefiting from it if we were born with a certain skin color or gender, or more resources, or if we have managed to avoid incarceration.

Dancing with others is never going to erase that baggage. Yet there is something equalizing in dancing—moving to music, feeling our own fluidity and awkwardness and beauty and rhythm. When I began to learn from the teachers facilitating dance as a way to heal—rather than as performance or training in expression of specific culture—I felt I was tapping my deepest spirituality.

An African proverb says, "To dance is to pray twice." Before I came to Kenya, I danced with women in jail. Here in Kenya, I danced with a family whose daughter was raped—talk therapy is not the way forward here—and dance offered a space for embodied healing. I have danced with peace practitioners from around the apprenticeship circle and from various parts of East Africa. I have danced with a group from one of Nairobi's informal settlements, "the Legends," who are working to turn away from crime and find new livelihoods, even as their neighbors reject the idea that they might be able to reform. I have seen that, somehow, the baggage of privilege and challenges of language do not disappear completely, but we meet each other in a way that is so human and true when we dance together.

Early in the apprenticeship, John Paul cautioned me, half-joking (at most, half), "Katie Mansfield, you'd better not try and make me dance." And then he proceeded to notice what a passion it was for me, and how I had tuned into learning more about healing through dance and movement. He encouraged me to learn as much as I could.

Our first apprentice retreat followed one of the trainings I attended—called JourneyDance—and so he suggested perhaps I might lead the group in a JourneyDance. I questioned whether he would participate, given his earlier warning. He not only participated in the first JourneyDance; he joined us when the group suggested we dance again the next day.

The following year, planning the agenda for the second full-group retreat, he gave me a different warning: "I hope you don't mind, I've put a JourneyDance on our agenda every afternoon." Immediately after the last dance, he guided us through a writing exercise as we listened to music and caught our breath, helping us find our poetic voices after moving our bodies.

During that recovery time, he wrote one of the more exquisite poems I have ever read, helping me know more deeply the value of bringing many forms of creativity to bear at once, and helping me see more clearly that I bring valuable gifts that can reignite spirits.

As a result of the encouragement from my mentor and fellow apprentices, I have taken that vocation seriously and am applying it to my own life and work, now pursuing a doctorate in Expressive Arts and Conflict Transformation.

Small Steps, Deep Exhales—Laura Taylor

I first found myself doing peacebuilding work in the highlands of Guatemala, thrown into an indigenous women's mental health and human rights empowerment program. Listening to their stories of war and loss, my heart, head, and whole self would get flooded. This was compounded by their current hardships in remote communities, largely forgotten by the state and often facing chronic poverty. I would experience a deep heaviness that could easily linger beyond those community dialogues. After two years I was burned out. While part of me felt weak and like I was abandoning these women, I decided to pursue a long-term vision to bring mental health into a conversation with peacebuilding. At the same time, my training in psychology allowed me to recognize that my own trauma was being carried forward from these experiences. Self-care is often talked about, and rarely practiced, by peacebuilders. To be effective in the long run, I needed to step away and consider their stories from a new angle. Looking back, I wonder if we had practiced walking while talking, if I may have had more life and peace in me to give and share.

I began the dual PhD in psychology and peace studies at the University of Notre Dame at the same time that the apprenticeship program was initiated. During those first three years, that experience in the program brought a number of new perspectives and potentials into my life. Being an apprentice provided a critical balance and complement to the traditional coursework, exams, and peer-reviewed publications I pursued. I learned, with some difficulty at first, how to simultaneously hold present the faces of those I have worked with in Guatemala or the mountains of Nepal, along with the new questions and new students that I teach. One of the ways that I was able to hold both of these disparate aspects of my work as a scholar-practitioner was by taking walks, side by side, with John Paul or my fellow apprentices. This embodiment of accompaniment, talking and walking shoulder to shoulder, frequently occurred around two beautiful lakes on our campus: two small, green pools bordered by trees and narrow dirt paths. Through the circles walked here, the physical movement along with the spiritual accompaniment helped me to see what was at the core of myself. For me, feeling centered was what freed me to hold the experiences of those facing the daily realities of the front lines of conflict along with the curiosity of those learning about these issues for the first time.

Staying rooted is a challenge because there are many times during peacebuilding work, and in academic pursuits, that I feel like I am spinning. Powerful emotions and a multiplicity of challenges overwhelm me, filling my head and heart so that I feel like I can hardly hear. But, on our walks around the lakes, I found I was able to be more aware of the person next to me, waiting patiently for a response, allowing the silence between us to ripen. This silence between us created a space for my inner voice to be more clearly heard through the cacophony of sounds created by pain, cruelty, naysayers, and structural barriers.

The walking and talking that we have done during the apprenticeship program, this simple practice, seems to take on almost a sacred space. It allows me to hear my inner voice through the noise of my spinning thoughts. In conflict settings, it is easy to be pulled into the next emergency, to respond to the constancy and the immediacy of need. At times it is what we must do: go all in and experience over and over the overwhelming heartbreak that so many face. But part of what makes us peacebuilders is the ability to see hope, even if only in brief glimpses. And for me, this sense of hope, this sense of inner peace, is cultivated by walking, by taking small steps and deep exhales. These subtle practices help me find more ways to be healthy and full in the long run. I think that we will find more clarity with each circle walked, and more daily peace with each step.

> circles, spinning 'round.
> all twisted up, stories
> reverberate.

In the final retreat of the apprenticeship program,[7] we worked with wood and sandpaper. We created talking sticks from the Aspen trees that had fallen in John Paul's backyard. These sticks now circle the globe. Mirroring the reverberation of talking, the movement of these talking pieces around a circle allows for deeper listening and opens spaces for fuller reflection (Pranis 2005). While coteaching an undergraduate community-based learning course on organizing around issues of violence in

Chicago's Latino neighborhoods, we used a circle process with our students. Each night of the week-long immersion, we started with simple prompts, such as "what was something that surprised you today?" and "what will you do differently when we get back to campus?" Across a diverse set of personal and political perspectives, we made ourselves vulnerable. By exposing my own pain, confusion, frustration, and joy in response to the people that we met, I think it helped the students do the same. With a shift in role from apprentice to facilitator, I was reminded that, as a professor or leader, we do not have to have all of the answers. Asking questions—especially of our own assumptions—is a critical pedagogical and personal practice. Through asking questions—whether inside or outside of a classroom—we can cultivate growth, reenvision the status quo, and foster our human spirit.

lake on our left
renewed hope, clear inner voice
welcomes the next step.

Now teaching in a master's degree program, our courses include an emphasis on skills and techniques. Because of my apprenticeship experience, however, my approach will add a third component: *compassionate presence*. I will expand, integrate, and weave in the practices we have used, such as collective reflective writing, walking together, and listening for creative haikus. My hope is that my students and I can work together to capture the simple complexity of the emotions, fears, hopes, and joys of the people and world around us.

Presence and Connection—Myla Leguro

I was an inspired yet very worn-out Mindanaon peacebuilder when I was invited by John Paul to become part of his circle of apprentices. For the whole of my eleven years prior to this interlude, I had journeyed across many conflict-torn areas; listened to stories of pain and suffering of those who bore the brunt of the war; witnessed the unfolding of many initiatives to heal, transform, and rebuild; and accompanied the brave attempts to reach out to the unlike-minded in my home context. In the push and pull of efforts at promoting peace and in the fluid context in which we live, sustaining hope was precious because we felt the urgent demands of creating and re-creating possibilities and alternatives to the unending violence. In these whirling dynamics I had always tried to commit myself to the view that I am in this work for the long haul. The vision of building peace in Mindanao is a lifetime engagement.

Yet it was perhaps serendipity that brought me to the apprenticeship program. My inner self needed respite from the demanding peace praxis on the ground, yet I wanted to honor my commitments. Even before fully experiencing the apprenticeship program, John Paul, as a mentor, had already gently invited me to take part in a vocational pause. This invitation to become part of a community of apprentices allowed me to much more deeply acknowledge the need to internally connect as I prepared myself for the next phase in my vocation journey.

Within our small community of mentor and apprentices, the nurturing of poetic listening through journaling and other creative expressions (such as writing haikus and little books) brought me to two defining themes in my vocation as peacebuilder—*meaningful presence* and *connection*. I have come to fully appreciate that presence and accompaniment may not always mean "being in action and in my own context at all times." I came to understand that genuine connection with people and communities emanates from a deep connectedness with oneself as a peacebuilder. These themes guided me to appreciate and learn from the experience of accompanying John Paul's own peace efforts in Nepal. It was my experience in Nepal that helped me to critically view and reframe issues of conflict, as well as peacebuilding responses, in my own context in Mindanao. It was also in Nepal that I was able to explore other facets of my own identity as a person and as a peacebuilder beyond the all too familiar markers of religion and ethnicity in Mindanao.

It was also through the apprenticeship program that I was able to appreciate the beauty of purposive walking and talking as an expression of connection and deep communication. I have come to explore with freedom my own questions about life, about vocation, about challenges, about directions, in my walks with my mentor and fellow apprentices. The walks and conversations took place at the Notre Dame campus, in the beautiful forest at the Fetzer Institute, in the streets of Kathmandu, in Chiang Mai, and in Mindanao. Every experience was made memorable with the comforting company and environment but, more importantly, the profound wisdom of the exchange. Walking to genuinely encounter the other and the self can provide care and nurturing to peacebuilders amid the constant challenges of the work.

The practices of poetic listening, walking and talking, and vocational pause fostered a new and refreshing resolve in me as a peacebuilder. Two years after the apprenticeship program was launched, I am now integrated back as a peacebuilder in the context of Mindanao. While continuing to be mentored by John Paul and nurtured by my fellow apprentices, I have also started to mentor others and to help cultivate peacebuilding vocations among young leaders. As I try to replicate and grow this alternative paradigm of accompaniment to nurture peace practice, I am assured of the fact that I belong to a community that truly supports my creative endeavors as an inspired peacebuilder.

Goldberg

Key Concepts

By now, you have read Lederach's goals and practices behind this program as well as some reflections on how they worked from the apprentices involved. This section develops those concepts in greater depth and includes four narratives similar to the student accounts, but all from Lederach. The information, unless otherwise noted, comes from the two interviews that I conducted with Lederach. Three narratives focus on how he saw the key concepts and the three practices at work with the apprentices, and one is about his own practice. I included the last because I wanted to explore how Lederach feels he personally has developed, in terms of wholeness, using these practices himself. In other words, I wanted a narrative about what a developed practitioner looks like, what the apprentices (and others using these practices) could hope to develop in themselves, and what kind of practitioner develops from these practices.

What are the key concepts? How do we teach peacebuilders to bring their full selves to bear? Lederach says it is neither easy nor something learned in an hour. He says that in some ways it is a lifelong undertaking of self-development. "I am really trying to figure out what these tools for being human are, and it seems to me they return over and again to our quality of presence. They form and are formed by what we may refer to as spiritual disciplines. At essence: How to cultivate openness, humility, and patience."[8] For Lederach, the goals for his apprentices are to be able to use that openness, humility, and patience to touch their own deeper selves; and then to bring that to bear in their work as tool and wellspring; and finally, to develop the compassionate presence that would enable them to touch compassion in those they work with. He feels these are part of being able to work from that place of wholeness so that their work moves beyond structures, tools, and processes to the inspired moment, the creativity, that brings our techniques and tools to life. I will start by exploring some of these concepts in greater depth, as well as expanding on the three practices (walking and talking, poetic listening, and vocational pause), before presenting the four narratives.

What is compassionate presence? In his own words, Lederach explains compassionate presence as follows:

> Compassion or a compassionate presence essentially reflects the capacity to really see yourself in the suffering of another and to notice how the divine is present in them as a gift to remember your own humanity. The great mandate of love in the Biblical tradition was to remember you were once a stranger. Compassionate presence functions like a pathway that permits us to find our way home, back to just being people, back to humanity.[9]

Why is creativity important? Creativity is important because the ability to be whole and creative, as well as to develop compassionate presence, is, for Lederach, what enables practitioners to touch a deeper place in those they work with. This is, for him, the difference between skills and presence, and the difference between a sterile plan and a truly transformative response or program. In his view, one of the distinctions is the difference between a tool and the very process of creation:

> One of the things that happens is that we have a new tool or approach—let's say transformative mediation. When Bush and Folger were initiating that, it came in bits and sparks and bits of insight and then they arrived at a way of framing it and then they shared it and people said "ah ha!" then they put it in a book and then workshops and then it was an approach. And what I'm after is not just to learn an approach but to learn this thing [of creation]: how does this process unfold?[10]

For him creativity connects with the concepts embedded in the words "respect" and "admire":

> The Latin root spec is "to look," so re-spect is the idea that you look and then look again—to be respectful is to slow down sufficiently to look carefully. And "admire" in Latin means to tend with great care—and again it implies, to go back a second and third time. The act of creativity is that act of careful attention to notice, to have the capacity to take account of and to do again and from that arise new ways of thinking about things that have always been there.[11]

He feels that this kind of creativity is connected to spirituality because "you have to live always at the edge of what is and to bring into existence something that does not yet exist. Creativity is very mystical. Most just want the tool, they don't want the invention process, they don't want to live in that scary space of not knowing."[12]

What does Lederach mean by humility? Another core concept is humility. F. Scott Fitzgerald, in one of his minor short stories, said, "It isn't given to us to know those rare moments when people are wide open and the lightest touch can wither or heal" (Fitzgerald 2008, 209). Lederach is working to make space for those moments to be seen and valued. He does this through modeling, sharing his own stumbling, showing that it is acceptable to falter and that it may lead to deeper insight. Among the things Lederach decided to do very intentionally with this group was to lay out an overview of all the things that he was currently involved in on practice side, walking them through the elements of what he was facing. He tried to give them a sense of his life as a practitioner:

> It's a complex mess, there is a lot that I'm involved in and some have been very long-term engagements; I have been in some places since 1988. I do not usually have those kinds of conversations about what I am doing, as there are sensitive, confidential elements that need enormous background if my listener is to get it. I give them a glimpse of what it is that I care about and what I'm trying to hold together and the difficulty of that and the lengths of time it involves.[13]

Part of what this accomplished was to help the students do their own vocational reflecting. It is also a form of compassionate presence, sharing with humility the challenges of his own work. For him, this process models how sharing one's own wounds through compassionate presence may elicit empathy and transformation in the other. Lederach also shows that it is important to keep asking questions and to follow them, experimenting and learning as you go; artistry is a developmental process—there is no point at which you are done, as a practitioner. Lederach says this kind of work is "a circle that gets repeated. Iterativeness is important in an ongoing way, making space over and over shows that this is an ongoing process and an important one."[14]

Lederach adds:

> I find humility a particularly challenging notion. Because especially in the field of conflict, humility more than anything requires a kind of attitude of [feeling] that you have not yet arrived, that you don't know, that you are not certain.
>
> The opposite of humility is arrogance, and that of course we know very quickly. We feel the presence of arrogance immediately. It says, "I am better than you. I know more than you. I am superior. I have a greater knowledge." In conflict settings, arrogance forms part of a protective façade and emerges as a weapon, not just as a tool—a weapon. The weapon comes out when I or we believe we have the Truth, so much so that we no longer need to search for it and that the searching is finished. Humility says: searching and truth-seeking are endless. I don't have the truth. And then of course you are in a place

where it is a bit disconcerting. How do you continue to have faith and believe when you don't have the truth? It is a kind of unnerving way to live, to be honest. But it has a lot to do with how you interact with other people . . . I also think . . . the capacity to see the divine in conflict and how you are working to develop it [is important].

For me, the important part is to develop the capacity to see [that] more regularly. That is, [on] a normal everyday basis, to be aware of the Divine in others and in our conversations. Sometimes it shocks you because you are in a context where you suddenly find that someone—this is why I come back to the notion of honesty and humility—has revealed a part of themselves at great risk, and in so doing, you felt moved in the connection you felt with that person in such a way that you experienced something that was simultaneously very human and very divine. And it is then, in that moment, that you notice something of God in the other.[15]

How do you help students develop presence? Most of these components are in aid of developing intervener presence. Lederach mentions several things that help support the below and beyond kind of presence, including talking deeply about presence himself and about how the work of a mediator is to "be able to transcend him/herself while being fully immersed in reality."[16] I thought it would be useful to summarize the ways Lederach helps apprentices develop presence before we hear his narratives. These include:

- stories about how he does this kind of work himself, including the challenges, and the movement forward;
- practices that elicit the kind of openness, humility, creativity, and deep human connection that equate to presence, including supporting students to work through their own vocational pauses as a gift of insight, not a moment of weakness;
- poetic listening to pull on the other places in us that speak and hear; and
- walking and talking, which makes space for the different kind of interactions needed to go to this deep, whole place, to explore vocational pause.

What made that kind of interaction possible was the trusted mentor relationship that had a regularity of contact and an openness to be available for a range of questions the apprentices themselves were not capable of understanding or generating. Lederach says, "They ask questions, but it's not really the question they really have and it takes a while to get at the root. The real questions are much deeper."[17]

Woundedness. Part of what these techniques open space for, Lederach believes, is the ability to look at and own our wounds as something transformative we can share, as compassion grows out of looking at our own wounds and seeing them mirrored in others (and their wounds in us). What creates these spaces is the kind of honesty and trust that grows out of long-term, committed relationships; that is what makes this kind of communication possible. He uses the same kind of alongsideness with the apprentices that he uses in his practice: the humility that comes from looking honestly at our own flawed nature and sharing that in a way that allows others to accept their own flaws, and that of their enemies, as fellow humans—to rediscover the depth of their humanity, and that of their enemies.

Poetic listening. Although Lederach covered this concept in his section, I found additional richness in my discussions with him. Lederach writes poetry himself and over time has learned to listen for the poetic in ordinary conversations. He listens for

> what appeared to me to be moments when a person spoke that touched something fairly deep about their understanding, and they shared it in public space, and that made an insight that reverberated and resonated in the group. It's listening on the one hand to where people seem to connect to their sense of their own insight, and sharing it out. And they may not themselves fully know or recognize the significance of what they said or what it means, but it has a resonance to it and seems to come from a fairly deep place in them and seems to touch others who are listening.[18]

Lederach also finds that this kind of listening has changed his work as a teacher and a practitioner. He finds that he is observant and attentive with people differently. "I think it has to do with your quality of presence—how am I with a class, how am I with another person."[19] In his words, he is also

> slower and faster. I am much slower in that to be attentive you have to slow down and it needs slowing down to notice a deeper quality of things that are happening in human relationships. But I am faster in that I have a greater capacity to capture and summarize the deep layers of things that may be emerging and quicker at capturing meaning, less reluctant to simply say "you know we are talking what but this conversation may really be about why."[20]

I also asked for more on how this worked in the program:

> In the apprenticeship program rather consistently I had them read poetry, and we reflected on it, and people wrote in their journals, and

I encouraged people to notice their own poetic voice. This is something that we all have—all of us are poets and have moments of insight in the way we interact with each other. Poeisis—in the Greek this is about the moment of creativity, not necessarily poetry. One of the reasons to take time each day to write or do so in the context of the opening of a class, the writing without stopping, is that it bypasses the internal nagging naysayer voice—"you haven't said that well," "it isn't right," "rewrite this," "it isn't well developed," all the things that may block you getting out the idea. [It helps] to create small, regular spaces where people are encouraged to just let come whatever comes. . . . Then maybe in other moments you can go back and underline a few things that you found particularly insightful and lift those things out onto another page, let them sit on their own and look at them and you can also go back over time—after three months or nine months or a year—and then reflect; notice that you may have been saying things to yourself over and again. You may notice a pattern, or something you haven't noticed before.

Over time, those little phrases will come out into a form [where you can see something emerging] where you had not noticed [it before in the] way that you said something. [It is] a kind of an insight, maybe [with] a creative, artistic flavor. And you can play with it; then work with poetry can become playful again. It may or may not become a poem in the more formal sense, but you notice the poetic instinct in you. We don't always find ways to listen to ourselves very well, and doing this in the group may be a way we can learn to listen to ourselves.

The reasons why you would take time to do this "poetic listening" in a class and in practice is not about the production of the product: a poem, but [about] a capacity to take note of how those things are emerging, to notice the artist, if you will, in one's everyday language and struggles.[21]

Examples of poems Lederach uses in class can be found on the Whole Practitioners website, which continues the work of this book (see the Acknowledgments), along with syllabi from the two courses he has taught using these methods. When asked about the prompt he created for a class assignment, he described how he asks students to do these reflective pages, writing in such a way as to "let come whatever comes," with a goal of them reflecting on what they write with poetic listening.[22]

Narrative Examples

I asked Lederach for instances of his practices, so that readers could get a better sense of how they worked, understand the known obstacles, and also when and how they succeeded. I wanted to know more about how to do these practices myself and thought others would seek the same level of insight. The goal is to help those who wish to use these methods to see how they work in greater depth. In practice, the three techniques and the key concepts overlap and reinforce each other, so the narratives do not go with one particular practice or concept in general but do illustrate all of them over the course of the narratives.

Narrative one.[23] Lederach used the reflective writing exercises to elicit both vocational pause and poetic listening. After the class took time to work on the reflective pages, they would "often take some minutes to share if anything felt sharable before we jumped into topics." This narrative comes from a time when Laura Taylor was in the first semester of her arrival at the Kroc Institute, after having achieved a master's degree in peace and justice studies and then having worked as a practitioner for three years on various initiatives. Laura was talking after one of these opening sessions, describing frustrations with the early part her current dual degree program. Lederach recalled:

> I don't remember what she said, but I remember a deep sensation that she was feeling very lost. I simply said, "Laura, it feels to me like you have lost your sense of voice." And she broke down. There were five of us in the room and it became clear that she was having difficulty knowing who she was; she was questioning: maybe this is not where I should be, I don't know if I'm supposed to be this person or that person, and [a lot of it was] about having lost voice. Laura's really regained her voice in significant ways and became the exemplar student of the whole PhD program.

Lederach explained how he had heard her real, underlying concern:

> It's a deep sense of myself having felt those same questions, empathy, deep intuition that she had lost a sense of herself. That she had come into something that she was so excited about, and the bottom had fallen out of it, and she was trying to portray outwardly a certain kind of strength but deeper inside she was dealing with a great deal of insecurity and disorientation, and I've felt that a lot in my life. I've taught for twenty-five years, but every time I walk into a classroom, my heart beats [with] a butterfly feeling, especially when first starting. That thing that I felt then with her was something that I have felt myself, struggling to regain my sense of self again, so I recognized it.
>
> More and more in recent years I just say what I think I'm observing, what I am guessing people mean but their voice is not getting it out. I stated it not as a question but as a small observation. Clearly it touched a chord that was very much there but not let out.
>
> So I accepted that space and let it sit for a bit, and then we went on with the class. I didn't go deeper at that time. That happened on and off over a year or two, and she gained her voice over those years.

By the second year or so Laura was much more balanced, feeling that she had found herself in this new geography. She felt more comfortable with what was emerging in her program; she was excitedly engaged in a number of research initiatives. We also went on long walks, 45 minute to an hour walks. She talked a lot about the world of quantitative psychology, that she's very gifted in, and the world of practical engagement with humans, that she is also very gifted in, and where would she end up, what career she could do, and the constraints and jobs available.

In her fifth year, Laura was asked to teach a course that took undergraduate students in and out of Chicago [to learn about issues] around diversity and conflict. She contacted me about this class and asked for advice over a year and a half after the apprenticeship program had formally concluded. Laura incorporated some aspects of the apprenticeship program into the course, like using talking sticks I had made for each of the four apprentices out of a single larger branch. Rooted in our reflections on Rilke's "ripen like a tree," I also use the metaphor of the talking sticks: we are all part of same tree. After the course, Laura sent me another e-mail, describing how things went. I saw a notable sense of joy and contentment—I felt she was saying, "I have a sense of who I am and what I bring."

For Lederach, this showed both what the program and the mentoring relationship could achieve and the way reflection on vocation is iterative; that these are all ongoing circles; and that this was the middle and end of just one circle.

Narrative two. Lederach's second story was about Kathryn Mansfield:

With Katie, her struggle was and has been for years trying to locate how to land well, [such] that she is really contributing and in ways that are exciting to her. One dilemma is that the people I have been working with are so gifted—and so many people I've worked with are so gifted. We have parts of ourselves that can be drawn out [in one setting], but when we are paying attention to one piece, another is silent, and we realize at one point in our life that we oriented everything around one piece and after a while it really doesn't feel very whole anymore.

In this narrative, Lederach shows an example of walking and talking and vocational pause. "We walked around the lake six or seven times, and over the course of the program it got to the place that these folks would just call me and e-mail me and all they would say is 'need a walk.'" What made this possible was the kind of relationship he created, "one of openness and trust and honesty, [such that] they came to a place where they could say they needed a walk, they were being honest with themselves: 'I'm struggling with something and I need somebody to say it aloud to so I can hear it.'"

Often these walks opened space for Katie to talk and reflect. But this story also shows some of the limitations of the practices:

> For Katie it has been a long journey with finding a way to what she really wants to give in her life. Some elements were fairly deep emotional expressions and it took longer for her to find ways to really arrive [at] and embrace some of her journey. Sometimes I felt that I wasn't able to help her as well as I could have. Part of it was that she is a much more emotionally expressive person. She was asked at Kroc to become a professional in an academic setting [in ways that meant she felt] she could no longer be her full self, and she found this deeply bruising. We do a lot of that in academia and it was painful for her. We never had a meeting where she didn't cry, and cry hard, until a year or two ago. I wasn't always sure how to help her, what would open up ways to understand that depth. Just recently she went on to work in a new job. One of her deeper pulls was to be a practitioner on the ground, and she realized that her very nature had a hard time responding to the NGO world. She has been trying to find a way to do what she wasn't sure she could do: she's a dancer and is now beginning a PhD program in expressive arts. Some forms of the arts people can more easily manage and there are others that people are not sure what to do with. So this very bubbly, enthusiastic person tries to get people to sing at a conference, gets her wings cut, and it is deeply painful.
>
> She wrote me an e-mail two or three months ago about her struggle—should she stay in Africa, do what she is doing, where she is starting to find a bit of herself, or do a PhD program on the expressive arts? She is starting to think about if she could really do the dance professionally, but her parents are concerned about her finding her way in life, and she had been vice president of one of the largest banks in London, so they are confused. She is competent in so many different kinds of ways. I felt it was really about one big decision, and I located one sentence that indicated a level of joy, lifted that sentence out and sent it back and said this is the only place where I hear your joyful self [resonating], and I think you're trying to talk to yourself, and you will never go wrong if you follow joy."

When apprentices go into poetic depth or vocational reflection, he pays attention, listening with the quality of his presence that he hopes to cultivate in others, in a deep and conscious, attentive way. That shows the students that these moments are important—that he values this—and it teaches them to pay attention to this, that it matters. Lederach says this means paying attention to "a small trigger internally" that allows one to be "cognizant that I need a different quality of conversation and such that I want to walk with someone so I can hear my own self, hear what I need to tell myself." During the walking and talking, he says he does not do a lot: "just listen and make small observations." His sense is that most of what he does is make space for them to talk it through for themselves.

When developing this chapter, Lederach wanted to be sure the students involved were comfortable with these narratives. Katie actually composed a reply to some of his comments above, which shows a great deal about the mentor relationship between them, so it is included here as written:

> John Paul has helped me immensely, to the point that sometimes now, when I talk to my mother about a challenge I'm facing, she suggests, "Maybe you should talk with John Paul about this."
> It's a surprise to hear he doesn't know if he was really able to help.
> It was also a surprise to me how much I cried with John Paul. He never told me to stop crying. He actually helped me accept the flood with some background that the Greek Orthodox view tears as a sign of compassion. Even with that positive spin, I still found myself wondering, "What is going on in me that I use this precious time with JP *crying* of all things?! He's a poet, a visionary, a storyteller, a teacher, one of the most renowned and insightful and sought-after peace practitioners alive, and I waste his time by crying? And what do I have to cry about, anyway? My life has been so full of blessings." Yet something about his patient, understanding presence somehow invited some of my deepest pain (which I don't yet understand fully) to pour out, not in words, but in tears.
> When I made the error of encouraging participants to sing at an academic conference (forgetting the decades-long struggle of some of the peace studies professors to be taken seriously within a conservative academic environment), I actually felt great about it. Then a few senior people set me straight on how inappropriate my behavior had been. I had been a student at the place and had felt encouraged to nurture creativity in myself and others. I felt like my little song was well placed as an after-lunch energizer before I gave a short presentation. Apparently I was incorrect. In being corrected, I felt very, very small.
> When I shared all this—along with various other moments when my idealistic vision of the Peace Institute and my experiences within it (as a staff member) were clashing—John Paul offered me questions and stories and channels for my frustration. He reminded me of a few small questions to ask myself about timing. He encouraged me to write about "things I like about where I am working" and "things I would change." One day, he suggested I might take a look at *Friedman's Fables,* in particular the one about the bottom-feeder. It's her job to swallow the waste of all the other fish in the tank, but one day she becomes fed up (Friedman 1990). On a walk, he told me the story of the eagle who thought it was a chicken, who only realized its eagleness when thrown from a very high cliff, where the wind forced its wings to open wide and allowed it to soar.

During the course of my time in Kenya, JP has continued to help me through e-mail and occasional chats. In response to my myriad questions and my decision to hand them over to God, he wrote: "So the amazing thing I found about God is she has big arms and a large lap. You are on a good path!"

Another exchange, which JP refers to here, was just a few months ago. I wrote John Paul an e-mail that began with "Dear Abby, Dear Abby." I proceeded to pour out a long e-mail about the horizon I could see, the knowns and the unknowns that were swirling within me—"questions, like stars, are good," he had advised in an earlier chat. Despite the enormous number of demands on this man, he responded with a touching, thoughtful, helpful e-mail, the essence of which was "Never doubt the step that follows joy (especially if it seems to come wrapped up in a PhD program)."

Before the apprenticeship, I'd been lucky enough to have John Paul as my faculty research adviser when I was in Mindanao. He would read my reflection journals (hundreds of pages), survey the messy jungle of my thoughts, and pluck out the one tree that seemed ready to bear fruit. Delivering a speech at our graduation a few months later, he highlighted insights from various classmates he'd read in our journals. He recalled my discussion of an interview where one of my informants, responding to a question about a particular group in Mindanao, said: "They are not educated. They only live in a forest."

He said, "Katie noted, though I am hesitant to report this with her parents in the audience, 'I think when I graduate I need to go live in a forest.'" He mused about whether the leadership of the institute would see that as an indicator of success or not, but encouraged us that "according to Henry David Thoreau, there is no greater or more important place to learn than a good long walk in the forest."

While I have not yet literally lived in a forest, I have begun a (low-residence) PhD program in Expressive Arts and Conflict Transformation, where one of our classrooms was the forest around Saas Fee in the Swiss Alps. Several of our classes involved silent walks, sitting and watching and catching poems, and, of course, walking and talking. Having recently returned from the first residential part of the PhD learning, I am walking and talking and listening and pausing in Kenya too, dancing joyfully, opening spaces for healing for myself and others, and not crying quite so much. I am comforted by the big arms and large lap, and I am learning many lessons from trees.

Narrative three. The final story broadens the discussion. I wanted to explore, even if briefly, how the kind of presence Lederach is fostering in his apprentices shapes his own work. In essence, if they develop this wholeness, how might it change what they can do as practitioners if he is the model? I asked him to discuss it in terms of a case:

My area of practice doesn't naturally fit with what people would call a case. I've been working on a process that dates back to 1992, so twenty years, and I don't have many colleagues who work on cases over that many years. I worked with at least two negotiating panels in the Philippines from work they've done since the Communist insurgency, and they had counterparts in Manila. There were one or two representatives on one side, and four or five on the other, and they have all been the same people [working together] over all that time. I never had a formal mediation role; I had a conciliation role. And I may not use those terms as others in the field would use them. Conciliation by my view is much more a form of accompaniment, unofficially focused. Among other things, I work at understanding the dilemmas people are facing at a particular moment and the way they are trying to attend to the preparation of themselves and the issues so that they may be more successful when they do formally negotiate.

I've had maybe fifty, sixty, I don't know how many, conversations, and while there are instances of very concrete things I am asked to do or reflect on around issues, if I were to convey the quality of presence that has been emergent for all of this time, it would be essentially that it has been a capacity for [me to help] them to maintain some kind of hope that it is worth trying again.

In some instances we have had times where we were actually exploring a concrete set of proposals and things that are more technical—how a cease-fire might be extended, whether prisoners can or cannot be released to relive an impasse. And in the course of the more technical discussion—how have others done this, how has it worked—what has invariably come out is that people who are involved in these kinds of difficult, protracted negotiations—they have little space to talk about their deeper personal frustrations and feel a loss of hope that anything is possible. So one thing I offer through my accompaniment and presence is to help them find hope.[24]

For Lederach, accompaniment is a commitment over years, decades even, and requires patience; through the conversations with the parties, they all find ways to preserve or nurture hope. What makes this kind of presence and accompaniment possible?

Expanded time frames, especially for settings that have experienced protracted, longer and deeper, conflict. For me it comes back to more of a relationship focus like Quakers and Mennonites have. A mentor for me was Adam Curle; for instance, he would have used the term conciliation the way I do. And another term Curle would use is befriending, to befriend people.[25]

For Lederach, the apprenticeship program is not about the preparation of people into "neat little categories or into the various roles we play, but [preparing to be] whole—whole relationships, whole people." He feels his work is really a kind of befriending, as in the case above: "What I did as an anchor-mentor, what I do for protracted conflict, is all a form of befriending that moves beyond what the field, for professional reasons, tends to segment into marketable slices."[26] For Lederach, the aim is to cultivate a sense of wholeness in healthy relationships and communities.

Conclusion

This chapter has focused on the promise of this kind of work. We will end with some of the lessons learned from the project that can be passed on to other institutions interested in implementing something similar, challenges involved in making such a thing happen, and some of the limitations of the techniques.

How Another Institution Could Duplicate This Kind of Work

One of the key findings was that success was tied to having "an expansive enough of a time frame that the relationships could develop in some depth. You can do some of this work in a shorter term—I do the same kinds of things in a workshop format—but it's not as significant as an ongoing space that is available through a relationship that has continuity in time."[27] In sum, if we want to develop whole peacebuilders, we need to recognize two things: "(1) It's about extending the nature of the relationship [so] that it is about [students'] deeper exploration, and (2) it's iterative and that means we meet more than 2–3–4 times so it permits a conversation to happen that is more intentional about their deeper questions and struggles."[28]

The expansive time frames are needed to develop the deeper relationship, thereby fostering the deeper reflection; everyone involved needs to keep making themselves open to this kind and level of work again and again. In Lederach's words:

> It's not a plateau—it's a job of continually retraining yourself to pay attention to these other parts of yourself and others. And we aren't good at passing this on yet in the field, and we don't talk about it. Part and parcel of this whole process is the ability to touch in ourselves, and open ourselves, to allowing something transcendent and spiritual to change the situation and ourselves.[29]

Specifically, for mentors, this means:

> Be true to yourself and give it time and be willing to be in relation-
> ships. You have to be willing to explore, experiment, and discover,
> because what works for me might not work for you. Another thing is
> that you have to have [a] willingness to notice things differently. Try
> and become more attuned to a deeper conversation with people rather
> than the technique or content of a particular activity that you are try-
> ing to do. While the techniques are useful—it's like, if you have ever
> seen very experienced, great Buddhist meditation teachers—they tell
> you to concentrate on your breath, but then they say that really it isn't
> the breath that matters, it's a way to hold space differently. There's a
> certain paradox that comes with this question—the thing that you
> could elicit at the level of do's and don'ts may not help you. It will
> really require a kind of attentiveness and listening to layers, to things
> that you are doing, as opposed to the content of a particular exercise
> or lesson.
>
>   If we were to pinpoint one or two of the elements [needed to
> mentor like this], one is that you commit in a different way. One way
> to understand this job is that you are a student and I am a teacher, and
> we have requirements that we need to fulfill, and in order to fulfill
> them we meet together for that purpose, which is somewhat crude, but
> it is one way of looking at it. This different model would suggest that
> you are committing to accompaniment with a student who in many
> regards is trying to open up a deeper vocational inquiry process—an
> understanding of their gifts, their niche, also parts of them that they
> have not always fully explored. It's a very different sense of what this
> job is.
>
>   What we produce now are technically proficient professionals
> who will apply techniques efficiently but will have little overall
> impact and will probably leave the field within a year or two or will be
> in a tenuous search for the next technique and will hop on whatever
> the next technique is and will try and apply it to their situation
> whether it works or not. We become very effective at forms of perpet-
> ual bureaucracy, and so when we hear about burnout or the latest ver-
> sion of impact assessment where people are lamenting that things are
> not as effective as they should be—these are clues and hints that there
> are other levels of things happening that have not been fully tapped.[30]

Challenges and Limitations

One set of issues associated with this type of commitment involves normal academic structures, such as a professor's time, classroom "seat
hours," and other academic norms. Duplicating this kind of work would
take institutional commitment and resources that are atypical at best,
complemented by dedication from both apprentices and mentors: "In
order to support the kind of peacebuilding we need, academic programs
may need to shift the way they think about doing what we do.[31]

Moreover:

> Teaching this deeper work is, necessarily, a much messier and more complex and harder thing to describe and undertake than just passing [on] theories and techniques and skills (although that is valuable and important, as well). And can we teach it? Maybe the best we can do is open space to encourage students to do the kind of self-reflective work necessary to become a different kind of practitioner.[32]

Lederach himself is the model for much of what he passes on, and the job seems to require senior, reflective mentors with a great deal of humility, who have struggled through their own vocational pauses and are willing to share those moments with apprentices. It also calls for those willing to be creative in a way that leaves out a lot of certainty and authority. Lederach affirms,

> very simply, that [apprenticeship] is different than what I typically experience in academic advising. There, you interact on a one- or two-time basis. Here the difference is committing to a relationship that flows in both directions—it's a time commitment, a more expansive interaction, being alongside for a period of time, alongsideness. It's a question of having sufficient trust so you can hear these observations—we don't always recognize the kinds of commitments that trust requires. Part of it is just being comfortable within your own skin and being a person with other people. Being a human being. I think it takes a commitment to being vulnerable; and as academics we aren't encouraged to be very vulnerable.

Another issue is that, currently, academic institutions are not designed to compensate this level of engagement as professors. Lederach notes:

> In the academic world we have credit hours, class hours, ways we organize time. What I am struggling with is that these [new] topics organize time as a flow more consistent with life exploration and so can be attended to in iterative forms, but have a quality of deepening that requires things that don't always fit the [ways] we organize time in academic settings.[33]

Another challenge is the interest and willingness of students to do this kind of self-exploration. Lederach explains, "On numerous occasions I attempted to open that other space with [other students] and I was not successful." For some students the intellectual enterprise is really the only one of merit. "These people will be a force to contend with intellectually, but almost everything we did that wasn't research would have been seen by them as not worthwhile. They could describe the importance of it—probably very well—and do it intellectually—but they didn't get it beyond the capacity to describe it."[34]

He goes on:

I think probably one of the things that is apparent—to me, at least—is that you need people who have some predisposition to explore these things. Where it's seen as inappropriate or not particularly important or central to what they think they need, it's likely to not work as deeply. So for María Lucía, when she came in, this spiritual exploration was an extra tool that she could add to her box. As it went on it became something that had much greater significance to her—she was predisposed to giving it a try—interested in the process they were developing. This is not something that she would have sought naturally, but something that she was open to.

I also find that, rather consistently, throughout a semester, around a third of my students end up asking for this deeper work, in one way or another. So, for instance, a group will come to meet with me, asking about a particular assignment or something they were struggling with. That is the presumed reason for me giving them an hour. Those students had a question that had to do with some theory or application or practice and *invariably,* 100 percent of the time—what snuck out in the middle of that conversation were questions that were much deeper—another conversation began to emerge—questions about who am I? Where am I going? What difference will I make in the world? What are the things that I am uniquely gifted to do? Why should I go this way and not that way? What do I do with having spent months in Palestine and I'm not sure what, if anything, seems any better—and people have been working here for decades and nothing seems to be fixed?

You notice in this person that is alongside of you, a rising scholar or practitioner, [that] while they are asking you a question about how to achieve a particular structural change or policy, there is another conversation that is happening, and it is about hopes and fears, the nature of who they are as a person, their voice and vocation. And when you notice that and you are alongside of that, even if for a short time—remember these are iterative moments, it happens again and again over time—you become part of a conversation they are having with you and with themselves.

The same thing happens with the reflective readings, as well. I always start with a short poem and a 5-10-minute reflection period, and on a regular basis, a few students will ask for additional readings so they can [continue to] do this kind of exploration. Around a third of the class is fiddling and don't seem to be doing more than catching up on an e-mail or two, and there are others that seem engrossed.[35] You will consistently find, if you open up a little bit of space for these things, a few people will gravitate and ask for more—and you can set up additional space. So I give these students the set of readings that I tend to suggest, and throughout the semester we would meet 3–4 times and talk about them.[36]

In the end, not every student will want, or be capable of using, this kind of mentoring, but those who do may be capable of sustaining and performing truly transformative peacebuilding work. For them, we may need to change our thinking about what mentoring really means. So, for instance, while mentoring is expected of all professors, most institutions do not use it as a major criterion for promotion or tenure. This model would place mentoring at the center, not the periphery, of our work.

This chapter ends, as it began, with Lederach's writing.

Lederach's Concluding Thoughts on Wholeness

The vocational pause is not exclusive to rising leaders searching for a place in our wider field and world that, somehow, those of us with more experience no longer face because we have arrived. To the contrary. The spiritual imagination provides a salve that softens the callus we develop over our heart's yearning as the years of work transpire. Whether in the form of cynicism or avoidance, the callus may prevent the pain, but this prevention diminishes our capacity to feel and listen deeply, to be fully present, to be whole.

Wholeness is not arriving at a place where everything is under control and understood. Wholeness is the embrace of our human condition without retreat or reaction, being fully who we are while fully aware of our need for continuous growth, acceptance, and love. These are not words we often hear expressed in our field, but they are the source of becoming and rebecoming healthy human beings and communities. And they form the heart and soul of spiritual awareness and imagination, the heart flow and source of constructive change.

Notes

The authors are arranged this way because John Paul Lederach was the author of the original version of this chapter. It has been revised extensively by Rachel Goldberg based on two interviews with him and through the use of additional materials. Yago Abeledo is listed as the third author because his blog interview with John Paul inspired the eventual rewrite, and we used some sections of that interview, with his permission, in this chapter. Abeledo's interview and many other wonderful interviews can be found at http://www.breathingforgiveness.net/search?q=lederach. The four apprentices are listed as coauthors because they wrote their experiences of the techniques discussed here, and are listed in alphabetical order.

    1. John Paul Lederach, interview by Yago Abeledo, *Breathingforgiveness*, http://www.breathingforgiveness.net/search?q=lederach, 2012. In order to avoid distracting the reader, all interview attributions will be annotated in this chapter.

    2. Ibid.

3. The locations included North America, the Southern Cone of Latin America, and Thailand. Each location differed in its organizational structure. The Kroc Institute, for example, is primarily an academic organization whereas those in the Southern Cone were exclusively practitioner-based initiatives.

4. Lederach, interview by Abeledo, 2012.

5. Ibid.

6. There is ample literature related to ADR. For more information please check the work of Robert A. Baruch Bush and Joseph P. Folger (1994); Roger Fisher, William Ury, and Bruce Patton (1991); William Ury (1993); Jayne Docherty (2005); and Mark Umbreit (1995).

7. The program held regular retreats, which brought together the different teams.

8. Lederach, interview by Abeledo, 2012.

9. Ibid.

10. John Paul Lederach, interview by Rachel Goldberg, April, 17, 2013.

11. Lederach, interview by Goldberg, April 2013.

12. Lederach, interview by Abeledo, 2012.

13. Lederach, interview by Goldberg, April 2013.

14. Ibid.

15. Lederach, interview by Abeledo, 2012.

16. Ibid.

17. Lederach, interview by Goldberg, April 2013.

18. Lederach, interview by Goldberg, May 3, 2013.

19. Ibid.

20. Ibid.

21. Lederach, interview by Goldberg, April 2013.

22. Lederach, interview by Goldberg, May 2013.

23. Lederach, interviews by Goldberg (2013). All quotes and information in this section are from both of Rachel Goldberg's interviews with John Paul Lederach (April 17, May 3).

24. Lederach, interview by Goldberg, May 2013.

25. Ibid.

26. Ibid.

27. Ibid.; John Paul Lederach (2010), report to Fetzer Institute.

28. Lederach, interview by Goldberg, May 2013.

29. Lederach, interview by Goldberg, April 2013.

30. Lederach, interview by Goldberg, May 2013.

31. Ibid.

32. John Paul Lederach, interview by Abeledo, 2012.

33. Lederach, interview by Goldberg, May 2013.

34. Ibid.

35. Of note, the readings he recommends are in the sample syllabi on the website.

36. Lederach, interview by Goldberg, May 2013.

8

The Inner Spirit of Peacemaking: A New Training Imperative

Louise Diamond

> Everything is interconnected. Therefore, *connect the disconnected*.
> Everything is energy. Therefore, *energize peace*.
> We are all simply Divine. Therefore, *relate to the ideal potential*.

These three core principles and their related action imperatives define the inner spirit of peacemaking. I say "inner spirit" because these principles reside within any good peacemaking process, regardless of the overt content, and because they require subtle and often invisible behavior by the peacemaker acting from his or her higher, or spirit-infused, self. In this chapter we will examine the three principles at play in the practice of peacemaking—whether at the micro level of two-party mediation or at the macro level of deep-rooted social or political conflict—and their implications for the training of peacemakers.

Everything Is Interconnected

From a study of living systems, from ancient mystical and wisdom traditions, and from cutting-edge science, we understand that everything exists in a giant web of interrelatedness. Nothing and no one exists by themselves, without relationship to others and their environment. This challenges and changes the predominant paradigm of the last several centuries in Western society, which assumed a reductionist, materialist worldview in which everything was seen as separate, disconnected. I believe that this sense of disconnection is actually our woundedness—it lies at the core of all our conflicts, whether intrapersonal, interpersonal, or intergroup, and is responsible for the many "isms" that have caused so much suffering in the human family: racism, sexism, colonialism, imperialism, and more.

If separateness is the wound, then the healing medicine is connectedness. This requires peacemakers to *connect the disconnected*. What exactly needs connecting? Externally there may be relationships that are broken and need mending, chasms between people(s) that call for bridges to be built, or ugly stereotypes that need rehumanization. The peacemaker's response is to bring together conflicting parties for dialogue; mediation; mutual understanding; reconciliation; joint, creative problem solving; negotiation; or whatever the appropriate method may be in any situation. And we must do so in ways that allow the parties to engage safely and fruitfully and to build new and better relationships. Most current training for peacemakers focuses on the theory and practice skills for these various processes.

Connecting the disconnected means also looking at the whole of the conflict system and noticing who and what may be missing from the peacemaking conversation, and introducing those absent elements into the process. The missing "who" are not usually difficult to identify.

Are women present when peace is discussed within male-dominant settings? Are the local recipients of aid equal partners in devising and implementing development programs? In peace processes between Israelis and Palestinians, what place is there for Palestinians who are citizens of Israel?

Discovering the missing "what" may be more challenging. In our work in Cyprus, we found the internationally recognized eighty-to-twenty percent division of resources to lack balance (with 80 percent going to the Greek-Cypriots, who comprised 80 percent of the island's population). We therefore required an even representation of Greek- and Turkish-Cypriots in our conflict resolution programs. The Turkish-Cypriots told us that this commitment to balance was deeply appreciated—it was the first time anyone had acknowledged them in this way—and was what convinced the authorities to allow our activities to go forward.

In many situations, what's missing is safety, so, for instance, in order to bring together Israeli settlers and Palestinians for dialogue, we had a "leave the guns at the door" rule. (The Israelis refused, so the dialogues were canceled.) In Bosnia after the war, what was missing was the ability to speak directly about people's experiences and feelings—it was just too much too soon—so we introduced the metaphor of gardening, allowing

Serbs, Croats, and Bosniaks meeting together for the first time after the Dayton Accords to speak of pulling weeds of hatred and intolerance, or preparing the soil for planting seeds of reconciliation, thereby addressing critical issues while maintaining a sense of emotional safety.

The ultimate quality often missing from conflict is love. Gradations of anger, fear, and sorrow usually cloud the relationship between the parties. Love is nurturing; anger, fear, and sorrow are depleting. Therefore, any suitable way the peacemaker can introduce nurturing into the conflict situation is a way to provide what is absent, and reminds the parties of what is possible—indeed, of what lies under the surface of the conflict, waiting to be remembered.

Introducing nurturing can take many forms: appreciation, caring, gratitude, empathy, compassion, and more. Giving parties our full and undivided attention when they speak is a form of nurturing, as is providing a pleasant and comfortable physical setting, and even good food when appropriate. One of our trainees in Cyprus launched the ultimate love-in-action project. He reunited Greek- and Turkish-Cypriots from villages that had previously been mixed but whose populations had been ethnically divided during the violent periods in the 1960s and 1970s. He arranged the permits, hired buses, found a neutral and welcoming place for the meetings, and made it relatively easy, at least at the physical level, for these estranged covillagers to meet again. Mostly older now, the people were so happy to reconnect with their old friends and neighbors.

Other ways to connect the disconnected externally include integrating theory with practice, and both with policy; linking the present with the past and with the future; helping conflict parties bring in their values, their visions, their hopes and dreams, their intention for change, their patterns; their unconscious core assumptions; and more. All of these transform separateness into connectedness.

I think of the first conflict resolution summer camp we did with teenagers from the Greek- and Turkish-Cypriot communities in Cyprus. We did a walk-through-history exercise, asking each group to lay out on the floor a map of the significant events in their conflict over time, then walk the timeline silently, looking to the right and to the left to see how each party identified key moments. The silence became dense and deep, until finally one young person spoke up. "They lied to us," she said. "All our lives, our leaders, our teachers, our parents, our media—they lied to us. They never told us there was another way to view these events, another perspective."

Finally, connecting the right and left brain is important in peacemaking, especially since these problems cannot be solved exclusively through the rational mind, through cognitive intelligence. Encouraging moments for poetry, drawing, movement, rituals, storytelling, skits, and other forms of creativity, as well as activating the somatic and emotional dimensions, can bring great benefit. I think of a workshop shortly after the war in Bosnia, where a Bosniak woman who had lost a son in the war found herself face-to-face with a Serb soldier. All her hatred and anger was projected onto him. He hid in a corner during one of our activities, and came back having written a poem in which he described how he had never wanted to be a soldier, only a poet relating to the natural world around him. Her heart opened to him, and their ensuing deep and lasting friendship became a beacon for the rest of the group.

As much as connecting the disconnected externally is critical to any peace process, doing so internally is equally important if not more so, and here is where training for peacemakers is sorely lacking.

To be maximally effective, the peacemaker needs to connect the inner cognitive, spiritual, and emotional dimensions to his or her whole self, especially those parts that we do not normally associate with a linear, rational approach to problem solving. In other words, the peacemaker has both an opportunity and a responsibility to access, integrate, and exhibit that "inner spirit" of peacemaking, for in doing so one awakens that same resource within the system, models its usefulness, and fills a void in the situation.

For instance, when things get especially tense and angry, is the peacemaker able to relate to his or her own experience with anger and bring empathy into the room? When dialogue becomes unusually fractious, can the peacemaker rely on his or her own commitment to unity to lead through the chaos instead of running from it? Is the peacemaker easily swayed to one side or another of a conflict along with the parties, or can a center of stability be maintained?

Understanding that mind, body, and spirit are interconnected, within and between individuals, how can the peacemaker use that knowledge? For one thing, paying attention to his or her own bodily sensations can be useful in understanding what's happening in the room for others. If I am feeling antsy and uncomfortable, perhaps that's a sign of discomfort with how the conversation is going between the dialogue participants.

When the parties are deeply distrustful of one another, can peacemakers trust themselves and the peace process enough to move forward? When peacemakers are feeling strong emotions, can they locate the source—are they expressing what's happening in the system, or are the feelings arising from one's own life experience? Does the peacemaker have a strong vision for what might be accomplished so that even if the outer situation seems to be falling apart, within there is a sure and steady promise of what could be?

I think of three times in my peacemaking activities when connecting the disconnected within myself was especially useful. The first time was as I was preparing to begin this work. I realized I had a strong aversion to violence, arising from my family and political history. I further understood that this aversion would make it difficult for me to operate effectively in war zones. So I undertook a concerted plan of desensitization. I forced myself to read war memoirs and watch war movies, moving through the first stage of antipathy, to the second stage of mild interest, to the third stage of deep interest. When I reached the fourth stage, of feeling within myself the ultimate thrill of the kill, or attraction to bloodlust, I realized I had achieved a level of empathy that would allow me to go anywhere and work with anyone, even the most vicious perpetrators of atrocity. By accepting that the seeds of peace and of violence are in all of us, I understood that, by the good fortune of my life circumstances, I could be an agent of choice and change for others whose lives might have presented very different conditions. The inner journey from aversion to attraction and back to balance was necessary for me to embrace the peacemaking path.

The second example comes from a time I was in Liberia during the war there. Our team was supposed to go up-country to meet with the leaders of one of the warring factions. I became ill very early in the morning, but was feeling better by the time we departed. However, my intuition said to wait another hour or more, and the team was willing to do so. We subsequently got a call saying there had been an ambush on the road we were to have taken at approximately the original time we would have been there.

The third example was life changing. In the early days of my work in Israel and Palestine, during the First Intifada, I found myself deeply torn between wanting to be a peacebuilder creating bridges of understanding between the two parties and feeling a strong pull toward becoming a human rights activist on behalf of the Palestinians. The two directions require a different set of tools and lead to different ways of interacting with the various conflicting groups. I agonized for several days, taking a profound personal inventory of my motivations, intentions, and talents. Finally I realized that my particular training and skills, personality, and long-term goals were best suited to the peacebuilder path. Knowing that there were others passionate and competent in the human rights side of the work allowed me to let that go for myself and embrace how I could make the greatest contribution. Connecting with that deep knowledge about myself launched me on the peacebuilder path, which then became the heart of my career for many years.

Everything Is Energy

Therefore, *energize peace*. Einstein told us that matter and energy are interchangeable. Quantum physics tells us that what we think of as solid is both particle and wave. Wave is frequency, and frequency is vibration. The conclusion I draw from this is that every thing, thought, feeling, and action emits vibration.

We instinctively know this. We speak colloquially of people or situations having "bad vibes" or "good vibes." What we often fail to recognize is that we too are constantly generating vibrations. Nor do we recognize that different states of being have different frequency patterns. Thus, for example, I experience the energy of peace as different from the energy of hatred or fear. Going through our lives conscious of this, and of its implications, is not always so. For the peacemaker, this becomes critically important.

Understanding energy is important in two directions: the peacemaker's energy affects the conflict situation and system, and energy in the conflict system or situation affects the peacemaker. We can leave the quantum physicists to plumb the secrets of this. What we as peacemakers need to do is understand the basic nature of the energy field.

At the simplest level, the energy field is that area around each person or object that holds the vibration at any one time. At the more complex level, there is a vast field of energy in which we are all connected. Some call this a field of consciousness or of potential. Scientists are still exploring its intricacies. What I know from my experience and my spiritual tradition is that like attracts like, energetically. Thus, for instance, if many people in a system are experiencing fear, others around them will harmonize with that feeling. In that way the field of fear grows infectiously until it becomes nearly impenetrable. Likewise, a single thought by a single individual can affect another individual—silently, mysteriously—through a process of energetic resonance.

How does this work? At the simplest level, we understand that energy follows thought. That is, we direct our energy through our actions and words, of course, but equally powerfully through our thinking. The potential or seed of peace (or of any human emotion or state of being) resides in each one of us. Because we are all connected in the web of life through the energy field, and because all humans share the same capacity for feeling, if any of these seeds is activated in one, a resonant chord is struck in others. If I see someone smile, I am likely to smile also. If I am around someone who is feeling sad, I am likely to "catch" that feeling as well.

So our thoughts are actually strengthening similar states in others. This is critically important in the general field of peacemaking because it means that what we resist persists. That is, if someone pushes me (physically or emotionally), and I push back in equal measure, I am actually escalating the conflict; I am energizing the same response in them.

We can easily see this pattern at the international scale. The United States was attacked on September 11, 2001, by terrorists. In our anger and sense of vulnerability, we struck back against the Taliban in Afghanistan, ejecting them from power. They regrouped, strengthened in their determination to defeat the infidel, and fought back, leading to more than ten years of war and destruction. So, too, in other conflicts: even as we find ever more effective ways of thwarting al-Qaeda and other terrorist groups, they find more ways to adapt and grow.

At the subtle level this pattern is less obvious but equally destructive. I once had a business partner with whom I had daily disagreeable interactions. He thought I was stupid in the ways of business; I thought he was ignorant in the ways of human relationship. I would go home every night playing over in my mind all the things I wished I had said to him to counter all the mean things he had said to me, and prepared myself to carry on with the battle the next day. He became a constant enemy presence in my head and heart, as well as in our business dealings, and this was especially painful because he was my best friend's husband, thus contaminating that relationship as well.

It was only when I was able to realize how I was contributing to the growing dysfunction by the thoughts I was feeding myself that I could begin to change the system. I practiced sitting quietly and imagining sending rays of love from my heart to his, breaking through the massed energies of vitriol and blame. It was not easy at first. My habitual response of anger ("Yes, but he did this or that to me!") would arise, and I would need to recenter myself back into the pure love stream. It took many days of concentrated practice, but finally as I shifted my thought patterns from resistance to acceptance, the dynamics between us were able to shift as well. We began to remember the caring that had brought us into the partnership in the first place. Then, acknowledging that our styles, skills, and personalities were not a good fit, we were able to dissolve the partnership in an amicable way, heal the damage done, and move on.

This has vast implications for the peacemaker, and is at the core of the inner spirit of peace. It means peacemakers need to be aware of and responsible for the energy they are generating into the conflict system at any point in time, and must know how to manage the energy they are receiving from the conflict system. Let us look at each of these in turn.

Harking back to the first section of this chapter, in which we discussed connecting the disconnected, what is often missing from conflict situations are particular energy streams or frequencies, such as calm, peace, love, openness, empathy, and more. The peacemaker is able to introduce these frequencies into the system, often at a most appropriate time. For instance, once I was facilitating a residential program of dialogue between key leaders of two conflicting parties that became highly contentious—so much so that the participants in their fury were ready to declare failure, pack their bags, and go home. I had no appropriate words to offer, so I simply went into a deep and quiet meditative space and generated a field of openness and calm. Within moments the group decided to stay together and use their animosity as an opportunity to reach for breakthrough. Though I cannot prove that my energetic state changed the behavior of the group, I believe it may well have made a difference.

Participants in my peacebuilding activities have often told me that, though my interventions and actions were skillful and useful, what mattered most was my quality of presence. In other words, our being is as vital as our doing. Yet peacemakers are not commonly trained in the skills of being. That is, we are not taught in our peace and conflict studies programs how to connect to our own center and higher self, and to radiate peace and associated qualities. Nor are we taught how to manage the energies of the conflict situations that we absorb.

Because of the energy field that we share, when we engage with a conflict system, we naturally are exposed to the energy patterns of that system. We may respond unconsciously, unable to distinguish what is arising from within us and what we are responding to from the outside. So, for example, I would sometimes find myself feeling highly judgmental of one side or the other. Only with reflection and introspection could I determine whether that was my own inner judge speaking or whether I was being carried on the wave of blame that permeated the system.

I recall a specific moment when I was especially affected by the energy in the system, even though there was a significant time lapse. In Bosnia after the war, I helped run a training program for young adult leaders from all three of the warring communities. The day of their graduation ceremony we were all in Sarajevo at the Holiday Inn, preparing for the special event. I went for a walk on the street, which, during the war, was dubbed Sniper Alley because of the clear view Serb snipers had to that particular spot from the hills surrounding the city.

I walked past buildings that, as in the rest of the city and indeed the country, showed the graphic signs of wartime destruction. Yet somehow this particular street evoked a different response in me. I was able to sense the terror of people who, during the siege of Sarajevo, found them-selves darting for their lives between one safe spot and another along this road, hoping to avoid the snipers' bullets. Many did not make it. I was struck by the fact that the people who lived through the actual events of that time were upstairs celebrating, while I, who was safely at home in the United States during that period, was trembling with the trauma of the situation that, though it was in the past, I experienced in the present.

As in this example, we as peacemakers are exposed to the whole range of feelings and energetic patterns in the conflict systems we engage with. Whether it is a divorce mediation or a negotiation process among violent warring groups, the situation has a strong energy field that we enter into and participate in. When we do this work frequently, some of the effects of that exposure can build up inside us. Some peace-makers are more sensitive than others, and can and do develop some reaction along the spectrum of secondary posttraumatic stress.

I found this was true for me after a dozen years of working in war zones. This was so even though I have a deep spiritual practice that pro-vides me with methods to clear my energy field, return to center, and ground myself in an aligned body, mind, and spirit. These skills are not normally taught to peacemakers.

I also found that most of my colleagues in the peacebuilding field did not want to discuss this. They dismissed me as somehow weak for acknowledging it. The relief and development communities have come a long way toward changing their organizational cultures so that staff are encouraged to debrief emotionally. In parts of Europe, a reentry process is required of state-sponsored development and peacemaking specialists. The peacemaking professions are tardy in adopting these perspectives and practices.

We Are All Simply Divine

Therefore, *relate to the ideal potential*. Once, during a dialogue I facili-tated between Israeli and Palestinian women, I opened the session by asking the group, "Why are you here?" One woman responded, "I'm here because I know there has to be a better way." Seeing from her approximate age and the history of the conflict that she could never have known real peace in her lifetime, I said, "How can you know about a bet-ter way? You have only lived with hatred, violence, and fear all around you." She put her hand on her heart, patting it softly, and said, "Because I just know." What I understood from the combination of her hand and her words was, "In my heart I know all about that better way, even if I have never seen or experienced it in my life." She did not know peace itself, but she knew from her very core the ideal potential of peace.

We all know about peace in our hearts, because peace is encoded within us as our spiritual DNA. How else to explain the fact that the major world religions all hold peace as the highest ideal; that those we hold in greatest esteem are the peacemakers of the world: Gandhi, Martin Luther King Jr., Nelson Mandela; that of all the Nobel prizes awarded, the one with the most prestige is the one for peace?

Let us explore that encoding. This third premise of the inner spirit of peacemaking follows from the first two. In the Judeo-Christian tradition we are told that "man is made in the image of God." In Buddhism we hear that all sentient beings contain innate Buddha nature. In some indigenous wisdom traditions we learn that all things and all beings are sacred. In the systems understanding that infuses this chapter, we have an explanation for this.

We understand that everything is interconnected through interdependence. Another aspect of that interconnectedness is that everything is both a whole in itself and also part of a larger whole. For instance, the cells in the human body coalesce into tissues, which join together into organs, which operate within digestive, circulatory, neurological, or other systems, which, taken together, make up the human body. That human body is part of a family, a neighborhood, a community, a religion or other affinity group, a nation, and so forth, to planet, solar system, galaxy, and beyond.

The further into the macrocosm we go with expanding wholes, the closer we get to that great mystery some call God. The largest whole we are capable of imagining is the all-encompassing One. This interconnected and universal fabric of life at its most cosmic scale is ineffable and awe inspiring. We attribute the finest qualities we can articulate to that One: infinite Power, Love, Presence, Peace, Wisdom, Perfection, Harmony, Balance, Beauty, Unity, Light, and more. But since we too are an integral part of that larger One, we share those qualities. I write them with capital letters here because these are values shared by and aspired to by religions and cultures all over the world.

If we innately share these qualities, how do we explain our behavior that is so often at odds with their expression? The story I tell myself to make sense of this is that Christ, Buddha, Muhammad, Moses, and others we consider to have attained a state of God-realization, or enlightenment, remembered who they were, their inherent divinity, 100 percent of the time, while most of the rest of us are struggling to do so in the 10 to 50 percent range.

Our task as human beings is to make increasing that percentage our life's journey, and when we inevitably fail, forget, or otherwise slip off the path, to gently and kindly forgive ourselves and step back on. Our task as peacemakers is to support others in doing the same.

Consider the acorn. It looks nothing like the oak tree, yet it contains the pattern of that tree within it, allowing it to grow into its fullest potential. We too are tiny seeds of the Divine, holding within us the spiritual DNA of perfection. And because we know that energy follows thought, if we relate to that potential for perfection in a person or situation, we are actually energizing or strengthening it. If we relate to the limitation being expressed through anger, hatred, fear, greed, and so forth found in conflict situations, we feed that instead.

Knowing that the seeds of peace, love, harmony, and similar qualities lie within everyone without exception (including ourselves), our job as peacemakers is to nourish those seeds with our thoughts, words, and actions. Understanding every person as sacred in their essence, regardless of their external behavior, allows us to hold every conflict situation and participant in a field of love and hope.

And so it is with all of us. We know Beauty, even if our lives are surrounded by ugliness. We know Harmony, even if we live in chaos. We more than "know" these qualities; we aspire to realize them. That is the evolutionary thrust of humanity, our spiritual journey.

If indeed these ideals exist as seeds within us, how do we, as peacemakers, nurture that potential with our thoughts, words, and actions? We do this first by recognizing this reality underlies any and all external behaviors to the contrary. Second, we address this ideal potential directly. Third, we generate the vibrations of these ideals, as discussed earlier in this chapter.

For example, peacemakers are trained to create "safe space" for mediation, dialogue, and negotiation events. We mostly think of this as arranging comfortable and neutral logistics. However, it also can happen energetically. For instance, before I meet with conflict parties, I first go deep inside to connect with the seed of Peace and radiate that into the room. Next, I imagine a stream of connection between my heart and the heart of each person in the circle, honoring the Divinity within each one and acknowledging those ideals that underlie why we have come together. Finally, I align myself with my own divine nature and dedicate my thoughts, words, and deeds and all the activities of our gathering to manifest those ideals in a concrete way, to alleviate suffering, and to do so for the benefit of all. I have no way of demonstrating, measuring, or proving any positive outcome from this, other than the fact that I feel whole and wholly lit up and available to do and be the best I can within the peacebuilding situation.

Once, when I was in a particularly vicious war zone, where so many people were suffering unspeakable atrocities, I felt a profound despair. How could human beings inflict such cruelty on one another? I was so discouraged that I had an especially hard time recalling any of the skills I have mentioned here. Then, as if from the Earth herself, the words came: "Peace is possible; peace is possible." Like a mantra, it kept cycling in my mind, and I was restored to my hopeful self. By remembering that the ideal potential of peace resides even in the worst of violent situations, I was able to energize that possibility once again. That country later concluded a peace agreement and is now well on its way to healing and thriving, proving the mantra to be true.

I would suggest that none of the skills associated with what I have described in this section are routinely taught—if at all—in our peace and conflict development programs (academic or professional), and that our field would greatly benefit if they were.

Conclusion

In this chapter I have presented three basic spiritual principles that I consider to comprise the inner spirit of peacemaking. I have explained the principles and given examples of how they operate externally in peacemaking settings and internally within the peacemaker. Finally, I have suggested that our professional training venues now need to support peacemakers in the skills associated with these principles.

Harking back to the first principle of interconnectedness and our charge to connect the disconnected, I believe that peacemaking on the outer, material level of processes and transactions is only one part of the equation. Without also aligning with that inner spirit of interconnectedness, energy, and the divine ideal potential—both within the peacemaker and in the conflict system—we doom ourselves to half measures and incomplete outcomes.

Finally, I would suggest that at the largest level of human evolution we are moving from a world based on separateness to one of interconnectedness. When peacemakers embrace the inner spirit of peacemaking, they become the leading edge of that evolutionary journey for humanity. They are actualizing Peace in its true whole and holy nature, for the well-being of all the family of life on, and with, this one planet we all call home.

9

Concluding Reflections

Brian Blancke

> He drew a circle and shut me out,
> Heretic, rebel, a thing to flout.
> But love and I had the wit to win:
> We drew a circle and took him In!
> *Edwin Markham, "Outwitted"*

In his concluding remarks in Chapter 4, M. Brandon Sipes said revealingly, "While facilitating, I can recall moments where spiritual language *crept in* and I encouraged participants to grasp onto hope and believe in change, despite their reality" (emphasis added). I was struck by the phrasing, as if the back door was left open by mistake, and spiritual language crept in where it should not have been. I think the field of conflict engagement has struggled for many years with whether and how spirituality and religion should be included. Some want to slam the door shut and keep it that way, while others leave it unlocked, not necessarily knowing when it might be ajar, or, if it is open, what is coming through. Others, as we have seen in this book, consciously and conscientiously have opened the door and invited it in.

And the importance of that "door ajar" approach is that it may be part of our more youthful development as a field, and no longer as appropriate as it once was. Much of the written work in this field deals with basic skills, processes, evaluation, and analysis. However, we are growing into a maturity that a demands deeper, self-critical analysis of our goals and how well we are meeting them. Mayer (2009), among others, has led the way in challenging us to broaden and deepen our understanding of our work. Bowling and Hoffman (2003) made the point that critical to a sense of the deeper, more complex sense of why we do and do not succeed in our goals as a field and in practice is an examination of not just what we do, but who we are—our presence as mediators. This book takes us the next step in this journey. Now that we have identified presence as key to the art and mastery of this work, how do we do it well?

The Multidimensional Framework introduced in Chapter 2 implies that drawing on multiple intelligences, and understanding how we bring our whole selves into the work, may be key to understanding how we bring our presence to bear as an asset. What follows is a look at how practitioners in this volume engaged the multiple dimensions of the work and themselves, reviewed through the framework. By doing this, we can begin to assess what we do and how we are as interveners that succeeds well, and explore what we might be missing (in the field and in the framework) that we should be attending to.

Building the Case for Spirituality and Faith in Conflict Engagement

One thing the framework offers is a way to counter the fears in the field around engaging faith. The fear—one that, as a practitioner, I have acted out of (in the example mentioned in Chapter 2 and analyzed more thoroughly in later sections here)—is that religion will creep in and derail the process by polarizing disputants even further than they already are. But as Sipes notes, spiritual language crept in precisely because other language could not, in his mind, do what it could—provide hope when it was most needed. This is not to say that only spirituality or faith traditions can provide hope. But they are one way—a powerful and important way, as Gandhi and Martin Luther King Jr. have shown—that is often underutilized and underappreciated.

Using the framework, we can see that rather than suppressing spiritual language, beliefs, concepts, or practices, the practitioners in this volume have offered different thoughts and life examples about how to incorporate them into conflict engagement, and they have done so in a way that is respectful of the self-determination of the disputing parties. Indeed, they are "models" in that way, whose work sparks our curiosity and "opens up prospects" that we have not seen or contemplated before (Adler 2003, 69).

Because of the strong (and real) fear that we, as conflict interveners or *third-siders*,[1] will impose our values and beliefs on the parties if we open the door, the models provided by these authors are important because they show that through self-awareness and integrity it is possible not only to respect the parties' rights to self-determination, but to enhance it. One wonderful example is Daniel Bowling's thorough self-reflection and personal accountability, which are part and parcel of his spiritual beliefs (as seen in Chapter 3).

These practitioners provide different examples of ways third-siders can respect their own faith and spirituality, as well as those of the parties, while still preserving party self-determination, which is not to say that this is easily done or without real challenges.[2] Piercing the veil of neutrality by bringing any part of yourself into the process is always a risk to party self-determination. But, every move we make—shaping language expression by using ground rules, restructuring discussion through reflective listening and reframing, structuring dialogue—to some extent, takes autonomy from the parties. And, of course, those moves are the way we assist parties in conflict. The goal, as stated in the first two chapters, is not to stop acting in ways that change conflict. The goal is to act in ways that are as respectful, sensitive, and as empowering as possible. That work is part of the process of becoming a better practitioner—becoming increasingly aware of your own biases and how they relate to the choices you make. Mastery is about making wise choices. The practitioners in this book raise the possibility that those choices are often cognitive and conscious, but also sometimes based on experience, intuition, inspiration, and soma, like Joy Meeker's use of the understanding of emotions as "embodied thoughts" (Chapter 6). It takes experience (to read the situation well, and to know what to say and do), sensitivity, and self-awareness to navigate this terrain well.

Using the Multidimensional Framework to Integrate Multiple Intelligences in Conflict Resolution

If you are willing to explore opening the door to faith and spirituality, emotions, and the body, how do you incorporate them in conflict engagement work (in a safe and effective way)? How do you move beyond technique to mastery? The Multidimensional Framework encourages us to reflect on this and several other questions: How, using the framework, can we better prepare to practice with a wholeness that leads to a positive presence and mastery and integrity in our work? How can we use the framework to make visible how practitioners can and have used multiple intelligences in the moment to make better choices (when those moves might otherwise be invisible or chalked up to abstract artistry)? And how can we use the framework to learn from our successes and failures so that we improve over time? In doing so, we can assess how useful the framework is (or is not) in helping us navigate the difficult terrain of bringing our own and parties' multiple intelligences to bear in conflict.

Using the Framework to Prepare for Practice

How do we, through being as well as our doing, "bring peace into the room" (Bowling and Hoffman 2003)? For surely how we carry ourselves, how we "show up" or "drop in," impacts parties perhaps just as much, if not more, than what we actually say or do (Diamond, Chapter 8; Bowling and Hoffman 2003; Fox 2004). One way is through our preparation in advance of the work and how we prepare who we are in the interaction. If we fail to prepare adequately, we will be hard-pressed to do well in the heat of conflict. Preparation helps us anticipate what might happen and what the needs are, and helps ameliorate surprises that arise in the moment. But how do we prepare in a systematic fashion? As with the other phases of conflict intervention, the Multidimensional Framework can help in this regard. We can prepare by thinking through a series of questions that explore the different intelligences (see Table 9.1). We hope that this kind of self-examination can help practitioners learn to be more whole in the interaction and to do so in a way that invites greater abilities to be open to, and to integrate, all the data in the room.

Bowling and Hoffman, in their seminal work on the role and place of personal qualities such as presence in mediation, speak of the importance of integration that underlies presence. Integration is "a quality of being in which the individual feels fully in touch with, and able to marshal, his or her mental, spiritual, and physical resources" (2003, 6). One way the framework can be utilized is as a compass to help third-siders think about when and how they are (1) in touch with and (2) marshaling their cognitive, spiritual, somatic, and emotional intelligences. The first step in preparing oneself to be capable of utilizing all available data is to become aware of, for instance, one's emotional reactions and what they are telling one about what is happening in a case, as Meeker demonstrated. The ability to effortlessly integrate "multiple sources of insight" (Bowling and Hoffman 2003, 7) into our work is a result of both the development of awareness and the ability to calibrate our intuition (see Chapter 2). Bowling's chapter (Chapter 3) is an excellent description of the kind of internal work he has done that enables him to become mindful during the chaos of a conflict case. Practitioners such as Bowling and Meeker are capable of mastery in their work not just because of their skills and techniques, but as a result of a level of self-development that changes who they are in the interaction.[3]

Thorough preparation—both long-term (with regular spiritual and somatic practice) and short-term—will help with raising self-awareness

Table 9.1 Preparation Sheet

Mind (vertical thinking) (lateral thinking)[a]	• What is the root cause of the problem? • What do I think logically should happen? • If I were to draw an analogy or describe the conflict using a metaphor, what would it be? How would I describe it using that metaphor? What insight does that give? • Can I use poetic or reflective writing to illuminate the conflict or my feelings about it?
Emotions	• What am I feeling? Any discomfort? Does this signal a gap between current reality and what is desired? What is the gap? • What do these emotions signal about what is cared about? • Is there creative discomfort? Are there asymmetries of power involved? • What perspective am I coming from that shapes my emotional response?
Somatic (body as bellwether and instrument of change)	• Where is my body tight? • Where am I holding the stress? • What is my current posture? • Am I centered? Grounded? • Can I feel the energy in the room? • What energy am I putting out? Do I want to put out? • Am I triggered (fight/flight/freeze)? Or relaxed/present? • Have I slept enough? • How can I lead with my body? • Can I walk (and talk) with the others, accompany them?
Spiritual	• How do I connect with my higher self, with God/Source/ guiding principles (through prayer, song, meditation, etc.)? • How do I plan on staying connected to the highest part of myself? • How do I invite others to connect with their higher selves? • What intentions do I want to set? • What guidance do I seek? • What support am I requesting/looking for from the sources of transcendence in my life? • How can I use my spiritual resources to transcend my own impulses or limitations? • How could I support the parties to draw on their resources to transcend their situation and assumptions?

Notes: a. To learn more about different kinds of thinking, see Gordon (1961) on lateral and vertical thinking and Hocker and Wilmot (1995) on metaphorical thinking.

to avoid countertransference in conflict situations and support healthy boundaries. The practitioners in this volume have provided a number of insights, questions, and advice that we can use to prepare ourselves for any conflict engagement, whether that is mediation, Playback Theatre, or a direct confrontation. Table 9.1, drawing on those insights and organized around the framework, is intended to help you think about if and how you are aware of your different intelligences, and how they might be used at different stages of the conflict so that you can bring your whole self to bear (and support the higher selves of the parties).

Using the Framework to Explain and Support Artistry

The Multidimensional Framework is also a way to think about and reflect on how practitioners and inside third-siders integrate multiple intelligences at different stages of conflict (entry, gathering perspectives, orientation, etc.) to create separation, transition, and incorporation. In this regard, the framework is useful as both a descriptive and a prescriptive tool. First, as analysts, we can use the framework to examine what practitioners actually do (and did here) and how their presence and actions impact the conflict (i.e., descriptive analysis). Second, the framework can be used to generate thinking about how we should use multiple sources of insight to produce good outcomes (i.e., prescriptive advice).

Let us look at two practitioners in particular who shared conflicts they were involved in—one as a conflict party and the other as a mediator—to see how we might use the framework to understand what they actually did, shown in Table 9.2.

From examining Table 9.2, we see how Bowling's Buddhist approach redefines the conflict from interpersonal to intrapersonal and thereby opens a new way out for him. His personal conflict with Mr. James shows the connection between his spiritual practices (for example, meditation and *metta* meditation) and his choices with regard to how he interacts with and reacts to Mr. James, and how that changed their working relationship (for the better). Here, we see how Bowling uses his spiritual intelligence to change the conflict even when the other party does not cooperate.

Second, we can use the framework prescriptively. Meeker explores explicitly what might have happened if she had located emotions within the conflict settlement perspective (presented in Chapter 6), treating them as obstacles to be removed rather than as touch points or signposts of deeper truths. If she had done this, the conflict would have been lim-

Table 9.2 Multiple Intelligence Framework of Conflict Intervention

Phase: Stage	Bowling	Meeker
Entry	Attorney postponed mediation and then cancelled.	Hired to mediate a conflict between a supervisor and an IT technician.
Gathering Perspectives	(from Bowling's perspective) • He would not return calls • Most difficult lawyer I've worked with • He left messages and did not try to cooperate or show courtesy by returning calls directly • I insisted on speaking with him (Lost all mindfulness: lost awareness of breath and body, of feelings, of mental state, and fundamental laws governing human behavior) • Call or else I will proceed and report you to the judge	(from parties' perspectives) • (Janet/technician): Never call me at home! • (Matt/supervisor): We're a family— I needed to make sure you were ok
Locate Conflict	• We were both angry—treating each other with contempt • I felt his greed drove his manipulative behavior • We both had the "wrong view"— believing what the other did was all about us • Did not notice anger was arising and was not mindful that "conflict feels like this" • Got lost in the events and identified with the anger • I was attached to "becoming," to be seen and respected • Didn't live/know the possibility that the conflict could cease between us.	• Boundaries between workplace and family • Janet's source of anger: she had to divide her and her partner's lives from their work, denying their family because of homophobia ("Don't' Ask, Don't Tell") • Subtext of homophobia in the office • With Matt, Meeker explored oppression, and gender differences and power relationships, and the metaphor of parent/child • Matt was positioning himself as the father
Arrange/Negotiate	• Reflected on truthfulness with others/recognized pattern (clinging to expectation of respect) • Recognized what freedom from obsession looks like • Invited Mr. James to meet to clear the air. To prepare for meeting, practiced *metta* meditation	• Asked Matt what other role he might take that Janet might welcome—such as being an ally • Discussed changes to the office culture—what kind of office they would like to leave (a vision)
Way Out	• Began with an apology— acknowledging anger and inappropriate behavior with his staff • Reached an understanding about working together	• Agreed not to speak of matters that are personal • Matt agreed to be an ally • Diversity workshop for the office

ited to the presenting problem, and she would have acquiesced to the parties' desire for "a thin resolution" rather than helping them achieve what they did. It took a heightened sense of emotional intelligence, along with her spiritual commitment to *ubuntu*, for Meeker to see and make space for the deeper truths of the conflict. However, a less emotionally aware mediator than Meeker could use the framework to learn to perceive critical dynamics like these. In other words, it assists us to ask: what might I be missing here?

One technique that Goldberg and I have used is to calibrate one intelligence against another, as mentioned in Chapter 2. Any one set of data can give a flawed or incomplete sense of a situation; however, using multiple intelligences can give a richer, sounder picture. So, for instance, if I can tell cognitively that the parties are stuck, but don't know why, I can quickly check other data streams. If I find that my body is tense, and looking around I see that the parties are holding themselves rigidly and my emotional reading of the room cues me into a sense that something important is happening, I can more reliably suspect we are getting close to something key, but difficult, for the parties. If, however, I get data from a single source, like hearing the parties say something is key for them, but the body language and emotional responses in the room (theirs and mine) read differently, then I may need to delve more deeply into the stated issues.

The examples shared previously in this chapter and the exercise in calibrating intelligences indicates how the framework can help us entertain counterfactuals based on a greater use of our many intelligences. It highlights turning points—opportunities—where the conflict might change direction if we choose to show up or act in a different way. It gets us to think about what we should be doing, not just what we are doing.

How does the framework help us understand what actually happens during artistry, and how might the framework be improved? In this section, I briefly describe some classic dynamics of conflict and how the framework helps practitioners during the dynamics of conflict, and then apply an integral approach (Lebovic 2013; McGuigan and McMechan 2005; McGuigan and Popp 2012, 2007; McGuigan and Popp 2015; Perloff 2010)[4] to show how the framework could be deepened and enhanced.

Some may be uncomfortable discussing spirituality and faith or the body and emotions, and their impact on conflict intervention because these can be seen as esoteric, nebulous, or hard to pin down. Some might call it too "woo-woo." The framework is offered as one way to begin to "de-mystify" and to provide insight into how and why these aspects impact and are important for our work. As Allen Nan aptly notes, "In conflicts, we may not only be 'in over our heads' but also emotionally exhausted, spiritually shattered and physically frozen" (2011, 247). It is this that we as outside and inside third-siders step into in order to support change. But what are we specifically trying to change? How does what we do and/or how we show up (i.e., our presence) achieve this? And what role does spirituality play in this change?

In conflict, when we perceive that we cannot get what we want or something bad has happened and we are being blamed for it, all sorts of conflict dynamics set in, leading us to be in "over our heads." Once we perceive a threat, we experience a physiological and emotional response—fight, flight, or freeze (Goleman 1995)—which is often counterproductive. If we end up fighting, we may take actions unilaterally to achieve our goals, which may cause our counterpart to respond likewise. An escalation dynamic takes hold (Senge 2006)—more extreme measures are taken by both sides, more issues or grievances are raised, more parties are drawn in, and/or our goals change from doing well for ourselves to hurting the other (Kriesberg and Dayton 2012; Rubin et al. 1994). As polarization sets in, communication decreases (in quality and often in quantity) and relationships suffer (Kriesberg and Dayton 2012; Rubin et al. 1994). Our worlds get smaller. Simply put, most of us, when we encounter conflict, regress or constrict cognitively, emotionally, physically, and spiritually. We often act out of our lower rather than higher selves: "He drew a circle that shut me out—Heretic, rebel, a thing to flout." (See Table 9.3.)

It is these conflict dynamics and regressions that we are trying to interrupt and reverse through our actions and presence. To see the connection between the regressions and the framework (how our interventions/presence can reverse them), see Table 9.2. With Bowling, during the gathering and locating conflict stage, we see him regress along a

Table 9.3 Conflict Regressions and Constriction

Cognitive	More black and white thinking, unable to hold paradox, reduced creativity
Emotional	Drops in self-awareness, self-management, social awareness (empathy) and social skills (influence and communication)
Somatic	Drawing in of the body, drawing in of energy fields, heart rate increases, breadth shortens, Fight/Flight/Freeze response
Spiritual	Losing a sense of the bigger picture, or connection with the source, increased zealotry and righteousness

Source: Nan 2011; Goleman 1995; and Senge 2006.

number of dimensions, including emotional, somatic, and spiritual. By adopting some of the somatic practices suggested by Julia Morelli and Christopher Fitz in Chapter 5, he could have used his body as bell-wether to detect the negative shifts that were occurring and recenter. Likewise, if he practiced *metta* meditation before his first meeting, he may have approached Mr. James differently from the start (especially given their joint history). The point is that at different stages of conflicts, we can use our multiple intelligences to both detect constriction and reverse it: "But love and I had the wit to win: we drew a circle and took him In!" As Allen Nan notes, "much conflict resolution practice can be seen as supporting shifts in consciousness" (2011, 249). Intentionally using multiple intelligences is one way to support shifts in consciousness.

Applying Integral Theory: Adding More to the Framework

Although the framework has a great deal to offer, it can, of course, be further developed. Here I will apply integral theory to explore ways the framework could be expanded. One aspect of integral theory is looking at conflict from all four perspectives of human experience (individual/collective and internal/external), which are irreducible (Esbjörn-Hargens 2009). For example, an environmental dispute over the use of a lake involves the individual's subjective experience of the conflict (see Table 9.4, upper left quadrant), how the different stakeholder groups see the conflict and how they interact (collective intersubjective experience; Table 9.4, lower left quadrant), the lake itself (its size, depth, amount of water, fish populations, etc.; Table 9.4, upper right quadrant), and the legal, economic, and political systems or inequalities that shape what the problem is and what can be done about it (Table 9.4, lower right quadrant).

To understand conflict from an integral approach, all four perspectives (known as quadrants) must be considered. Consequently, to intervene effectively in conflict requires that all four perspectives be considered (during the gathering perspectives and locating conflict stages), as they are connected to each other. To focus conflict intervention on only one or maybe two quadrants is to invite failure due to not understanding the bigger picture, and explains why conflict engagement is often ineffective. So, for example, parties engaged in an environmental conflict around the use of a lake might fail to succeed in negotiation because parties cannot agree on the data about the lake (upper right quadrant), or because they have very different values about how we, as humans,

Table 9.4 Integral Approach to Conflict: Lake Dispute Example (Four Quadrants): Where might you locate the conflict (Stage 3 of the Multidimensional Framework)?

	Internal (subjective)	External (objective)
Individual	Conflicting individual interests, needs, fears, feelings, identity, etc.	Conflicting or insufficient data about the lake (pollution levels, state of the lake's ecology, etc.)
Collective	Conflicting group perceptions, group identity Clashing cultures/ values (worldviews): • How we should relate to nature • How we should dispute	Structurally violent social systems • Legal system/inequality • Political system/inequality • Economic system/inequality

should relate to the lake (lower left quadrant), or because their interests are not met (upper left quadrant). And often, all these quadrants need to be addressed before the conflict can be resolved.

Do this quick thought experiment: based on your training and conflict intervention orientation, did you focus on any one quadrant more than another when you read Table 9.4, or did you treat them all equally? If not, how might that emphasis impact which perspectives you might gather and your view of how the conflict is located? How would this, in turn, impact arranging a way out? Are there some intelligences that you would immediately recruit (such as vertical and lateral thinking, or empathy), at the individual and/or group levels, to foster resolution? Did you think about group somatic practice?

Integral theory helps us see why Meeker's mediation was successful. First, she surfaced and aired some underlying anger (upper left quadrant) that resulted from systemic homophobia (lower right quadrant). Drawing on shared values (lower left quadrant), the parties reached an agreement that improved not only their relationship (lower left quadrant), but the organization as well.

Integral theory can be used to build on the Multidimensional Framework and show how we can better understand what these practitioners are doing in their work.[5] The framework relies on looking at intelligences—what integral theory calls lines or developmental capacities (Esbjörn-Hargens 2009)—to understand how we might more effectively engage conflict. To be truly effective, the framework needs to consider how third-siders marshal multiple intelligences—emotional, spiritual, and somatic (i.e., lines)—to interrupt the regressions (which are changes in levels) and foster consideration of all perspectives (i.e., quadrants) through separation, transition, and incorporation (i.e., stages) in order to reach some kind of resolution or new synthesis.

Adopting an integral perspective allows us also to see the importance of faith and spirituality for conflict engagement. Faith is experienced in all four quadrants: from individual experience with it (upper left), to collective beliefs and rituals used to alter states of consciousness (lower left), to buildings and sacred sites (upper right), and to hierarchies and power structures (lower right). So, how can we combine our experiences with faith traditions and spirituality across these four quadrants to effect positive change in conflict situations?

What we see in the practitioner chapters is that it is not just about what intelligences we use (and using more of them), as we see with Bowling and Meeker. It is also about how we use them to change levels (to deeper, more expansive consciousness and organization), induce different states (of being, in self and others), and leverage different personality types so that we engage conflict in all quadrants. This broadens our understanding of what success in conflict intervention looks like. Are we hitting, in our practice, all five elements (quadrants, levels, lines, stages, and types) or just some, and how does that account for our success or lack thereof?

Assessing Our Work:
Learning from Our Successes and Failures

Critique, Adler says (2003, 71), is about fostering intellectual honesty, being self-critical, and learning from mistakes. If we are to improve as practitioners or as inside third parties, we need to reflect on what we do and how we show up in conflict. Here, as suggested above, the framework can help as a way to systematically reflect on what was done, what was present, and what was missing.

To start, are we happy with the results we are getting? If so, there is little incentive to either change what we are doing or to change the underlying assumptions guiding our choices. But if we are not, we need to consider either changing what we are doing and/or changing those underlying beliefs that are guiding our choices. The former is *single loop learning* while the latter is *double loop learning* (Peppet and Moffitt 2006).

Often we just experiment with changing what we say or do (our behavior) to see if that will get different results (single loop learning). But frequently what gets in the way of the results we are looking for are the underlying assumptions we have about what is going on that guide our behavior. If we can change our working assumptions (our mind-sets), those changes will cascade through our being and doing to impact the outcome. This surfacing, disrupting, and replacing of assumptions or mind-sets is what double loop learning is about.[6] Bowling's Chapter 3 exemplifies how changing fundamental assumptions changes behavior and outcomes.

What this volume and books before it, such as *Bringing Peace into the Room* (Bowling and Hoffman 2003), are attempting to do is double loop learning: showing how the predominant mind-set makes assumptions about the role and place of spirituality, faith, emotions, the body, and reason in our practice—assumptions that shape the choices we make, whether we are disputants ourselves or we are helping others.

One useful tool for exhuming and examining these underlying mind-sets is the "left hand column" exercise (Senge et al. 1994). I present it here as a useful tool for self-assessment for practitioners, first explaining the process so you can use it yourself and then presenting examples from my own practice and from that of the book's other authors. On a piece of paper, draw a line down the middle of the page. In the right column, note a piece of dialogue that you want to reflect on (for example, a mistake perhaps that you feel you made in a mediation or in a coaching session). Write out what you said and what the other person said for three or four lines. Then in the left column, write down what you were thinking, feeling, experiencing in your body or any spiritual experience. Be as honest with yourself as possible, realizing that you have a full range of feelings, sensations, thoughts, and motives that are animating you. Then look at and analyze your thinking. How were you using cognitive (logical-mathematical and linguistic), emotional, somatic, and spiritual intelligences, for example, to read what was happening in the moment? This might reveal what beliefs or emotions were shaping your reasoning process; or were disconnects between your frame of reference and that of the parties; or were ways in which you made assumptions based on your own experience that got in the way of your understanding the key dynamics in the room; or were a clue to something key but hidden.

For example, many years ago, as described in Chapter 2, I was comediating a congregation dispute that involved over twenty parties. I was wrapping up the opening remarks in the first session when the following exchange happened (presented in Table 9.5). Here I focus only on emotions and cognition for the sake of simplicity in demonstrating the technique. The reflection is richer, of course, if all dimensions, including the somatic and spiritual reactions, are recorded.

My training was in community mediation. I, along with other staff, spent an hour doing an intake interview with each of the twenty parties

Table 9.5 Left-Hand Column Exercise—Examining Failure

Thinking and Feeling	Saying and Doing
	One party said: "We want to offer a prayer."
Oh G-d, they are going to use the prayer to attack the other side. We've got to stop this.	I said: "Each person will have a chance to speak during the mediation process."
	Another party (from the other side of the conflict) said: "Yeah, we want to offer a prayer, too."
This is going to spiral out of control. We need to put a stop to this.	I said: "Let's stick with the process as we explained it."
	They said: "We won't continue unless we can offer a prayer."
{Bleep} What do we do now? I'm afraid this could derail everything before we even get started. Should we give in?	I said/did: I stared at my comediator and hunched my shoulders.
	Other side said: "Yeah, us too."
Mentally crossing my fingers and holding my breath.	I said: "Ok."

to understand what their concerns were, what they were looking for from mediation, what they thought the problem was, and whether they were interested or ready to participate in mediation. It never occurred to me, as part of the intake process, to explore how they wanted to incorporate their faith into the process. We could have vetted any prayers ahead of time and stressed the need to set a positive intention and tone, respecting what was important to the parties, and using it as a way to support shifts in consciousness (Nan 2011).

And, I consider myself a spiritual person. But that part of me was completely divorced from my professional role. Nowhere in my mediation training, other than at the beginning of my training—when we discussed what got us interested in mediation in the first place, and I responded that mine was a spiritual call to be a peacemaker—did we ever talk about faith traditions or spirituality. At the time of this congregational mediation, I was acting out of fear; there was no place for spirituality (other than as a threat) in my mediation worldview.

In the end, one side offered a heartfelt prayer, and the other side reciprocated, and the mediation began with the highest intentions of both groups. But my attempt to prevent faith from "entering in the door" almost scuttled the mediation, until the parties seized back the process and insisted that their will, not mine, be followed. (Here, interestingly, my lack of openness to the parties' need for bringing faith into the process denied their right to self-determination, until they threatened to walk away.)

This is an example for me of not just changing my practice (for example, by asking about faith during the intake process), but exploring the assumptions I have about the role of religion, faith, and spirituality in mediation. In many ways I carry the assumptions of the Spock approach (Meeker mentions this in Chapter 6)—the omnipotence and omnipresence of reason and civil discourse as the basis for conflict resolution. This is the mind-set that I am struggling to change and working to replace with a different or expanded set of governing assumptions.

When To Raise Matters of Faith and Spirituality

There is still the practical matter of when, if, and how to raise spirituality and use faith traditions in conflict interventions explicitly, if they are already not obviously present, as they were in the congregation dispute.

Many of the practitioners have spoken openheartedly about how important faith and spirituality are for their practice—for how they conceive of what they are doing, for what motivates them, and for what guides them (e.g., Bowling, Sipes, Diamond). Indeed, take away their spirituality and they would be very different practitioners. But their faith and spirituality are not expressed publicly. Unless they told you, you would not know that faith or spirituality was playing such a significant role in what they do and how they show up. Sipes, who does a great deal of religious identity–related conflict work, reveals: "as both a Christian and as a practitioner, I can say that I have had very few instances where I have explicitly used the theological frames discussed" (see Chapter 4).

And this is often appropriate. Are there times when it is useful to raise faith directly? Sipes suggests in Chapter 4 that we take three things into consideration when making this decision: the context that we work in, the makeup of the disputants, and the relationship between the intervener and the parties. When working with Christian communities, it makes sense to be explicit because they do not need to be persuaded of their faith's merits, and faith is key to their approach to conflict. That being said, Goldberg and I argue that the clients should determine if faith is an explicit part of the process or not and that simple intake questions can make space for clients to tell us what they want (2011).

In Chapter 4 Sipes proposed that revealing his faith was appropriate when he knew the parties, and when it would help make the conversation richer and deeper. When theological concepts might be grasped by the parties or provide energy to help the parties move forward, they may be appropriate.

But what this book challenges us to do is to push our collective thinking on this front. If faith traditions and spirituality are important resources for transcending limitations, are there ways to explicitly support those resources? We need to, as Gold (2003) argues, think about how we can marshal not only all of our own resources, but the other parties' as well, calling all of us to act from our higher selves. Maybe that means raising transcendent resources explicitly, or maybe it means involving spiritual or faith concepts (such as forgiveness and compassion) but not the language of faith traditions. Regardless, the challenge remains—how do we sensitively and respectfully engage all intelligences, including spiritual intelligence?

We know that religion, faith, and spirituality can interrupt conflict dynamics and reverse the cognitive, emotional, somatic, and spiritual regressions that drag people down and apart. And, as Sipes argues in Chapter 4, avoiding them runs the real risk of avoiding "the fullness of its capacity to provide exactly the conciliatory elements we strive to recreate."

What is needed, as Sipes notes, is a more nuanced and balanced approach to faith and conflict. One way to help develop this approach is to look at our past interventions and engagements through the lens of the framework and learn what worked and what did not. Maybe we should have raised spirituality and faith but did not (as in the congregation mediation), or the reverse. This speaks to the importance of reflecting on our practice to achieve more integration and to discern when is the right time to use our own multiple intelligences or to support parties to use theirs.

Developing Mastery: Or, Where Do We Go from Here?

The framework thus offers several windows into what the practitioners in this book are doing that reflects how the multidimensionality of their work is effective, and raises some questions for us as a field about how to continue to develop into whole practitioners striving for mastery. Bowling and Hoffman speak about three stages of professional development for mediators, which are applicable to all third-siders: (1) studying technique, (2) intellectual inquiry and understanding how and why mediation (or any conflict engagement process) works, and (3) a growing awareness of how personal qualities influence the process (2003, 15–16).

The practitioners in this book have collectively taken a step into the third arena to examine presence, its connection to mastery, and how that can be achieved. By helping the field of conflict resolution take a more sophisticated view of the role of the third-sider in the process, they help the field consider the potential benefits of marshaling all our resources— especially spiritual, emotional, and somatic, which are often ignored—to constructively engage conflict. And while there is no one right path to mastery (Bowling and Hoffman 2003), we can learn from others who have broken ground when it comes to multidimensional work. Mastery does not have to be mysterious. In this regard, the previous chapters are not merely a collection of anecdotes about how some individual practitioners have achieved their portions of mastery, which offers little help or guidance for the rest of us. Instead, each author has also offered concrete, practical skills and techniques, and we have tried to provide, with the Multidimensional Framework, lenses through which to consider mastery that combines both professional and personal development (integration). By utilizing all our intelligences to help ourselves and others to achieve greater awareness and understanding (so that we are no longer in over our heads, shattered or frozen), we can draw that circle and take them in.

Notes

1. If a conflict has, for simplicity's sake, two sides (the antagonists), the third side is made up of outsiders and insiders who support a peaceful resolution, one that meets the need of the disputing parties and the larger community (Ury 2000, 14). To accomplish this, third-siders can play any number of roles including providers, teachers, bridge builders, mediators, arbiters, equalizers, healers, witnesses, referees, or peacekeepers (190).

2. Indeed, one colleague presented a great example of a challenge in a community mediation between husband and wife—the husband, an evangelical Christian, thought his wife should be obedient to him (as the Bible says so) and should let him make all the decisions about the household finances (a policy the wife opposed). How, if at all, does a community mediator engage this? Are community mediators prepared, with their basic forty hours of training, to handle religious conversations in a constructive way? Lederach et al. (see Chapter 7), and Diamond (see Chapter 8) propose responses that train and educate at a different level.

3. Spiritual self-development and its importance is explored in much greater depth in the Lederach et al. and Diamond chapters (see Chapters 7 and 8, respectively).

4. Ken Wilber, the philosopher, describes what is meant by integral this way: "the word integral means comprehensive, inclusive, non-marginalizing,

embracing. Integral approaches to any field attempt to be exactly that: to include as many perspectives, styles, and methodologies as possible within a coherent view of the topic. In a certain sense, integral approaches are 'meta-paradigms,' or ways to draw together an already existing number of separate paradigms into an interrelated network of approaches that are mutually enriching" (Esbjörn-Hargens 2009, 1).

5. There are five core elements to integral theory, including quadrants (perspectives), lines (human capacities), levels (developmental stages), states of consciousness (normal, altered, etc.), and types (personality, gender, etc.): "These five elements signify some of the most basic repeating patterns of reality. Thus, by including all of these patterns you 'cover the bases' well, ensuring that no major part of any solution is left out or neglected" (Esbjörn-Hargens 2009, 2).

6. For example, a lot of positional bargaining in negotiation is driven by a competitive mind-set: the pie is fixed and I have to manipulate or coerce the other to get the larger slice. This thinking undermines the creative, collaborative, and value-expanding aspects of negotiation. To really change the behavior of how parties bargain, we need to help them replace those underlying framing assumptions. Otherwise, attempts to move from positions to interests will be abandoned or the information gained will be used against the other negotiator.

Bibliography

Aarja, H. 2014. ISIS enforces strict religious law in Raqqa. *Al-Monitor: The pulse of the Middle East*. March 21. http://www.al-monitor.com/pulse/security /2014/03/isis-enforces-islamic-law-raqqa-syria.html (accessed June 20, 2014).

Abeledo, Y. 2012. Anti-slavery campaign interview series: John Paul Lederach; Mysticism, new physics, and peacebuilding: Towards a new spirituality on the field. *Breathing Forgiveness* (blog), December 12. http://www.breathing forgiveness.net/search?q=lederach.

Abernethy, A. D., T. R. Houston, T. Mimms, and N. Boyd-Franklin. 2006. Using prayer in psychotherapy: Applying Sue's differential to enhance culturally competent care. *Cultural Diversity and Ethnic Minority Psychology* 12: 101–114.

Adler, P. 2003. Unintentional excellence: An exploration of mastery and incompetence. In *Bringing peace into the room*, eds. D. Bowling and D. Hoffman. San Francisco: Jossey-Bass.

Adler, R. S., B. Rosen, and E. M. Silverstein. 1998. Emotions in negotiation: How to manage fear and anger. *Negotiation Journal* 14 (2): 161–179.

Ahmed, S. 2004. *The cultural politics of emotion*. Edinburgh: Edinburgh University Press.

Alexander, N., and M. LeBaron. 2013. Embodied conflict resolution: Resurrecting roleplay-based curricula through dance. In *Educating negotiators for a connected world*, eds. C. Honeyman, J. Coben, and A. Wei-Min Lee. St. Paul, MN: DRI Press.

Amory, K. K. 2010. Acting for the twenty-first century: A somatic approach to contemporary actor training. *Perfformio* 1 (2): 5–20.

Anzaldúa, G. 2002. Preface: (Un) natural spaces, (un) safe spaces. In *The bridge we call home: Radical visions for transformation*, eds. G. Anzaldúa and A. Keating, 1–5. New York: Routledge.

Appleby, R. S. 2003. Retrieving the missing dimension of statecraft: Religious faith in the service of peacebuilding. In *Faith-based diplomacy: Trumping realpolitik,* ed. D. Johnston. New York: Oxford University Press.

197

————. 2000. *The ambivalence of the sacred: Religion, violence, and reconciliation*. New York: Rowman & Littlefield.

Appleby, R. S., and J. P. Lederach. 2010. Strategic peacebuilding: An overview. In *Strategies of peace: Transforming conflict in a violent world*, eds. D. Philpott and G. F. Powers. Oxford: Oxford University Press.

Arendshorst, Thomas R. "Drama in Conflict Resolution." In *Beyond Intractability*. April 2005. http://www.beyondintractability.org/essay/drama/Drama in Conflict Transformation.

Aten, D. J., and M. M. Leach, eds. 2009. A primer on spirituality and mental health. *Spirituality and the therapeutic process: A comprehensive resource from intake to termination*. Washington, DC: American Psychological Association.

Avalos, H. 2005. *Fighting words: The origins of religious violence*. New York: Prometheus Books.

Barr, A. 2006. "An investigation into the extent to which psychological wounds inspire counselors and psychotherapists to become wounded healers, the significance of these wounds on their career choice, the causes of these wounds and the overall significance of demographic factors." PhD diss., University of Strathblane. http://issuu.com/imran_manzoor/docs/wounded _healer_research_alison_barr_part_1_of_2; http://issuu.com/imran_manzoor /docs/wounded_healer_research_alison_barr_part_2_of_2 (accessed July 24, 2015).

Bazerman, M. H. 1991. *Negotiating rationally*. New York: Free Press.

Benjamin, R. D. 2003. Managing the natural energy of conflict: Mediators, tricksters, and the constructive uses of deception. In *Bringing peace into the room: How the personal qualities of the mediator impact process of conflict resolution*, eds. D. Bowling and D. Hoffman. San Francisco: Jossey-Bass.

Bhukhanwala, F. A. 2007. *Pre-service teachers' perspective on the use of pedagogy and theatre of the oppressed in teaching and teacher education: Outcomes and potential*. PhD diss., University of Georgia.

Bishop, Bill. 2008. *The big sort: Why the clustering of like-minded America is tearing us apart*. New York: Houghton Mifflin.

Blancke, B., and B. Wulff. 2002. Whose land is it anyway? The Third side's response to Indian land claim conflicts in upstate New York. In *When spider webs unite*, ed. J. Weiss et al. Cambridge, MA: PON Books.

Boal, A. 2002. *Games for actors and non-actors*, 2nd ed. New York: Routledge.

————. 1985. *Theatre of the oppressed*. New York: Theatre Communications Group.

Bodhi, B. 1998–2012. Purification of mind. In *Access to insight: Readings in Theravada Buddhism*. http://www.accesstoinsight.org.

Bodhi, B., trans. 2000. *Samyutta nikaya: The connected discourses of the Buddha*. Boston, MA: Wisdom Publications.

Bodtker, A., and J. K. Jameson. 2001. Emotion in conflict formation and its transformation: Application to organizational conflict management. *International Journal of Conflict Management* 12 (3): 259–275.

Boler, M. 1999. *Feeling power: Emotions and education*. New York: Routledge.

Bowland, S. Y. 2008. What is justice in conflict resolution practice? In *Re-centering: Culture and knowledge in conflict resolution practice*, 303–315. Syracuse: Syracuse University Press.

Bowling, D., and D. Hoffman. 2000. Bringing peace into the room: The personal qualities of the mediator and their impact on the mediation. *Negotiation Journal* 16 (1): 5–28.

———, eds. 2003. *Bringing peace into the room: How the personal qualities of the mediator impact process of conflict resolution.* San Francisco: Jossey-Bass.

Brashear, M., B. Sipes, and M. Sternberg. 2012. Social transformation in conflict and the Kumi method. *Embedding mediation in society*, eds. S. Manichev and A. Redlich. St. Petersburg Dialogues, International Training and Practice of Mediators in the Light of European Experience, December 16–17, 2011. http://www.sorryebooks.org/27p45c_pdf-book-embedding-mediation-in-society-theory-research-practice-training-saint-p.pdf.

Brown, H. 2002. The Navajo Nation's peacemaker division: An integrated community-based dispute resolution forum. *Dispute Resolution Journal* 57 (2): 43–50.

Brueggemann, W. 1978. *The prophetic imagination.* Minneapolis: Fortress Press.

———. 1976. *Living toward a vision: Biblical reflections on shalom.* Philadelphia: United Church Press.

Bush, R. A. B., and J. P. Folger. 2012. Mediation and social justice: Risks and opportunities. *Ohio State Journal on Dispute Resolution* 27 (1): 1–52.

———. 1994. *The promise of mediation: Responding to conflict through recognition and empowerment.* San Francisco: Jossey-Bass.

Cahn, R. B., and J. Polich. 2006. Meditation states and traits: EEG, ERP, and Neuroimaging studies. *Psychological Bulletin* 132 (2): 180–211.

Cannon, W. B. 1929. *Bodily changes in pain, hunger, fear, and rage.* New York: Appleton-Century-Crofts.

Chené, R. M. 2008. Beyond mediation—reconciling an intercultural world: A new role for conflict resolution. In *Re-centering: Culture and knowledge in conflict resolution practice*, 32–36. Syracuse: Syracuse University Press.

Chiesa, A., and A. Serretti. 2009. Mindfulness-based stress reduction for stress management in healthy people: A review and meta-analysis. *Journal of Alternative and Complementary Medicine* 15 (5): 593–600.

Ciarrochi, J., T. Kashdan, and R. Harris. 2013. The foundations of flourishing. In *Mindfulness, acceptance and positive psychology: The seven foundations of well-Being*, eds. T. Kashdan and J. Ciarrochi. Oakland, CA. Context Press.

Clark, M. 1993. Symptoms of cultural pathologies: A hypothesis. In *Conflict resolution theory and practice: Integration and application*, eds. D. J. Sandole and H. van der Merwe. Manchester and New York: Manchester University Press, 43–54.

Cloke, K. 2013. *The dance of opposites: Explorations in mediation, dialogue and conflict resolution systems design.* Dallas, TX: Good Media Press.

———. 2009. Bringing oxytocin into the room: Notes on the neurophysiology of conflict. http://www.kennethcloke.com/articles.htm and http://www.mediate.com/articles/cloke8.cfm.

———. 2006. *The Crossroads of conflict: A journey into the heart of dispute resolution.* Québec: Janis Publications.

———. 2004. Journeys into the heart of conflict. *Pepperdine Dispute Resolution Law Journal* 4 (2): 241–249.

————. 2001. *Mediating dangerously: The frontiers of conflict resolution.* San Francisco: Jossey-Bass.

Cobb, S. 2004. Witnessing in mediation: Toward an aesthetic ethics of practice. *Institute for conflict analysis and resolution working paper 22.* Washington, DC: George Mason University.

————. 2003. Fostering coexistence in identity-based conflicts. In *Imagine coexistence: Restoring humanity after violent ethnic conflict,* 294–310. San Francisco: Jossey-Bass.

————. 2001. Dialogue and the practice of law and spiritual values: Creating sacred space: Toward a second-generation dispute resolution practice. *Fordham Urban Law Journal* 28 (4): 1017–1031.

————. 1993. Empowerment and mediation: A narrative perspective. *Negotiation Journal* 9 (3): 245–260.

Cobb, S., and J. Rifkin. 1991. Practice and paradox: Deconstructing neutrality in mediation. *Law and Social Inquiry*: 35–62.

Cohen, C., R. Gutierrez Varea, and P. O. Walker, eds. 2011. *Acting together: Performance and the creative transformation of conflict.* 2 vols. Oakland, CA: New Village Press.

Coleman, P. 2011. *The five percent: Finding solutions to seemingly impossible conflicts.* New York: PublicAffairs.

Coser, L. A. 1956. *The functions of social conflict.* New York: Free Press.

Crumb, T. 1987. *The magic of conflict: Turning a life of work into a work of art.* New York: Touchstone Books.

Curle, A. 1995. *Another way. Positive response to contemporary violence* Oxford: Jon Carpenter.

————. 1971. *Making peace.* London: Tavistock Limited.

Daly, E., and J. Sarkin. 2007. *Reconciliation in divided societies: Finding common ground.* Philadelphia: University of Pennsylvania Press.

Davidheiser, M. 2006. Rituals and conflict transformation: An anthropological analysis of the ceremonial dimensions of dispute processing. In *Beyond intractability*, eds. G. Burgess and H. Burgess. Boulder: Conflict Research Consortium, University of Colorado.

Davidson, R. J., and S. Begley. 2012. *The emotional life of your brain: How its unique patterns affect the way you think, feel and live—and how you can change them.* New York: Plume.

Davis, M., E. R. Eshelman, and M. McKay. 1995. *The relaxation and stress reduction workbook.* 4th ed. Oakland, CA: New Harbinger Publications.

De Gelder, B., J. Snyder, D. Greve, G. Gerard, and N. Hadjikhani. 2004. Fear fosters flight: A mechanism for fear contagion when perceiving emotion expressed by a whole body. *Proceedings of the National Academy of Sciences* 101 (47): 16701–16706.

Della Noce, D. J. 1999. Seeing theory in practice: An analysis of empathy in mediation. *Negotiation Theory* 15 (3): 271–301.

Demasio, A. 1994. *Descartes' error: Emotion, reason, and the human brain.* New York: Putnam's Sons.

Diamond, L. 2004. *The courage for peace: Daring to create harmony in ourselves and the world.* Berkeley, CA: Conari Press.

————. n.d. Bio. Louise Diamond. *Global Systems Initiatives.* http://www.globalsystemsinitiatives.net/BioLD.pdf (accessed July 16, 2010).

Diamond, L., and J. McDonald. 1996. *Multi-track diplomacy: A systems approach to peace.* West Hartford, CT: Kumarian Press.

Docherty, J. S. 2005. *The little book of strategic negotiation.* Intercourse, PA: Good Books.

Donlon, S. 2001. *The use of somatics to integrate body, mind and emotions in conflict resolution interventions.* PhD diss., George Mason University.

Dubuisson, D. 2007. *The Western construction of religion: Myths, knowledge, and ideology.* Trans. W. Sayers. Baltimore, MD: Johns Hopkins University Press.

Dukes, F. E., J. B. Stephens, and M. A. Piscolish. 2009. *Reaching for higher ground: Creating purpose-driven, principled, and powerful groups.* Book-Surge Publishing.

Eddy, M. 2009a. The role of dance in violence prevention programs for youth. Vol. 7 of *Dance: Current selected research,* eds. L. Y. Overby and B. Lepczyk. Brooklyn, NY: AMS Press.

———. 2009b. A brief history of somatic practices and dance: Historical development of the field of somatic education and its relationship to dance. *Journal of Dance and Somatic Practices* 1 (1): 5–27.

Emmonds, R. A. 2000. Is spirituality an intelligence? Motivation, cognition, and the psychology of ultimate concern. *International Journal for the Psychology of Religion* 10 (1): 3–26.

Esbjörn-Hargens, S. 2009. *An overview of integral theory: An all-inclusive framework for the 21st century.* https://sites.google.com/site/integralconflict resolution/integral-theory (accessed July 27, 2014).

Fenton, W. 1985. Structure, continuity and change in the process of Iroquois treaty making. *The history and culture of Iroquois diplomacy: An interdisciplinary guide to the treaties of the six nations and their league,* eds. F. Jennings, W. Fenton, et al. Syracuse, NY: Syracuse University Press.

Fetherston, B., and R. Kelly. 2007. Conflict resolution and transformative pedagogy: A grounded theory research project on learning in higher education. *Journal of Transformative Education* 5 (3): 262–285.

Fisher, R., and D. Shapiro. 2005. *Beyond reason: Using emotions as you negotiate.* New York: Viking.

Fisher, R., and W. Ury. 1981. *Getting to yes: Negotiating agreement without giving in.* Boston. MA: Houghton Mifflin.

Fisher, R., W. Ury, and B. Patton. 1991. *Getting to yes: Negotiating agreement without giving in.* 2nd ed. New York: Penguin Books.

Fisher, W. R. 1985. Narrative paradigm: In the beginning. *Journal of Communication* 35 (4): 73–89.

———. 1987. *Human communication as narration: Toward a philosophy of reason, value, and action.* Columbia: University of South Carolina Press.

Fitzgerald, F. Scott. 2008. *Babylon revisited: And other stories.* New York: Simon & Schuster.

Fogel, A. 2009. *The psychophysiology of self-awareness: Rediscovering the lost art of body sense.* New York: W. W. Norton.

Foucault, M. 1980. *Power/knowledge: Selected interviews and other writings.* New York: Pantheon Books.

Fox, E. A. 2013. *Winning from within: A breakthrough method for living, learning, and lasting change.* New York: HarperBusiness.

————. 2004. Bringing peace into the room. *Negotiation Journal* 20 (3): 461–469.

Fox, J. 2004. *Acts of service: Spontaneity, commitment, and tradition in the nonscripted theatre.* New Paltz, NY: Tusitala Publishing.

Frasier, R. E., and N. D. Hansen. 2009. Religious/spiritual psychotherapy behaviors: Do we do what we believe to be important? *Professional Psychology: Research and Practice* 40 (1): 81–87.

Freire, Paulo. 2011. *Pedagogy of the oppressed.* 30th ed. New York: Continuum International Publishing.

Friedman, E. H. 1990. *Friedman's fables.* New York/London: Guilford Press.

Fronsdal, G., trans. 2008. *The Dhammapada: Teachings of the Buddha.* Boston, MA: Shambhala.

Galtung, J. 2004. *Transcend and transform: An introduction to conflict work.* Boulder, CO: Paradigm Publishers.

————. 1996. *Peace by peaceful means.* Oslo: International Peace Research Institute.

Gardner, H. [1983] 2011. *Frames of mind: The theory of multiple intelligences.* New York: Basic Books.

Garland, E., and B. Fredrickson. 2013. Mindfulness broadens awareness and builds meaning at attention-emotion interface. In *Mindfulness, acceptance and positive psychology: The seven foundations of well-being,* eds. T. Kashdan and J. Ciarrochi. Oakland, CA: Context Press.

Gold, L. 2003. Mediation and the culture of healing. *Bringing peace into the room: How the personal qualities of the mediator impact the process of conflict resolution,* eds. D. Bowling and D. Hoffman. San Francisco: Jossey-Bass.

————. 1993. Influencing unconscious influences: The healing dimension of mediation. *Conflict Resolution Quarterly,* 11: 55–66.

Goldberg, R. 2009. How our worldviews shape our practices. *Conflict Resolution Quarterly* 26 (4): 405–431.

Goldberg, R., and B. Blancke. 2012. Wisdom and conflict resolution: A possible framework for integrated practice. *Cardozo Journal of Conflict Resolution* 13 (2): 437–465.

————. 2011. God in the process: Is there a place for religion in conflict resolution? *Conflict Resolution Quarterly* 28 (4): 377–398.

Goldstein, J., and J. Kornfield. 1987. *Seeking the heart of wisdom: The path of insight meditation.* Boston, MA: Shambhala.

Goleman, D. 2011. *Leadership: The power of emotional intelligence: Selected writings.* Northampton, MA: More than Sound.

————. 1995. *Emotional intelligence: Why it can matter more than IQ.* New York; Bantam Books.

————. [1995] 2006. *Working with emotional intelligence.* New York: Bantam Dell.

Goleman, D., and J. Gurin, eds. 1993. *Mind-body medicine: How to use your mind for better health.* Yonkers, NY: Consumer Reports Books.

Gopin, M. 2009. *To make the Earth whole: The art of citizen diplomacy in an age of religious militancy.* Lanham, MD: Rowman & Littlefield.

————. 2004. *Healing the heart of conflict: 8 crucial steps to making peace with yourself and others.* Emmaus, PA: Rodale.

————. 2000. *Between Eden and Armageddon: The future of world religions, violence, and peacemaking.* New York: Oxford University Press.

Gordon, W. 1961. *Synectics: A new method of directing creative potential to the solution of technical and theoretical problems.* New York: Harper & Brothers.

Gunning, I. R. 2004. Know justice, know peace: Further reflections on justice, equality, and impartiality in settlement oriented and transformative mediation. *Cardozo Journal of Conflict Resolution* 5 (2): 87–95.

————. 1995. Diversity issues in mediation: Controlling negative cultural myths. *Journal of Dispute Resolution* (55): 55–93.

Hall, D. 2005. *The spiritual revitalization of the legal profession: A search for sacred rivers.* Lewiston: The Edwin Mellen Press.

Hanna, T. 1970. *Bodies in revolt: A primer in somatic thinking.* New York: Holt, Rinehart and Winston.

Hanson, D. H., and I. J. Grand. 1998. *The body in psychotherapy: Inquiries in somatic psychology.* Berkeley, CA: North Atlantic Books.

Harpviken, K. B., and H. E. Røislien. 2008. Faithful brokers? Potentials and pitfalls of religion in peacemaking. *Conflict Resolution Quarterly* 25 (3): 351–373.

Harris, K. 1995. *Collected quotes from Albert Einstein.* http://rescomp.stanford .edu/~cheshire/EinsteinQuotes.html (accessed May 17, 2007).

Harris, S. 2004. *The end of faith.* New York: W. W. Norton.

Harvard Law Bulletin. 2004. *Getting to Wisdom.* Spring. http://www.law.harvard.edu/news/bulletin/2004/spring/bf_02.php (accessed July 27, 2010).

Hathaway, W. L., and J. S. Ripley. 2009. Ethical concerns around spirituality and religion in clinical practice. *Spirituality and the therapeutic process: A comprehensive resource from intake to termination,* eds. D. J. Aten and M. M. Leach. Washington, DC: American Psychological Association.

Hew Len, I., and C. Brown. 1999. *Self I-dentity through Ho'oponopono.* October. http://hooponopono.org/Articles/self-i_dentity.html (accessed June 22, 2006).

Hitchens, C. 2007. *God is not great: How religion poisons everything.* Lebanon, IN: Twelve/Hachette Book Group, Warner Books.

Hocker, J., and W. Wilmot. 1995. *Interpersonal conflict.* 4th ed. Madison, WI: WCB Brown and Benchmark.

Hosseini, M., H. Elias, S. Krauss, and S. Aishah. 2010. A review study on spiritual intelligence, adolescence and spiritual intelligences, factors that may contribute to individual differences in spiritual intelligence, and related theories. *International Journal of Psychological Studies* 2 (2): 179–188.

Hugo, V. 1943. *Les miserables.* New York: Blue Ribbon Books.

Hurdle, D. E. 2002. Native Hawaiian traditional healing: Culturally based interventions for social work practice. *Social Work* 47 (2): 183–192.

Jaggar, A. M. 1989. Love and knowledge: Emotion in feminist epistemology. In *Gender/body/knowledge: Feminist reconstructions of being and knowing,* ed. A. Jaggar and S. Bordo, 145–171. New Brunswick, NJ: Rutgers University Press.

Jameson, J. K., A. Bodtker, and T. Linker. 2010. Facilitating conflict transformation: Mediator strategies for eliciting emotional communication in a workplace conflict. *Negotiation Journal* 1: 25–48.

Jarymowicz, M., and D. Bar-Tal. 2006. The dominance of fear over hope in the life of individuals and collectives. *European Journal of Social Psychology* 36 (3): 367–392.

Jones, D. 2009. The role of spirituality in the mediation process. *Conflict Resolution Quarterly* 27 (2): 145–165.

Jones, T., and A. Bodtker. 2001. Mediating with heart in mind: Addressing emotion in mediation practice. *Negotiation Journal* 17 (3): 207–244.

Jones, T. S., and R. Brinkert. 2008. *Conflict coaching: Conflict management strategies and skills for the individual.* Los Angeles, CA: Sage Publications.

Jones, W., and S. Hughes. 2003. Complexity, conflict resolution, and how the mind works. *Conflict Resolution Quarterly* 20 (4): 485–494.

Juergensmeyer, M. 2003. *Terror in the mind of God: The global rise of religious violence.* 3rd ed. Los Angeles, CA: University of California Press.

Kahneman D. 2011. *Thinking fast and slow.* New York: Farrar, Strauss, and Giroux.

Kaner, S. 2007. *Facilitator's guide to participatory decision-making.* 2nd ed. San Francisco: Jossey-Bass.

Kashdan, T., and J. Ciarrochi, eds. 2013. *Mindfulness, acceptance and positive psychology: The seven foundations of well-being.* Oakland, CA: Context Press.

Kelly, T. L. 2000. The case of the missing Shaman: A general comparison of problem-solving and transformative perspectives on conflict resolution. Unpublished graduate paper. Portland State University, Portland, OR. http://web.pdx.edu/~psu17799/shaman.htm (accessed July 24, 2010).

Kimball, C. 2002. *When religion becomes evil.* San Francisco, CA: Harper Collins.

King, D. 1989. *Beyond traditional means: Ho'oponopono.* http://www.xplore heartlinks.com/hooponopono.htm (accessed June 22, 2006).

King, M. L., Jr. 1981. *Loving your enemies; Letter from a Birmingham jail; Declaration of independence from the war in Vietnam* 1. New York: A. J. Muste Memorial Institute.

Kriesberg, L., and B. Dayton. 2012. *Constructive conflicts: From escalation to resolution.* 4th ed. Lanham, MD: Rowman & Littlefield.

Ladd, P. 2005 *Mediation, conciliation, and emotion: A practitioner's guide for understanding emotions in dispute resolution.* Lanham, MD: University Press of America.

Laue, J., and G. Cormick. 1978. The ethics of intervention in community disputes. *The ethics of social intervention,* ed. G. Bermant et al. Washington, DC: Halsted Press.

LeBaron, M. 2003. *Bridging cultural conflicts.* San Francisco: Jossey-Bass.

———. 2002. *Bridging troubled waters: Conflict resolution from the heart.* San Francisco: Jossey-Bass.

LeBaron, M., and C. MacLeod. 2012. *Dancing at the crossroads: Body-based ways of tranforming conflict across cultures.* Preconference workshop presented at the Association for Conflict Resolution (ACR) annual conference, New Orleans, LA.

LeBaron, M., C. MacLeod, and A. Acland, eds. 2013. *The choreography of resolution: Conflict, dance and neuroscience.* Chicago: American Bar Association.

LeBaron, M., E. McCandless, and S. Garon. 1998. *Conflict and culture: A literature review and bibliography, 1992–1998 update.* Fairfax, VA: George Mason University, Institute for Conflict Analysis and Resolution.

Lebovic, H. 2013. Towards a coherent unity of perspectives on peace: Burton, Lederach and the philosophy of Ken Wilber. *Integral Review* 9 (1): 3–33.

Lederach, J. P. 2015. Spirituality and religious peacebuilding. *The Oxford handbook of religion, conflict, and peacebuilding*, eds. A. Omer, R. S. Appleby, D. Little. New York: Oxford University Press.

———. 2011. Narratives of care: The social echo of community transformation. Unpublished paper. Eastern Mennonite University Attachment Conference, March 31–April 2.

———. 2010. End-of-pilot progress report. Peacebuilding apprenticeship pilot program, Initiative No. 2435. Unpublished report, December.

———. 2008. Re: Draft 1—short version of the peacebuilding apprenticeship proposal. Unpublished memo to Tom Callahan and Mark Nepo, February 19.

———. 2005. *The moral imagination: The art and soul of building peace*. New York: Oxford University Press.

———. 2003. *The little book of conflict transformation*. Intercourse, PA: Good Books.

———. 1997. *Building peace: Sustainable reconciliation in divided societies*. Washington, DC: US Institute of Peace Press.

———. 1995. *Preparing for peace: Conflict transformation across cultures*. Syracuse, NY: Syracuse University Press.

———. 1986. The mediator's cultural assumptions. *Conciliation Quarterly* 5 (1): 2–5.

Lederach, J. P., and A. J. Lederach. 2010. *When blood and bones cry out*. Oxford: Oxford University Press.

LeResche, D. 1993. Editor's notes. *Mediation Quarterly* 10 (4): 321–325.

Levine, P. A. 1997. *Waking the tiger: Healing trauma*. Berkeley, CA: North Atlantic Books.

Lincoln, B. 2006. *Holy terrors: Thinking about religion after September 11*. 2nd ed. Chicago: University of Chicago Press.

Lincoln, Y. S., and E. G. Guba. 1985. *Naturalistic inquiry*. Newbury Park, CA: Sage Publications.

Linden, P. 2007. *Embodied peacemaking: Body awareness, self-regulation and conflict resolution*. Columbus, OH: CCMS Publications.

———. 2003. *Reach out: Body awareness training for peacemaking—five easy lessons*. Columbus, OH: CCMS Publications.

Lipton, B. 2005. *The biology of belief*. San Francisco: Hay House.

Lutz, C. 1988. *Unnatural emotions: Everyday sentiments on a Micronesian atoll and their challenge to Western theory*. Chicago: University of Chicago Press.

Maise, M. 2006. Engaging the emotions in conflict intervention. *Conflict Resolution Quarterly* 24 (2): 187–195.

Malchiodi, C. 2005. Expressive therapies: History, theory and practice. *Expressive therapies*, ed. Cathy Malchiodi. New York: Guilford Publications.

Mayer, B. S. 2015. *The conflict paradox: Seven dilemmas at the core of disputes*. San Francisco: Jossey-Bass.

———. 2009. *Staying with conflict: A strategic approach to ongoing disputes*. San Francisco: Jossey-Bass.

———. 2004. *Beyond Neutrality: Confronting the crisis in conflict resolution*. San Francisco: Jossey-Bass.

McGuigan, R., and S. McMechan. 2005. Integral conflict analysis: A comprehensive quadrant analysis of an organizational conflict. *Conflict Resolution Quarterly* 33 (3): 349–363.

McGuigan, R., and N. Popp. 2015. *Integral conflict: The new science of conflict.* New York: SUNY Press.

———. 2012. Consciousness and conflict (explained better?). *Conflict Resolution Quarterly* 29 (3): 227–260.

———. 2007. The self in conflict: The evolution of mediation. *Conflict Resolution Quarterly* 25 (2): 221–238.

McKee, A., R. Boyatzis, and F. Johnston. 2008. *Becoming a resonant leader: Develop your emotional intelligence, renew your relationships, sustain your effectiveness.* Boston: Harvard Business Press.

McTernan, O. 2003. *Violence in God's name: Religion in an age of conflict.* Maryknoll, NY: Orbis Books.

Mediators Beyond Borders. n.d. *Who we are.* http://www.mediatorsbeyondborders .org/who/index.shtml (accessed July 16, 2010).

Meeker, J. 2012. *Engaging emotions and practicing conflict: Emotions and teaching toward social justice.* PhD diss., California Institute for Integral Studies.

Menkel-Meadow, C. 2001. Commentary: And now a word about secular humanism, spirituality, and the practice of justice and conflict resolution. *Fordham Urban Law Journal* (April 28): 1073–1086.

Mensinga, J. 2011. The feeling of being a social worker: Including yoga as an embodied practice in social work education. *Social Work Education* 30 (6): 650–662.

Merry, S. E. 1987. Cultural aspects of disputing. *PCR Occasional Papers Series*: 1987-2. Program on Conflict Resolution. Manoa: University of Hawaii.

Mitchell, C. 2006. *Religion, identity and politics in Northern Ireland: Boundaries of belonging and belief.* Aldershot, UK: Ashgate Publishing.

———. 2002. Beyond resolution: What does conflict transformation actually transform? *Peace and Conflict Studies Journal* 9 (1): 1–21.

Moffitt, P. 2008. *Dancing with life: Buddhist insights for finding meaning and joy in the face of suffering.* New York: Rodale Press.

Moore, C. W. 2003. *The Mediation Process.* 3rd ed. San Francisco: Jossey-Bass.

Morelli, J. 2012. Conflict, space and movement. Conference workshop presented at the Association for Conflict Resolution annual conference, New Orleans, LA.

———. 2002. The mind, body and conflict. Conference workshop presented at the Association for Conflict Resolution annual conference, San Diego, CA.

Moreno, J. L. 1951. *Sociometry, experimental method and the science of society: An approach to a new political orientation.* New York: Beacon House.

Nachmias, C., and D. Nachmias. 1992. *Research methods in the social sciences.* 4th ed. New York: St. Martin's Press.

Nan, S. A. 2011. Consciousness in culture-based conflict and conflict resolution. *Conflict Resolution Quarterly* 28 (3): 239–261.

Nanamoli, B., and B. Bodhi, trans. 1995. *Majjhima Nikaya: The middle length discourses of the Buddha.* Boston: Wisdom Publications.

Napoli, M., and R. Bonifas. 2011. From theory toward empathic self-care: Creating a mindful classroom for social work students. *Social Work Education* 30 (6): 635–649.

Nic Craith, M. 2003. *Culture and identity politics in Northern Ireland*. Hampshire, UK: Palgrave McMillan.

Noble, C. 2014. *Conflict mastery: Questions to guide you*. Toronto: CINERGY Coaching.

Palmer, P. J. 1999. *Let your life speak: Listening for the voice of vocation*. San Francisco: Jossey-Bass.

Pargament, K. I., and E. J. Krumrei. 2009. Clinical assessment of clients' spirituality. *Spirituality and the therapeutic process: A comprehensive resource from intake to termination*, eds. D. J. Aten and M. M. Leach. Washington, DC: American Psychological Association.

Park-Fuller, L. 2005. Beyond role play: Playback theatre and conflict transformation. Paper presented at the International Playback Theatre Symposium. Tempe, AZ. February 27.

Peppet, S., and M. Moffit. 2006. Learning how to learn to negotiate. In *The Negotiator's Fieldbook*, eds. A. K. Schneider and C. H., 615–626. Washington, DC: American Bar Association.

Perloff, F. 2010. Ken Wilber's integral theory applied to mediation. *Conflict Resolution Quarterly* 28 (1): 83–107.

Pranis, Kay. 2005. *The little book of circle processes: A new/old approach to peacemaking*. Intercourse, PA: Good Books.

Pukui, M. K., E. W. Haertig, and C. Lee. 1971. Ho'oponopono. *Nana I Ke Kuma*, eds. M. Kawena, M. K. Pukui, E. W. Haertig, and C. Lee. Queen Lili'uokalani Children's Center Series.

Rack, C. 2000. The effect of culturally-based fairness norms on disputant negotiations in mediated small claims cases. Paper presented at the Peace Studies Association Conference. Austin, TX.

Rahula, W. 1974. *What the Buddha taught*. New York: Grove Press.

Rainey, D., and L. Wing. 2012. ODR and the development of theory. In *ODR theory and practice: A treatise on online dispute resolution*, eds. E. Katsch, M. Wahab, and D. Rainey. The Hague: Eleven International Press.

Reilly, P. 2010. Mindfulness, emotions, and mental models: Theory that leads to more effective dispute resolution. *Nevada Law Journal* 10: 433–460.

Reiman, C. 2004. Assesing the state-of-the-art in conflict transformation. *Berghof Research Center for Constructive Conflict Management*. http://www.berghof -handbook.net/uploads/download/reimann_handbook.pdf. (accessed May 1, 2007).

Reitman, J. W. 2003a. *The Allagash: A case study of a successful environmental mediation*. Mediate.com (accessed March 12, 2009).

———. 2003b. The personal qualities of the mediator: Taking time for reflection and renewal. In *Bringing peace into the room: How the personal qualities of the mediator impact process of conflict resolution*, eds. D. Bowling and D. A. Hoffman. San Francisco: Jossey-Bass.

Riccio, D. R. 2000. *Settlement master's report, submitted to U.S. District Court Judge Neal P. McCum*. Syracuse, NY, February 25. http://www.uticaod .net/site_html/Oneida_nation_archive/11march_3.htm (accessed July 18, 2012).

Richards, P. S., and A. E. Bergin. 2004. Theistic perspectives in psychotherapy: Conclusions and recommendations. *Casebook for a spiritual strategy in counseling and psychotherapy*, eds. P. S. Richards and A. E. Bergin. Washington, DC: American Psychological Association.

Richards, P. S., J. M. Rector, and A. C. Tjeltveit. 1999. Values, spirituality, and psychotherapy. *Integrating spirituality into treatment: Resources for practitioners*, ed. W. R. Miller. Washington, DC: American Psychological Association.

Rickard, R. L. 2008. Authentic lawyering: Engaging your head and your heart. *Michigan Bar Journal*, June.

Ringer, J. n.d. Hidden gifts: What aikido can teach us about conflict. http://www.judyringer.com/resources/articles (accessed March 28, 2015).

Riskin, L. 2002. The contemplative lawyer: On the potential contribution of mindfulness meditation to law students, lawyers and their clients. *Harvard Negotiation Law Review* 7 (1): 1–66.

Rollins, W. 2007. The myth of redemptive violence or the myth of redemptive love. *The destructive power of religion: Violence in Judaism, Christianity, and Islam*, ed. J. Harold Ellens, 219–228. Westport, CT: Praeger.

Rosaldo, M. Z. 1985. Toward an anthropology of self and feeling. In *Culture theory: Essays on mind, self, and emotion*, eds. R. A. Shweder and R. A. LeVine. Cambridge: Cambridge University Press.

Rothman, J. 1997. *Resolving Identity-Based Conflicts in Nations, Organizations and Communities*. San Francisco: Jossey-Bass.

Roy, B. 2002. For white people, on how to listen when race is the subject. *Journal of Intergroup Relations* 29 (3): 3–15.

Rubin, J., D. Pruitt, and S. Hee Kim. 1994. *Social conflict*. New York: McGraw-Hill.

Runde, C., and T. Flanagan. 2013. *Becoming a conflict competent leader: How you and your organization can manage conflict effectively*. San Francisco: John Wiley & Sons.

Ryan, E. 2006. Building the emotionally learned negotiator. *Negotiation Journal* 22 (2): 209–225.

Salas, J. 2011. Stories in the moment: Playback Theatre for building community and justice. In Vol. 2 of *Acting together: Performance and the creative transformation of conflict*, eds. C. E. Cohen, R. Gutierrez Varea, and P. O. Walker. Oakland, CA: New Village Press.

———. 1993. *Improvising real life: Personal story in Playback Theatre*. New Paltz, NY: Tusitala Publishing.

Salzburg, S. 2002. *Lovingkindness: The revolutionary art of happiness*. Boston: Shambhala.

Saunders, C. n.d. *100% responsibility and the possibility of a hot fudge sundae: Cat Saunders gets the scoop on Haleakala Hew Len.* http://hooponopono.org/Articles/100_percent_responsible.html (accessed September 8, 1997).

Scalmer, S. 2012. Mohandas Gandhi. In *The Ashgate research companion to religion and conflict resolution*, ed. L. Marsden, 337–352. Burlington, VT: Ashgate Publishing.

Schirch, L. 2015. Ritual, religion, and peacebuilding. *The Oxford handbook of religion, conflict, and peacebuilding*, eds. A. Omer, R. S. Appleby, D. Little. New York: Oxford University Press.

———. 2005. *Ritual and symbol in peacebuilding*. West Hartford, CT: Kumarian Press.

———. 2004. *The little book of strategic peacebuilding: A vision and framework for peace with justice*. Intercourse, PA: Good Books.

Schön, D. A. 1983. The reflective practitioner: How professionals think in action. New York: Basic Books.

Segrest, M. 2002. *Born to belonging: Writings on spirit and justice.* Rutgers, NJ: Rutgers University Press.

Senge, P. 2006. *The fifth discipline: The art and practice of the learning organization.* New York: Currency Doubleday.

Senge, P., A. Keller, C. Roberts, R. Ross, and B. Smith. 1994. *The fifth discipline fieldbook: Strategies and tools for building a learning organization.* New York: Currency Doubleday.

Serlin, I., M. R. Berger, and R. Bar-Sinai. 2007. Moving through conflict: Understanding personal and cultural differences through movement style. *Journal of Humanistic Psychology* 47 (3): 367–375.

Shank, M., and L. Schirch. 2008. Strategic arts-based peacebuilding. *Peace & Change* 233 (2): 217–242.

Shaw, M. L. 2005. Style schmyle! *Dispute Resolution Magazine* 11 (3): 17–20.

Shook, V. E. 2000. *Ho'oponopono: Contemporary uses of a Hawaiian problem-solving process.* Honolulu: University of Hawai'i Press.

Sibley, M. Q. 1984. Religion and law: Some thoughts on their intersections. *Journal of Law and Religion* 2 (1): 41–67.

Siegel, D. 2010. *Mindsight: The new science of personal transformation.* New York: Bantam Books.

———. 2007. *The mindful brain.* New York: W. W. Norton.

Sisk, D. 2002. Spiritual intelligence: The tenth intelligence that integrates all other intelligences. *Gifted Education International* 16: 208–212.

Spelman, E. V. 1989. Anger and insubordination. In *Women, knowledge, and reality*, eds. A. Garry and M. Pearsall, 263–274. New York: Routledge.

Sperry, L., and E. P. Shafranske. 2005. Future directions: Opportunities and challenges. *Spiritually oriented psychotherapy*, eds. L. Sperry and E. P. Shafranske. Washington, DC: American Psychological Association.

Sternberg, P. 1998. *Theatre for conflict resolution: In the classroom and beyond.* Portsmouth, NH: Heinemann.

Sternberg, R. 2003. A duplex theory of hate: Development and application to terrorism, massacres, and genocide. *Review of General Psychology* 7 (3): 299–328.

Stone, D., B. Patton, and S. Heen. 1999. *Difficult conversations: How to discuss what matters most.* New York: Penguin Books.

Strozzi-Heckler, R. 2014. *The art of somatic coaching: Embodying skillful action, wisdom and compassion.* Berkeley, CA: North Atlantic Books,

———, R. 2007. *The leadership dojo: Build your foundation as an exemplary leader.* Berkeley, CA: Frog.

Taylor, L. K., and J. P. Lederach. 2014. Practicing peace: Psychological roots of transforming conflicts. *Global Journal of Peace Research and Praxis* 1 (1): 12–31.

Taylor, S. E., L. Cousino Klein, B. P. Lewis, T. L. Gruenewald, A. R. Gurung, and J. A. Undegraff. 2000. Behavioral responses to stress in females: Tend-and-dance wozney magazine befriend, not fight-or-flight. *Psychology Review* 107 (3): 411–429.

Thera, N., and B. Bodhi., trans. and eds. 1999. *Anguttara Nikaya: The numerical discourses of the Buddha.* Walnut Creek, CA: AltaMira Press.

Thompson, Becky W. 1994. *A hunger so wide and so deep: A multiracial view of women's eating disorders.* Minneapolis: University of Minnesota Press.

Tillich, P. 1990. *Theology of peace.* Louisville, KY: John Knox Press.

Trujillo, M. A., S. Y. Bowland, L. J. Myers, P. M. Richards, and B. Roy, eds. 2008. *Re-centering culture and knowledge in conflict resolution practice.* Syracuse, NY: Syracuse University Press.

Turner, V. 1969. *The ritual process: Structure and anti-structure.* Chicago: Aldine.

———. 1967. *The forest of symbols: Aspects of Ndembu ritual.* Ithaca, NY: Cornell University Press.

Umbreit, M. S. 1995. *Mediating interpersonal conflicts: A pathway to peace.* West Concord, MN: CPI Publishing.

Ury, W. 2000. *The third side: Why we fight and how we can stop.* New York: Penguin Books.

———. 1993. *Getting past no: Negotiating with difficult people.* New York: Bantam Books.

Van Gennep, A. 1960. *The rites of passage.* Chicago: University of Chicago Press.

Vaughan, F. 2002. What is spiritual intelligence? *Journal of Humanistic Psychology* 42 (2): 16–33.

Volf, M. 2006. *The end of memory: Remembering rightly in a violent world.* Grand Rapids, MI: Wm. B Eerdmans.

———. 2005. *Free of charge: Giving and forgiving in a culture stripped of grace.* Grand Rapids, MI: Zondervan.

———. 1996. *Exclusion and embrace: A theological exploration of identity, otherness, and reconciliation.* Nashville, TN: Abingdon Press.

Volkan, V. 1997. *Bloodlines: From ethnic pride to ethnic terrorism.* Boulder, CO: Westview Press.

Weed, W. S. 2004. Why we hate. *Yale Alumni Magazine,* September/October.

Westbrook, A., and O. Ratti. 1970. *Aikido and the dynamic sphere.* Tokyo: Charles E. Tuttle Company.

What is Huna: Basic Huna, Ho'oponopono. http://www.huna.com/ho'oponopono.html (accessed June 22, 2006).

What is Huna: Basic Huna, The basic teaching of the three selves. http://www.huna.com/ho'oponopono.html (accessed June 22, 2006).

What is Huna: Basic Huna, four bodies, The bodies of mankind. http://www.huna.com/ho'oponopono.html (accessed June 22, 2006).

Wiggins, M. L. 2009. Therapist self-awareness of spirituality. *Spirituality and the therapeutic process: A comprehensive resource from intake to termination,* eds. D. J. Aten, D. J. Leach, and M. M. Leach. Washington, DC: American Psychological Association.

Wing, L. 2009. Mediation and inequality reconsidered: Bringing the discussion to the table. *Conflict Resolution Quarterly* 26 (4): 383–404.

———. 2008. Wither neutrality? Mediation in the twenty-first century. In *Re-centering culture and knowledge in conflict resolution practice,* eds. M. A. Trujillo, S. Y. Bowland, L. J. Myers, P. M. Richards, and B. Roy. Syracuse, NY: Syracuse University Press.

Winslade, J., and G. Monk. 2008. *Practicing narrative mediation: Loosening the grip of conflict.* San Francisco: Jossey-Bass.

Wolf, F. A. 1986. *The body quantum: The new physics of body, mind and health.* New York: Macmillan.

Wozny, N. 2006. Somatics 101. *Dance Magazine* 80 (7): 24–24.

Wright, N.T. 2008. *Surprised by hope: Rethinking heaven, the resurrection, and the mission of the church.* New York: HarperCollins.

———. 1999. *The challenge of Jesus: Rediscovering who Jesus was and is.* Downers Grove, IL: Intervarsity Press.

Yoder, C. 2005. *The little book of trauma healing: When violence strikes and community security is threatened.* Intercourse, PA: Good Books.

Yontef, G. M., and L. Jacobs. 2007. Gestalt therapy. In *Current psychotherapies*, eds. R. Corsini and D. Wedding, 328–367. 8th ed. Belmont, CA: Thomson Brooks.

Zohar, D., and I. Marshall. 2000. *SQ: Connecting with our spiritual intelligence.* London: Bloomsbury.

The Contributors

Yago Abeledo was born in Oñate, Basque Country, Spain, where he studied architecture. He served for fourteen years in Africa (Zambia, Kenya, and Tanzania) as a Catholic priest. He is the creator and editor of the blog *Breathing Forgiveness* (www.breathingforgiveness.net).

Brian Blancke is a content consultant and trainer in negotiation, difficult conversations, and influencing without authority for Vantage Partners, and has, in this capacity, worked with a number of Fortune 500 companies in many different industries. He has more than twenty years of experience in the field of conflict analysis and resolution as a mediator, trainer, and researcher.

G. Daniel Bowling, former executive director of the Society of Professionals in Dispute Resolution and CEO of the Association for Conflict Resolution, is staff mediator/trainer for the Alternative Dispute Resolution Program, US District Court for Northern California. A mediator since 1986, he has taught at US, Australian, and Canadian universities. He is also board president for Spirit Rock Insight Mediation Center.

Louise Diamond is one of the founders of the field as we know it today and brings her background in applied human behavior, organizational transformation, and systems dynamics to work all over the world. With Ambassador John McDonald she cofounded the Institute for Multi-Track Diplomacy (IMTD) in Washington, DC, and in 2008 founded Global Systems Initiatives, where she brings a transformative whole systems perspective on complex global issues to the policy community. For more than thirty years she has been a student of Native American and Tibetan Buddhist ancient wisdom.

Christopher Fitz—a trainer, scholar, and performing artist—uses theater, movement, and other embodied exercises for creative community change. With a background in mediation and group facilitation, his work now draws heavily from improvisational disciplines including playback theatre, theatre of the oppressed, and contact improvisation. He is the founder and director of River Crossing Playback Theatre in Pennsylvania.

213

Rachel M. Goldberg has been active in the fields of conflict resolution and peace studies for more than twenty years and is an experienced and proficient scholar, practitioner, researcher, teacher, and trainer. She is the supervisor of the Restorative Justice Program and assistant professor in conflict studies at DePauw University and head of her own consulting business, RMG Resilience.

John Paul Lederach is professor of international peacebuilding at the Kroc Institute for International Peace Studies at the University of Notre Dame. He is internationally known for his pioneering work in conflict transformation and is involved in conciliation work in Colombia, the Philippines, and Nepal, and countries in East and West Africa. He has helped design and conduct training programs in twenty-five countries across five continents.

Myla Leguro is a peacebuilding and development practitioner with twenty-four years' experience in Mindanao. She has conducted peacebuilding trainings with more than sixty organizations of different faiths. She has worked with John Paul Lederach on his work in grassroots peacebuilding efforts supporting the Nepal peace process. In 2005 she was nominated with twenty-seven other Filipino women for the Nobel Peace Prize in recognition of her work in peace building.

Kathryn Mansfield has worked in conflict transformation for the past ten years after departing from eight years work with a multinational bank. She recently began a PhD study in expressive arts and conflict transformation, following studies at the Kroc Institute for International Peace Studies at the University of Notre Dame and Harvard University.

Joy Meeker has taught conflict resolution and peace studies for the past two decades, and she is faculty at Saybrook University Graduate School with their social transformation concentration. She also has extensive experience as a conflict practitioner and trainer.

Julia Morelli is president of Holistic Solutions, Inc., and president of the George Mason University Instructional Foundation, Inc. She has two decades of experience as a mediator, facilitator, and trainer. Whenever it is appropriate, she incorporates mind-body practices such as conscious breathing and qigong into her conflict engagement work.

M. Brandon Sipes is a theologian and founder of ReFrame, LLC, a US-based organization specializing in conflict engagement and collaborative visioning processes. He has worked across Europe, Israel, the West Bank, and Tunisia with a particular focus on conflicts that contain religious issues.

Laura K. Taylor is assistant professor at the University of North Carolina at Greensboro in the Department of Peace and Conflict Studies. Her research examines the impact of political violence on children, families, and communities. She also has field experience and knowledge in conflict transformation, mental health, and transitional justice.

María Lucía Zapata is a lawyer from Bogotá, Colombia. She has extensive experience in peacebuilding, conflict transformation, and restorative justice in Colombia, Canada, and the Philippines. Currently, she is working toward her PhD in peace and conflict studies at the University of Manitoba in Canada. Her main research interests are grassroots peace building and postliberal peace.

Index

About the Book

WHAT WOULD THE WORK OF CONFLICT RESOLUTION LOOK LIKE if practitioners not only recognized that it is impossible for them to be neutral—and that there are dangers in believing otherwise—but also brought their whole selves to the negotiation table?

Focusing on this question, the authors of *Faith and Practice in Conflict Resolution* introduce the work of pathbreaking individuals who have successfully moved beyond the constraints of the objectivist paradigm to tap into the insights that their spiritual roots, their emotions, and even their bodies can contribute. The book presents an important new framework for whole, multidimensional practice, along with concrete techniques for promoting peace.

Rachel M. Goldberg is assistant professor of conflict studies at DePauw University.